A wealth of praise for
# ME AND THE BOY

"Nature may be literature's greatest vehicle for self-discovery. Thoreau uses it at Walden's Pond as a background for his most eloquent essays; Hemingway at the big two-hearted river to soothe his trouble mind, and in this book, Paul Hemphill uses nature as a way of getting in touch with himself and working out his troubled relationship with David, his son by his first marriage. . . . Hemphill . . . has five other books under his belt. None . . . are as risky as this one. Not only did he have to bet that his untested body would carry him far enough for there to be time for revelation, but that his son would open up enough for there to be be any revelation at all. In this case he won the bet."
*Chicago Tribune*

"*Me and the Boy* is not as much a nature piece as it is a human-nature story, of intimate talks about hurts and grievances, failures and forgiving, of self-discoveries that go far beyond a long walk through the woods by a son and middle-aged man." *The Philadelphia Inquirer*

"Indeed a first-hand account of a father and son climbing the crest of eastern America from Georgia to Maine fires the imagination. . . . Hemphill is excitingly vivid at capturing the experience of overland hiking, as well as the variety and idiosyncracies of the characters he and David meet on the trek. And he's superb at concisely depicting the places they drop into." *The Atlanta Journal-Constitution*

(more . . .)

# ME AND THE BOY

"It is a tribute to Hemphill's writing that you can sense the impending tension and the inevitable blowup before it happens, by the terse dialogue between the two. Finally, though, they achieve that area equilibrium of relating more as friends than as father and son."

*San Francisco Examiner-Chronicle*

"A touching essay of a last-ditch effort of a father and son to get to know each other . . . There is another journey going on beneath it all, a journey of discovery between father and son, and that journey is a success. Little by little, the two come to a realization of their mutual love and need. We are left feeling that, though losing their physical objective, they gained each other for life. Hemphill's work merits continued watching."

*The Kirkus Reviews*

"It wasn't just a walk in the woods and meals of rice and canteen water. The book is the brilliant account of a redemptive journey, filled with the resonance of laughter, the anguish of self-discovery, mud-packed hiking boots hitting the trail, and the newfound emotional embrace of father and son."

*The Chattanooga News–Free Press*

## PAUL HEMPHILL

# PAUL HEMPHILL

"*Me and the Boy* shows that a sometimes troubled 48-year-old can confront his demons—and emerge all the better for it. By the end of the book, one cares about the Hemphills, failures and success alike."

*Atlanta*

"In succinct, observant prose, Hemphill describes the trip with gutty precision, sidestepping the gloppy romanticism like a slippery rock while looking for the most direct, revealing path to recount what occurred. . . . But the forest is plainly viewed in this work, as are the trees. Like walking the trail, this book can be savored as a monumental accomplishment rich with smaller pleasures."

*Nashville Banner*

"Ultimately, it is the intriguing and insightfully confessional tone of Hemphill's narrative, as he delicately balances painful candor, ruthless self-examination, and outright self-pity, that gives *Me and the Boy* the power, pathos, and enlightenment of a finely written, well-paced novel."

*The Baltimore Sun*

# ME AND THE BOY

# ME AND THE BOY

*A Father and Son
Discover America—
and Each Other*

## Paul Hemphill

IVY BOOKS • NEW YORK

Ivy Books
Published by Ballantine Books
Copyright © 1986 by Paul Hemphill

Library of Congress Catalog Card Number: 86-106

ISBN - 0-8041-0142-6

This edition published by arrangement with Macmillan Publishing Company, a Division of Macmillan, Inc.

Manufactured in the United States of America

First Ivy Books Edition: June 1987

For David; for better, for worse, forever.

# Contents

# Acknowledgments

THE BOOK'S BEEN DEDICATED TO DAVID—WHO ELSE?—
and somewhere in there I jotted a note to him in Birmingham, where I could sense he was sitting about with a fair amount of trepidation, to tell him it was my guess that he wasn't going to begin to halfway appreciate what's in here until he was thirty or I was dead or whichever came first. There's no doubting that I violated a lot of confidences here and there's no doubting that my son will, for a few years at least, feel as though he got used. In anticipation of that reaction from him, all I could do was feebly quote Joan Didion's warning that "writers are always selling somebody out."

Acknowledgments. I don't want to let this get out of hand, so I will keep the list short. I can't for the life of me understand how a nice former Catholic girl like Susan Alice Farran Percy Hemphill, the "SAFPH, *qui a racheté une génération perdue*" dedicatee of *The Sixkiller Chronicles*, can continue to put up with this cowboy; nor why Bob Hannah keeps trying to show me how to beat the devil; nor, most amazing of all, why Sterling Lord keeps acting

more like my best friend rather than a mere literary agent.
I got me some True Believers out there.

P.H.

*Atlanta, 1985*

# Introduction

When I'm playing writer-in-residence at a little private women's college up in the foothills of the Southern Appalachians, which is an altogether civilized way for a writer to survive financially while writing his or her books, hardly a lecture passes when I fail to mention the importance of what my first boss in the newspaper business once called "getting out there amongst 'em." As one who received his basic training as a writer not by hanging out at libraries but by being forced into the streets to produce a 1,000-word column six days a week for a newspaper, in sickness or in health, I say that's how you learn to write. There would be no bottom to *The Grapes of Wrath*, which is still, to my way of thinking, *the* Great American Novel, if John Steinbeck hadn't bothered to get out there amongst the Okies.

The germination of the idea for this book occurred on a rather liquid Memorial Day weekend in 1983 when I went deep into the mountains of north Georgia with an old friend, a writer and editor named Billy Winn, on a camping expedition. Over the course of the weekend, bivouacked on a mice-infested island in the middle of a hard-charging trout stream, Billy and I caught a few trout and drank a lot of whiskey and did some reading (Che Guevara's *Guerrilla Warfare* made me wonder why we didn't read that before we went to Vietnam) and somewhere in there got to talking about how I really ought to be doing this with my son rather than with a friend. David had just turned eighteen and I was forty-seven. I had divorced his mother when he wasn't quite ten—had run away from home, as it were—and I had missed out on his most formative years. How would I ever catch up?

"Why don't y'all walk the Appalachian Trail?" Billy said.

"Godamitey, Billy. That'll take forever."

"About six months. Twenty-one hundred miles."

"Walking and camping for six months? You're crazy."

"You want to know your boy, that's the way to do it."

Well, yes. Backpacking 2,142 miles from Georgia to Maine along the spine of the Appalachian Mountains *would* be the ultimate in father-son togetherness. So I locked onto the idea and wrote David and my literary agent, who both agreed that it was a noble adventure, and one day in August I walked away from a two-hour lunch with a publisher in Manhattan and we shook hands on a book contract. On paper it looked simple: buy some equipment, get into shape, start hiking and see what happens. I didn't fully realize what I'd gotten myself into until that day around dusk, sipping martinis on a Delta jet headed back home to Atlanta, when I looked out window and saw what was happening 30,000 feet below in the Smokies. In progress was the quintessential late-summer thunderstorm, a violent laser show of hail and lightning and howling winds probably making toothpicks out of century-old virgin balsams, and even at that altitude we were being advised to cinch our seat belts due to turbulence. *Holy shit.* In less than a year I was going to be walking through that.

My preparation for the odyssey included some reading so I could be sure I had something fresh to say. There was a glut of backpacking books (the best being *Appalachian Hiker* by Ed Garvey and *The Compleat Walker* by a dry-witted Englishman named Colin Fletcher) and some motorized travelogues such as William Least Heat Moon's wonderful *Blue Highways* and Steinbeck's own *Travels with Charley* and Robert Pirsig's *Zen and the Art of Motorcycle Maintenance* (father and son on a biking excursion) and, of course, Thoreau's *Walden* and Robert Ruark's novelistic *The Old Man and the Boy* and Peter Jenkins's *A Walk Across America*. All were variously instructive and entertaining but I felt that if I pulled this thing off I would have a hybrid: some adventure, some backpacking, some turmoil, some philosophy, some mid-life crisis and some teenagery.

But at bottom the book is about fathers and sons. The Appalachian Trail, fierce and wonderful as it may be, is a mere prop for telling how this father and this son came to know each other at a critical point in their lives. It wasn't easy. It wasn't a walk in the woods. Many times I heard Ernest Hemingway talking to me: "In going where you have to go, and doing what you have to do, and seeing what you have to see, you dull and blunt the instrument you write with. But I would rather have it bent and dull and know I had to put it on the grindstone again and hammer it into shape and put a whetstone to it, and know that I had something to write about, than to have it bright and shining and nothing to say, or smooth and well-oiled in the closet, but unused." It got dull and blunted, all right, Papa. But me and the boy, we learned some things.

I went to the woods because I wished to live
  deliberately,
to front only the essential facts of life, and see if I
  could
not learn what it had to teach, and not, when I
  came to die,
discover that I had not lived.
—HENRY DAVID THOREAU, Walden

It is a wise father that knows his own child.
—WILLIAM SHAKESPEARE, The Merchant of Venice

"Dad, do you understand what we're about to
  do?"
"Not really, son, but I say let's get on with it."
—Me and the boy, on the eve of departure

# Into the Woods

HIS NAME IS DAVID,

David Nelson Hemphill (the David because I like the solid old names, the Nelson for my mother's side of the family), and of course he knows only through family lore that at dawn on Sunday, March 7, 1965, beneath the stark fluorescent lighting of the delivery room at Georgia Baptist Hospital on the ragged fringes of downtown Atlanta, doctors exhorted a woman named Susan Milliage Olive Hemphill to push hard one more time. And she, legs suspended from stirrups, sweating and grunting and doing whatever they told her to do, having already been through this one time before, strained and yowled and pushed—*okay, now, Susan, push hard, push-push-push, there you go*—until finally a matted furry head appeared and was followed by a tangle of gooey gangly flesh. Those were the days before Lamaze when fathers, rather than being allowed on the scene to bear witness, were more or less under house arrest, bragging and chain-smoking in the unspeakable limbo of a grim holding cell called the "Fathers' Waiting Room." Then one nurse whapped life into the kid and another

*3*

daubed the mother's forehead with cold sponges and somebody else began cleaning up the mess. And finally, while
I nervously bantered with the half dozen other men sitting
there with me, a doctor strolled down the corridor to the
waiting room and said from the doorway, "Mr. Hemphill?
It's a boy. Mother and son are just fine."

"Hey, Hemp, what color cigars you got?" That would
have been Hank, the jackleg plumber, the one who had
two daughters already, the spidery fellow with a pack of
Luckies rolled up under the sleeve of a T-shirt with FOR-
GET HELL!!! splayed across the front.

I said, with a silly grin, "I got some pinks and I got
some blues."

"Pink cigars taste like candy, you ask me," Hank said.

"Personally, I like the blues best, too."

"Well, goddam, what you waiting for? Pass 'em out.
Might bring the rest of us some luck."

Hope and joy stirred the airless linoleum-floored room
full of men praying for sons. By now we were friends.
Now "Hemp" had struck oil. Maybe we were on a roll.
*Man needs a boy*, was the consensus. So from one jacket
pocket I pulled the half dozen cigars with pink cellophane
wrapped around them, discarding them on a table in case
somebody might need them later in the morning, and from
the other I produced blue-wrapped cigars imprinted with
IT'S A BOY!!! and gleefully began tossing them to Hank
and Ernie and Jay and Howie and the others. *How big is
he, Hemp?/Hell, I forgot to ask/He gon' be a writer, too?/
Shit, no, baseball player.* And then I drifted out into the
bitter overcast Sunday-morning light and found my worth-
less old Thunderbird and roared back home to the apartment, through empty streets beginning to see light traces
of snow, to tell the news to Susan's sister and brother-in-
law, who had been left in charge of our two-year-old Lisa,
and to ponder the universe from the bottom of a magnum
of champagne.

Larger events would occur in the world that day. Only three hours after David's birth, some two hundred miles west in a little Alabama town called Selma, scores of state troopers and assorted other redneck bullies would riot against six hundred civil-rights protesters at the Pettus Bridge, causing such an outrage around the world that the incident marked the beginning of the end of the Deep South's own peculiar brand of apartheid. And *eleven* hours after David's birth, halfway around the world, 3,500 United States Marines waded onto the beaches of Da Nang, in a country called South Vietnam, signaling the United States' official entry into a war it would never win. But later that night, having telephoned everybody I knew and gone back to the hospital to kiss the mother and squint through glass windows to see the boy for the first time, those momentous historical events I was seeing and hearing about on the television set before me at the apartment ("There is no doubt that if they are shot at they will shoot back," said Secretary of State Dean Rusk of the Marines) meant little to me. For unto Paul James Hemphill Jr., himself the only son of an Alabama truck driver, a son had been born.

I WAS A TWENTY-NINE YEAR-OLD NEWSPAPER COLUMNIST at the time, about to jump across town to the *Atlanta Journal* from the dying *Atlanta Times*, and the former Susan Olive was a twenty-three-year-old whose life was committed to mothering. We had met each other four years earlier—in Birmingham, Alabama, hometown to us both, where I was a rookie sportswriter for the *Birmingham News* and she a bank teller who had dropped out of college for lack of interest after only one quarter—and we did not marry under false pretenses. We lusted for each other, naturally, but also we shared the dream of what I would, in later years and with some bitterness, refer to as the White Picket Fences: neat little yellow bungalow, station wagon, *a boy*

*for you and a girl for me*, PTA meetings and Little League
and Girl Scouts, barbecue pit in a trim backyard Daddy
would mow every Saturday morning, dishwasher and or-
gandy curtains for her, Naugahyde recliner and a fireplace
for me, color television in the "den," maybe a wet bar
featuring one of those clocks with the number 5 at every
hour and a sign saying BAR OPENS AT 5, cats and dogs,
vacuum cleaner, canopy bed; everything "nice" and orderly, the American Dream of the Early Sixties, a whole
fantasy world out there in the suburbs, all encircled by
white picket fences. Now I had my boy, to go along with
her girl, and we would continue to pursue the dream.

We'd been chasing it for nearly four years already and
the results were mixed. Right after the marriage I was ac-
tivated into the Air Force and she followed me to live in a
little French village for a year (where Lisa was conceived).
Then I decided to try public relations for a while, as sports
information director at Florida State University, and we
lived in a duplex in Tallahassee long enough for her to
birth Lisa and for me to find out that I wasn't cut out for
PR. There followed then a succession of towns and
newspapers and rental houses and apartments (once I leap-
frogged from Augusta to Tampa, swapping one sports-ed-
iting job for another, dragging Susan and the barely-walking
Lisa with me for a ten-dollar-a-week raise) and although
we still loved each other, and we still shared the dream,
cracks were appearing.

The problem is that most newspapermen and writers can
neither afford nor, after a while, care to pursue the White
Picket Fences. When David was born, in the spring of
1965, I was being paid something like $150 every Friday
morning. That wasn't going to put a man with a wife and
two children into a dream house on the outskirts of a build-
or-bust town like Atlanta. Nor was I particularly lusting for
it so much anymore, not when six days a week I had to
scour the bars and the locker rooms and the all-night diners

and the bus stations (and even the airport to meet pine boxes holding the remains of kids killed in Vietnam) in order to produce a 1,000-word human drama, because with such constant exposure to that world of casual violence and broken dreams and big-time swindling and all of that new world I was exploring—while she, it must be remembered, was sitting at home alone with the children and her dreams—I was fast losing my desire, once tightly held, to barbecue chicken out back on Saturday afternoon.

*Labor Day, my parents visiting for the first time in our first house, kids playing in their rooms, Susan boiling corn in the kitchen, Mama sewing something in the den. Pop and I are sipping Scotch and watching chicken barbecue on the grill in the backyard when we get into it about something and he says,* Well you know you married below your class. *Soon I'm raging through the house, a madman telling his own parents to get packing, and it is right there in David's room, right below the model airplanes the kid has made and I have hung from the ceiling, that the old man dares me to take off my glasses and fight like a man. I run them, the chicken burns, the kids are crying, I grab the bottle and take it out to the darkest corner of the new-mown lawn and wonder how much longer I can hang on.*

David was nine, going on ten, when I finally ran away from home. I would like to say that I gave every effort to endure what had become an unsatisfactory marriage, on the grounds that a son needs a father more than a father needs a son, but I'm not so sure about that. What I do know is that when I left the former Susan Olive and our three kids in the lurch on a little island off the coast of Georgia named St. Simons (a third child, Molly, had been added to the brood and was two when I took my leave) I went into a tailspin that was even worse than what I had abandoned. I joined the dark underworld of the runaway father: booze, sleepless nights of contrition, vague addresses, strange women in strange beds, haggles with lawyers, wild thoughts of kidnapping David, the kids being withheld from me by their mother for "as long as you owe me a single penny." More whiskey. Less writing. More threats from Susan, who had taken the kids back "home" to Birmingham, more booze. (About the best piece of writing I did that year, in fact, was a long letter to the kids, apologizing and trying to explain that I had left their mother, not them; but she intercepted it, I would learn, and never let them read it.)

Sanity returned after a year of that when I met another Susan—Susan Farran Percy—while teaching an adult-education writing class at Florida A&M University in Tallahassee. We had both just ended painful long marriages and when I lit out for San Francisco to write a newspaper column for a year she followed (she was the first Phi Beta Kappa I'd met, I would say flippantly, and I figured some of it would rub off on a truck driver's son who had learned to write by the seat of his pants) and we married. The kids and even their mother took a liking to her, to the extent that David, at the age of twelve, was allowed to fly out there by himself and join us for the 3,000-mile drive across America to Atlanta where Susan and I began our real life together. It is likely that my drinking had crossed over the bridge into alcoholism by then, attributable to the pressures and my age (forty) and my old man's genes, but that is a moot point. Susan would become a magazine editor and I would somehow continue to write books and magazine articles.

A measure of calm thus restored to my life (meaning, in part, that I was managing to take care of the child-support payments and Lisa's forthcoming foray at the University of Alabama), now only 150 miles rather than 3,000 miles away from Birmingham, I was able to make up for some of the time lost with David. We might go to Florida during his spring break while I wrote a magazine piece on, say, Pete Rose. There might be a weekend jaunt to Nashville for the Grand Ole Opry or a camping expedition into the Southern Appalachians or a fishing-and-canoeing adventure on the wild Chattooga River of *Deliverance* fame. Of the kids, I was worried most about David because he, like I, was awash in a sea of women. I figured the women could fend for themselves. During the summer of his seventeenth year, when I had an assignment from the *Reader's Digest* to profile the Arkansas River, we spent one month and 5,000 miles in my car together as we followed the river from the eastern slope of the Rockies, camping out for three nights at 9,200 feet and catching so many native trout that I got sick of eating them, all the way back to the Mississippi. It was a remarkable father-and-son experience, even though he did most of the driving and I did most of the drinking, and it represented the most consecutive nights we had awakened in the same room since my exile. And then, in the spring of the following year, there was this:

On the morning of the night he would graduate from high school I awoke at five o'clock. The night before I had laid out my uniform. There was the seersucker suit and the black wing-tipped shoes and the knee-length black socks and the white button-down shirt and the bow tie. *The bow tie.* So at daybreak I slid into my wasted '70 Olds Cutlass, the one they laugh about at the bank when I try to present it as collateral, and she cranked and I headed giddily west on I-20 to see my boy enter another orbit. It is exactly 151 miles from my house in downtown Atlanta to the apartment in Birmingham where he lives with his mother and his two sisters. That's three hours and nine minutes, door-to-door, and I can't say how many times I've driven it since his mother and I split.

The kid was sitting on the stoop with a smirk on his face. He had just been accepted by the University of the South—we call it "Sewanee" down here—on the basis of an astonishing Scholastic Aptitude Test score of 1,295 (I had no idea where that came from; but his grandfather, the trucker who never finished high school, can work the Sunday *New York Times* crossword with a ballpoint pen). He had finally finished converting his '67 Volkswagen squareback to a twelve-volt system and putting in a new steel floorboard, working all day at the Piggly-Wiggly Supermarket on weekends and hunkering over the car's innards at night beneath arc lights in the apartment parking lot, and now he was set to drive away to southern Colorado to dig postholes and ride horses on a ranch out there for the summer. I asked him if he knew anything about riding horses and he said, "No more than Pop knew about driving trucks until he tried it."

So there he went that evening, this long-gaited blue-eyed insouciant Southern rascal—son of a writer, grandson of a trucker, great-grandson of an Appalachian coal miner—and what I saw was an unbroken bronco about to be let out of the corral. My life, it was occurring to me as some dry fellow in a black gown read alphabetically from the list of the two hundred-odd graduates, has been dominated by women. You had Mama Nelson, the matriarch, and my own mother and sister and all of those aunts. I've had four children and three of them were girls. I've got a wife and an ex-wife. Even my current wife was an only child.

Soon they are calling David's name. I'm sitting there among these women: Lisa, a senior at Alabama who makes A's and B's through sheer grit; Molly, who is eleven and will punch out the first teacher who gives her anything short of an A; and the mother of the brood, the former Susan Olive, who was born to mothering. We are all in a group, dressed to the nines, the father and his women, and it is I who makes an ass of himself when they say "David Nelson Hemphill" and the boy lopes across the stage to collect his piece of paper. The women don't know why I'm acting like this. But the women haven't walked behind that lope in the rain, in January, in the Joyce Kilmer National Forest when the sleet is about to come.

I had about made up my mind at that point that I was going to walk the Appalachian Trail and write a book about it. That takes some five months and 2,100 miles. I wanted David to do it with me. That's five months without the American amenities—whiskey, cigarettes, TV, women, cars, the whole number— and what that was all about was fathers and sons together. David is very good at that stuff. I would be forty-eight and he would be nineteen when we did it. Just get outfitted and split, was my thinking as the ceremony at the high school ended. Five months on the road, I get healthy and we get to know each other again, quit leaning on women, think Thoreau, catch some trout, press on to the Smokies where the bears are mugging backpackers for their M&Ms, do the Reinhold Messner because-it's-there number. All of that. Me and the boy.

"Dave," I said down the corridor when they were shucking their gowns.

"Ceremonial gift?" he said.

"Come and get it."

He gave his gown to somebody and burst past his mother and his sisters and came to me on a balcony.

I told him I wanted to make this private and he looked around and said, "It's okay." With some drama I stripped the bow tie from my neck and draped it around his. I told him, "It's our own private signal. Don't wear it unless things are going very good or very bad. I don't want to hear about it if your life's just okay. I don't want my son to be just 'okay.' " When his English teacher saw the bow tie and asked about it she was bemused. "But I think he ought to wear it," she said, "when things are *fine*." We told her about walking the Appalachian Trail and she walked away.

The Appalachian Trail. Those are magic words to anybody who has ever so much as spent a night sleeping in the woods. The "AT" is Yankee Stadium and the Rose Bowl and the Kentucky Derby and the Grand Ole Opry: the oldest and longest blazed footpath in the world, more than 2,000 miles of walking from the southern end of the Appalachian Mountains range in northeast Georgia to the northern end at a mountain called Katahdin high up in Maine near the Canadian border, a test of strength and will and endurance that only 1,250 or so backpackers have conquered since both ends were connected in the mid-thirties. Millions of hikers have experienced the AT in lighter doses—simply parking the car and walking a couple of miles to a pleasant knoll for a picnic overlooking the Shenandoah Valley in Virginia, maybe putting aside ten days or two weeks to "do the Smokies" with a pal, or just taking an overnighter in one of the three-sided shelters found spaced every ten to twenty miles apart—but then you have the "through-hikers." They are the ones who rigorously prepare themselves, mentally and physically, in the manner of runners prepping for the Boston Marathon, and carefully chart the number of miles they will hike each day, and buy the latest in expensive lightweight equipment, and learn at least the rudiments of living and moving in the deep woods, and become expert amateur dieticians when it comes to knowing how to get the most calories and proteins out of the smallest (i.e., lightest) amount of food.

The AT has its legendary figures, naturally, two of them being Warren Doyle and Emma (Grandma) Gatewood. Doyle did the entire distance during the seventies in seventy days, made possible by having a "team" of helpers (led by his father) serve more or less as a pit crew by hauling the heavy stuff while he literally raced up and down the mountains, a record that the Appalachian Trail Conference is still reluctant to recognize ("The AT's not supposed to be a competition, anyway," is the official ATC response). Grandma Gatewood, though, lives in the hearts of all AT hikers because when she was in her seventies, a rawboned Southern mountain woman who was curious about what the fuss was, simply slapped together some things—ragged sneakers, duffel bag, raincoat, mittens, whatever she could find around the house—and walked the entire trail in one stretch. And then turned around and did it again.

David and I, by the summer of '83 when he was working on the ranch in Colorado and I was beginning to write my second novel (*The Sixkiller Chronicles*,, which itself had partly to do with the encroachment of civilization on the last corners of the Appalachian frontier), had already made up our minds that we would take on the hundred-to-one odds of hiking the AT in one unbroken stretch. I wanted to whip my alcoholism once and for all, for my part, and one doesn't have to ask a teenaged boy with cowboy instincts how he'd like to take an expenses-paid crack at through-hiking the AT. At bottom, though, we saw it as the ultimate father-and-son journey. As we moved into the fall, David now at Sewanee while I began buying some of the equipment we would need, I came across an interesting piece in a medical journal about some studies made by a clinical psychologist named O. W. Lacy: "Himself a 2,000-miler on the Appalachian Trail, Lacy has so far studied 96 men and 27 women who have also completed the trail. 'The 2,000-miler is typically an introvert and more likely to be intuitive.' [That type], for example, makes up about ten per cent of the hikers sampled, yet account for only 2.5 per cent of the general population. And although 11.2 per cent of men and 16.9 per cent of women in the general population are [extroverts who take heed of immediate practical realities], 'not a single [extrovert-realist] has surfaced as a 2,000-miler so far. . . .'" If I read through all of that correctly, David and I were perfect candidates to make it all the way. Both of us were foggy poets merely curious about what lay on the other side of the next hill.

And then I received an interesting letter, in response to mine, from a new friend of mine, an unusual man in the fact that he had just gotten his law degree one morning and swore into the Marine Corps that afternoon:

> You said in your letter that you will not be the same man when you return from the hike. I can assure you that you will be completely 100% the same man as the one who left initially. The only difference is that you will know yourself better. . . . As an artist you understand that every life is an epic tale of its own. The vast majority of lives do not seem epic to those who perceive them or by those who actually live them; the vast majority of mankind is blind to the prospect that life is a rich adventure—not always happy (in fact seldom happy) but always of some sort of potential substance. The artist finds the substance by looking beyond the surface. . . .
>
> You call it a folly, that you want the opinion of another who has also engaged himself in a folly. I could not agree more that I have, in fact, engaged in

a folly. Why else would a slickly-educated South of Broad [Charleston] resident with a law degree decide to enter the Marine Corps as an infantry officer? . . . I wanted to do something different, something that would make my life richer. . . .

You said that the trip will make you a better man than others. The trip will perhaps make you better than some, but to even think of evaluating your position relative to others on such a question is preposterous. The trip, as you have defined it, is to be an inner journey. Yes, you may be better than others because you have looked harder at yourself. . . .

You must walk. You said that you had even toyed with the idea of asking your father along so there would be the three generations together on the trail. You must take your father as far as he can go. If he makes it all the way, so much the better. . . . [But if he doesn't], tell your journal that his inability to finish the trip only symbolizes the fact that the next generation must carry on. In the big picture, no generation ever really completes the journey. But make the trip. At least begin it and don't hamper yourself with fears of falling short. *Plan* to complete the trip. . . .

In the meantime, while David was in the process of being intimidated by Sewanee and on the verge of failing nearly all of his first-semester courses, "the artist" my friend spoke of in his letter had a seizure from alcoholic withdrawal. Once before I had tried to quit whiskey on my own—without the help of Alcoholics Anonymous, being heavily promoted on me by an actor friend of mine named Bob Hannah, I dismissing AA out of my atheism and my cowboyism—and I had made it okay for ten solid months. But then, in the fall of '83, with a novel to write and a body to whip into shape, I abruptly quit cold turkey and

this time wound up in the hospital. ("There's no fool like
an old fool," joshed my doctor, Zeb Morgan, "but at least
you had enough sense to quit.") Then, two months later,
I went under the knife for a hernia I had been walking
around with for ten years. Some preparation.

Finally David came to Atlanta in late February, a week
or so after my forty-eighth birthday and two weeks before
his nineteenth, and the countdown began. I left much of
the preparation to him, since I had the novel to finish before we could go and he was the more knowledgeable about
those matters of equipment and nutrition and logistics, and
I was boggled by the money and time that goes into preparing for a five- to six-month expedition along the whole
of the AT. Even though he already had a tent and a stove
and a parka, and I had managed to collect assorted items
such as a sleeping bag and a good lightweight wool sweater
and a balaclava (ski mask), still we had to lay out more
than $3,000 on equipment: boots for each (around $100 a
pair), Polypro lightweight long johns, wool socks and rayon
inner socks, nylon rope, cook-pots (Swiss, lightweight,
very expensive), mittens and fingerless wool gloves, camera and film (I overindulged and bought a $500 Nikon FA
with a zoom lens), backpacks ($200 for David's internal-
frame alpinist's model, $150 for my many-pocketed exter-
nal-frame JanSport), bandannas, Sierra cups, waterproof
matches, Tylenol III prescribed by Dr. Morgan for dire
emergencies, snakebite kit and other first-aid items, a complete set of guidebooks from the ATC (ten of them, covering the fourteen states the AT passes through, $144), a
harmonica for David and a penny whistle I intended to
master before it was over, water-treatment tablets. So much
stuff that I couldn't keep up. Blue Ridge Mountain Sports
and a couple of other outdoor-equipment places in Atlanta,
even the Old Sarge war-surplus place on the edge of town,
loved to see us coming.

We kept running into a delightful ruddy gnome of a fellow, name of Dan Bruce, at every turn. Bruce had been planning *his* throughhike of the AT for about five years now and he had the selection of equipment and food down to such a science that he weighed everything on a pair of baby scales he had bought at a yard sale. Every time he bought a new piece of equipment he would pack it and go off to Springer Mountain, where the AT begins in Georgia, and spend a weekend trying it out, even if it were no more than a plastic trowel the discerning backpacker uses to dig a hole before and after he shits.

"Damn, Dan," I said to him one night when we ran into him again, the Phantom of the Outdoor Stores, at Blue Ridge Mountain Sports. "You'd drive me crazy. Why don't you just pack up and go?"

"You haven't walked very much, have you?" he said with a twinkle.

"I think maybe Dave and I covered twenty-five miles one weekend."

"Pack got kinda heavy, too, didn't it?"

"The sleet didn't make it any lighter."

"Gotta get you some baby scales," he said. "Weigh stuff right down to the gram." He showed us the voice-activated micro-cassette tape recorder of his that would be strapped to his backpack cinch so he would never have to slow down to take notes.

I was cranking out five to ten double-spaced pages of copy every day on *The Sixkiller Chronicles* as we moved into March. For the most part David spent his days sleeping in the back bedroom until noon, plugging in the headset he had brought with him to groove through the afternoon on his rock tapes and albums, eating like a steer headed to slaughter, sunning on the front porch, making notes on places along the route of the AT where we could count on detouring from the trail to resupply with food and the white gas necessary to operate the Peak I hiker's stove, calling or writing the two women who had turned his head at Se-

wanee before he took a leave of absence; crawling the
walls, really, anxious for me to finish the book and get it
in the mail so we could shove off. (One night four Sewanee
friends, one of them a spunky sophomore named Maggie,
came down to get him so they could go to a rock concert
at the venerable Fox Theatre in Atlanta; at ten o'clock the
next morning he called collect from Sewanee, ten bucks in
his pockets, claiming to be a kidnap victim, saying he might
hang around up there a few days; all I could say was,
"Shit.")

Details, details, details. I'm writing feverishly but I'm
also having to make my own preparations: type up a list
of everything from our blood types to phone numbers of
friends we would visit on the way (the writers Roy Blount,
Joe McGinniss, Jim Dodson of *Yankee* magazine; my agent
and my editor, whom we intended to meet over steaks on
the trail where it passes barely an hour's drive from Manhattan), learning how to detect "hot spots" before blisters
develop, how to set up the tent, how to hang food bags
from trees, how to handle basic first-aid crises such as
snakebites. Pondering how my acrophobia would treat me
when crossing a slippery log bridge with forty pounds of
stuff on my back. *Five pages on the novel today, need eight
tomorrow. How 'bout if we call ourselves Redneck Express, as a rail moniker, in the logs they say you find at
every shelter?*

And in the last week, of course, it seemed like every-
body else was suddenly interested. Fellow named John
Harmon called from the *Atlanta Constitution* for a story
and, because he walked the AT himself in '79, to advise.
They were putting together a pool both at the Old New
York Book Shop (Atlanta's answer to Sylvia Beach's
Shakespeare & Co. in the Paris of the twenties) and at
Manuel's Tavern, my neighborhood watering hole for
twenty years, the sort of place where now that Hemphill
wasn't drinking anymore he would get "eighty-sixed" if

he even *thought* about ordering a beer. Farewell parties ("Hemphill, I'm so scared of the dark I won't even sleep in the backyard," said Pat Conroy, a good friend, the novelist. "Why don't you just walk a few days and write a novel; call it 'Murder on the Appalachian Trail' or something?"). An appearance at a community college on "Appalachian Heritage Day," with some advice from my fellow panelist James *(Deliverance)* Dickey: "You're crazy. Noble. But crazy. You're gonna freeze to death up there." Conversation at Manuel's Tavern over lunch one day with a full-blooded Cherokee by the name of Ken Two Trees, believer in levitation and mind-over-matter, who had just dropped in for a beer from the reservation in western North Carolina on the edge of the Smokies: "It's all in the head, even broken leg. A man can walk on a broken leg if he thinks the pain away. If that doesn't work, I can give you some roots to carry in your pocket and rattlesnakes will get up and begin to run from your presence."

THEN, FINALLY, IT WAS TIME TO GO. BY DUSK ON THE last Sunday in March I had made multiple copies of the manuscript and boxed them up for mailing to New York in the morning. David and I and Susan, a curious bystander, were sprawled about the living room amid all of the stuff we would soon begin stuffing into our backpacks. The food he had rounded up for the first leg sounded perfectly awful to those who are accustomed to a good steak or a pot roast from time to time: Minute Rice, Ramen noodles, powdered soup mixes, peanut butter, dozens of high-protein-and-caloried Snickers bars, M&Ms, peanuts, raisins, tea bags, margarine.

"Tell you boys one place where I envy you," Susan said.

"You want to go along?" I said. "Not too late."

"I have commitments, thank you. Besides, the bugs bite."

"But you envy us?" said David.

"No television for five months. You know what that means? That means five months you won't have to hear that ugly little woman in the commercial scream, 'Where's the beef? Where's the beef?' "

And then, nearing one o'clock, too anxious to go straight to bed although we couldn't be certain when we would next sleep on a real bed, David and I were packed—including the box of resupply we would leave at a lodge four days up the trail in order to cut down on the load we would have to carry at the very beginning of the shakedown period— and there really wasn't much for us to say. It was D-Day.

"Maybe we should've gotten Ken Two Trees to come along," David said. "Ward off the evil spirits."

"Christ, he's too busy making appearances."

"Can't think of anything else, can you?"

"Wouldn't have room for it if I did," I said.

"The AT," he said.

"Yep. Ready or not."

"Dad?"

"Yo."

"Do you understand what we're about to do? I mean, *really*."

"Not really, son. But I say let's get on with it."

# The Trek

# 1

WHEN THE GE RADIO/ALARM BESIDE OUR BED POPPED alive on the morning of March 26, the red digits on the clock showing 7:00, I found myself fully alert in an instant. "I shall go to Katahdin," I announced, propping up against the headboard and stretching both arms and tensing the legs to make sure everything was in order, getting a "Whatever you say, Ace" from Susan as she flipped the down quilt over her head for a few extra minutes of half-sleep, then lighting the first of the last Camels while a fellow in a helicopter described over the radio the usual Monday-morning mess on the streets below. "An accident involving a tractor-trailer on the Northeast Expressway at Monroe Drive has traffic backed up to Shallowford. Motorists might want to take the Buford Highway as an alternate route to the downtown area. . . . Meanwhile, inbound on I-20 East, there's a stalled vehicle in the center lane. . . ." *A fool and his automobile*, I thought, the sniffy superiority of the born-again naturalist already taking over. I bounced out of bed and, in my Jim Palmer briefs, went through my knee bends and push-ups and sit-ups in front of the full-length mirror. "Don't you ever die, you sonofabitch," I said, quoting Stud Cantrell, the vain wasted ballplayer of my first novel. On the radio Willie Nelson began singing "On the Road Again." I swear.

It would be a day full of odd sensations. *This must be the "heightened awareness" the dope-smokers talk about*, I mused as I went through the morning rituals, performing each little task with the full knowledge that it might be a while before I came this way again. *Last crap on my own john. Last bubble bath. Won't shave again until August. Thank God I won't be opening cat food again anytime soon, but I am going to miss the Mr. Coffee machine, and if this linoleum floor seems cold in the morning just wait until I roll out of the tent onto frosted stubble at 5,000 feet*. A condemned man, taking his last meal before being hustled off to the electric chair, must wonder why he never really appreciated a good steak before. No woman of my knowledge had ever looked so desirable as Susan when I returned to the bedroom to bribe her awake with a neck massage and a cup of coffee. No five-year-old had ever seemed so precious as Martha, asleep in a pile of teddy bears and other treasures, when I kissed her and whispered "Good morning" into her ear. No teenaged boy seemed as bushy-tailed as my son, sprawled akimbo like the victim of a serious accident, when I jolted him awake with a kick at the sofa bed in the front room.

"Aw, man," he said, abruptly wide awake. "I was catching trout on this perfect stream in Vermont. Incredible."

"Yeah, too bad we can't take poles. Sleep okay?"

"Not really. How's the weather look?"

"Perfect," I said. "Rain's coming, but not today."

" 'I went to the woods . . .' "

" '. . . because I wished to live deliberately.' Thoreau, 1906. Also, 'Get your ass in gear.' Hemphill, 1984. Let's hit it."

The next two hours were a blur. Martha, eating her Cheerios and watching "Popeye" on television, complained about not going to preschool and asked one more time about the bears in the mountains. I dressed myself for that first day out with the sacred solemnity of a matador—first the Polypro long johns, then the virgin wool sweater, then the two pairs of socks (making sure there were no wrinkles), the cotton bush pants and finally the boots—while David, with an insouciance that unnerved me for a moment, slapped on his tattered hiker's shorts and slumped barefooted into the kitchen in search of the Cheerios supply. "The first thing I'm going to do when you gentlemen leave," Susan announced, "is put the ashtrays up and the toilet seats down." I gathered up the two boxes containing copies of my novel, one for the publisher and one for my agent, and drove them to the neighborhood post office to be Federal-Expressed to New York. When I returned the foyer was clogged with the neighborhood carpenters and electricians, who had chosen that morning to begin remaking the house in my absence. David loaded the trunk of the '70 Olds with our packs. Nancy, the carpenter from next door, opined that the most dangerous part of the trip would be "driving that heap to Springer Mountain." At 9:30, a half hour after mailing off one book, I was leaving home for another.

Spring was about to burst upon the lowlands as we left the haze and the ubiquitous "highway improvements" of Metro Atlanta behind us, Susan driving and David fooling with his harmonica and Martha sleeping and I rummaging through my pockets to be sure I had everything ($100 in traveler's checks, $55 cash, American Express, the typed card listing everything from Joe McGinniss' phone number in Massachusetts to our blood types), the car leaving the interstate and going around the busy little city/town of Gainesville before finally heading up into the moonshine-country foothills of Southern Appalachia. *Deliverance.* Pickup trucks with gun racks.

PREPARE TO MEET THY GOD. White clapboard Pente-
costal churches and weathered graveyards. Muddy, smashed
stock cars ("White Lightnin' " hand-painted on both sides)
being towed home from the Sunday-night races. George Jones
and Merle Haggard singing on the car radio about whiskey
and women and jail. Stray dogs, circling buzzards, gourds
and honey and questionable "antiques" for sale, three rusting
Fords in the front yard being cannibalized to keep another
one running. Somebody had taken a can of spray paint to the
"L" and now we had a sign welcoming us to Bumpkin
County. And looming up ahead, like the backbone of a whale
arched against the cobalt-blue sky of the Appalachian spring,
there they were. The mountains.

*It's my first time out with him on a long haul through
the mountains, Birmingham to Cumberland and back
in a week, and we've got cotton and we'll bring tires
back and I'm maybe fifteen and before we leave my
mama says,* Now Paul I don't want you to make a
truck driver out of him. *And my old man says,* It's
good enough for me and I notice you ain't starving,
*and we're gone. Just me and my old man. And some-
where up there around Roanoke at four o'clock in
the morning we're chugging up a hill doing maybe
three miles an hour when a man with blood all over
him is out in the road crazy and waving a flashlight.
My old man follows him down the hill through the
laurel thickets and rocks and rhododendron and when
he comes back in a half hour he's shaking.* Gotta go
tell the troopers, *he says,* fella's brakes burned out
and his partner and a girl your age they'd run off with
got crushed dead under the truck. Damn mountains,
they'll kill you.

First we would drive beyond the takeoff point of the
Appalachian Trail and stop at Walasi-Yi to drop off the

cache of food we would pick up four or five days later. Plumbers were everywhere, it seemed, and it looked like today would be the first time since the freeze of Christmas Eve that there would be running water throughout the place. David and I heaved the cardboard liquor box full of ten days' worth of supplies into the solid old lodge made of native brick and timbers, and Susan and the kid followed. It was 11:45 in the morning. Jeff and Dorothy Hansen, the twenty-ish couple who ran the lodge now, were busy orchestrating the plumbers and selling picture postcards and snacks and trinkets to a carload of tourists.

"The traffic picked up yet?" I asked Jeff Hansen.

"Hikers?" he said. "You're among the first. Going all the way?"

"That's the plan. Can't wait to get started."

"I know how you feel."

"You walked it yourself?"

"Some of it. But Dorothy, she went all the way. By herself."

"No kidding?"

"Yeah," he said. "In '79. She's been consoling that fellow over there. The one in the parka." A tall bronzed man with silvery hair, maybe sixty years old, stood on the far side of the lodge near a display of camping gear and talked in a low voice with Dorothy Hansen. Now and then he would throw out his hands in disgust.

"What happened?" I said.

"He quit."

"How long was he out?"

"Since Friday. Three, four days." Hansen shook his head. "Poor guy. He's from Huntsville, Alabama. Says he's been planning a throughhike for a year and a half and has eighteen food boxes back home in his garage ready for his wife to mail ahead on the trail. Now he's waiting for her to come get him. Said he didn't enjoy it, got bored. Said he's been seeing 'scenic overlooks' all of his life."

"Bored," I said.

"First time I ever heard that one."

Two hours later David and I stood at the narrow foot-bridge over Amicalola Falls to say goodbye to the women. "Tell'em I said, 'God, I love it so,' " I said to Susan. Martha said, "Susan, I think I'm going to be sad." And we hugged, all the way around, and the '70 Olds slithered away back down the hill to civilization and David and I cinched our packs and I said, "Take 'em to Missouri, men," and the father and the son slid into the woods.

Any hiker will tell you that you will never feel so alive again, not in your entire life, as you do in that first hour. You are neither tired nor hungry nor thirsty nor, God forbid, bored. That comes later. But for now you are thoroughly in touch with all of your senses. You feel every muscle in your body. You smell the piney woods. You hear the startled *whump-whump-whump* of a grouse frightened from a laurel thicket by the dull tromping of your boots on the footpath. You taste the salty sweat gathering on your upper lip. You wiggle your toes, checking for "hot spots," in the stiff new boots. You fine-tune the various straps and cinches in your fresh-out-of-the-box backpack. *What's that muscle there in the shoulder, I never felt that one before.* If it's a cliché, so be it: this is what the poets meant when they said "alone with nature."

The boy leading, the father following in his steps along the three-foot-wide path, we slowly walked where the blazes took us. The blazes were blue here, two inches wide and six inches high, painted ten feet up the sides of the trees, the next blaze always in sight, put there by weekend volunteers for the Georgia Appalachian Trail Club (formed, we would learn, exactly fifty years earlier in the midst of the Depression in the era of the Civilian Conservation Corps and the Works Progress Administration of Franklin Roosevelt). With each step there was the sound of water sloshing in the loaded canteens and the muted clunk of cook-pots and the squeak of new leather. No talking. Only walking. Says the hand-held blue-jacketed official Appalachian Trail Guide for North Carolina-Georgia: "Continue climb on road . . . Turn right off road . . . Cross USFS road, climb steeply through laurel thickets to ridge top . . . Cross abandoned road . . . Reach Cemetery Road. (To left, road leads to old cemetery; to right, road leads about 2 mi. to Amicalola Falls-Frosty Mtn. Road, USFS 46.) Cross Cemetery Rd. and start ascent on forest trail, following the blue blazes . . . Trail begins steep ascent of Frosty Mtn. . . . Miles 4.8. Reach site of old fire tower and Frosty Mtn. Rd. . . ." Better to walk it than to read about it. Also harder.

We took our first official rest stop at the site of the abandoned fire tower. Only the four-cornered concrete foundation of the tower remained. We released the catches and shook out of our packs and took out canteens and ziplocked bags bulging with mixed peanuts-and-raisins and flopped out on the ground in the clearing. Free at last.

"Only two thousand, one hundred and thirty-seven to go," David said. He flipped a peanut in the direction of a squirrel, the squirrel poising upright for a moment and then pouncing on it.

"Don't mention it," I said. "Any hot spots yet?"

"No. You?"

"Nothing. Maybe the socks are okay after all."

"We shall see."

I said, "I don't see how we can make Springer tonight, but I don't guess it matters. Guidebook shows a gap between Black Mountain and Springer, about 3,400 feet. Got a campsite there. Might as well stop there and do Springer in the morning."

We reached the gap at dusk, having walked the first seven miles in a leisurely first-day four hours, and the campsite was right out of a Sears Roebuck Catalogue: smooth, grassy, protected by trees showing the first bright green signs of spring, surrounded by sharp ridges. Hikers, we would hear later, consider this approach to Springer a fairly fierce test. But we were fresh and the weather was ideal and we felt no pain. For the first meal there was rice covered with mushroom soup, *lots* of rice covered with *lots* of mushroom soup, washed down with steaming tea-and-honey, Snickers bars for dessert. There was no need to set up the tent. We lay back in our sleeping bags after we had scoured the pots and utensils and built a fire and strung up the food bags to frustrate the critters. The dark blue sky was clear and we could see all of the stars and the contrails of jets making their approaches into the Atlanta airport. It was a fine roof to be shared by a father and his son. We didn't think to wish each other a good night.

# 2

*Red sky at morning, sailor take warning.* If the adage still held, and there was no reason to think such matters had changed since the time of the Ancient Mariner, we were about to get baptized on only the first full day out. When we stirred at daybreak the ridges around us were silhouetted against an ominous magenta backdrop and there was the musty smell of impending rain in the forest. From a close distance came another rhythmic *whump-whump-whump*, not from grouse this time but from helicopters attached to the Army Ranger training camp near the old gold-mining town of Dahlonega, and I was reminded of my stint as a newspaper correspondent in Vietnam as we hurried about a breakfast of oatmeal-and-honey and hot chocolate. We rearranged our packs so the rain gear would be handy. Evidence of our encampment gone—fire out, grass smoothed, garbage in a plastic bag inside my pack—we cinched up and prepared to move along.

"First phone we see, I got to call Winston-Salem," I

said. I had taken a ceremonious last drag on the last Camel and now I was grandly field-stripping it.

"Winston-Salem," said David.

"Yeah. R. J. Reynolds Tobacco Company. Camels."

"What, you gonna have some more airlifted in?"

"No, this is it. I quit. No more until Katahdin, and I'm not so sure there'll *be* anymore."

"Okay," he said. "I got you. 'I'd walk twenty-one hundred miles for a Camel.' "

"Finance the whole expedition," I said.

By 8:15 we had zipped up the short steep ridge to Springer Mountain's summit. "Bare rocky ledges afford excellent views of almost unbroken mountain range," the Trail Guide promises, but not on this day with the gray clouds rolling in from all sides. This is where it all begins or ends for a through-hiker. Some poor devil who for five or six months has stumbled and swum and crawled and bled and frozen and sweated over an obstacle course of 2,142 miles, starting from Maine in hip-deep snow, has every right to expect a brass band and a magnum of champagne when he falls across the finish line at Springer. No such luck. All he will find is an old-fashioned black rural mailbox, holding a spiral notebook where he can write his name and the date and something poetic ("I beat the sonofabitch," is my favorite), and a stark marker, white letters on bronze, mounted on four-by-four posts six feet high.

SPRINGER MOUNTAIN
ELEVATION 3,820
Southern terminus of the
Appalachian Trail. A mountain
footpath extending 2,000 miles
to Mt. Katahdin in Maine.

We dropped our packs and opened the mailbox and found a note addressed to us by John Harmon ("AT '79"), the correspondent in north Georgia for the Atlanta newspapers, saying he had waited until dusk the day before to meet us ("It's one hell of a 8.8 miles ain't it?") and giving his phone numbers in case we had any problems between there and the Smokies. Then there was the spiral notebook, the log, which began on December 23 with salutations from a geologist from the Adirondacks who had just finished grad school. Somebody had stopped by on January 1 to write "Happy New Year" and our friend Dan Bruce, the phantom of the outdoor-equipment stores in Atlanta, had drifted by shortly after that "just checking things out." Then came "Slow Joe from Md." and "Binky" and the Jesus People: "I came to the mountains to seek the Lord. He inhabits all of Creation and it's beautiful." (In ensuing weeks the same hikers would become more worldly as the AT ground on and on. "Okay," wrote one of them after shinnying up the sheer face of Albert Mountain, "who's responsible for the goddam rocks?") And only the day before there had been seven people to sign in. There had been two couples and three loners, all of them signifying they were "GA-ME" through-hikers, from Vermont and Florida and Indiana and Georgia. They were our crowd. We signed in and took the obligatory snapshots of each other posing beside the marker and pointed ourselves toward Maine.

We hadn't been walking an hour when we caught up with one of the couples who had signed in at Springer the day before. It was raining and turning colder by then and we had ducked into a bramble of rhododendron to put on our rain gear. Now, as we overtook the couple, we saw them being blown all over the trail by the whistling wind and rain. He weighed no more than 150 pounds and she may not have topped 100 and they were carrying far too much weight in their packs and they held hands to keep from going airborne in their shiny new yellow bat-winged ponchos. They stopped to rest and escape the wind behind an oak next to the trail. He was Jimmy from Rhode Island and she was Terry from

Ohio, they said, but they were married and lived in Sarasota now and they had a lawn-care business and they worked in restaurants at night. No kids.

"Is it always like this?" she said to no one.

"Worse," David said. "Wait 'til it snows."

"Aw, don't say that," I said. "We're as new as you are."

"We can double back to the shelter, hon," Jimmy told her.

"I'll be all right. It was just so, you know, so *sudden*. It's okay." She made some adjustments with the straps of her poncho. She looked at me and said, 'Jimmy always wanted to do this, so here we are. It'll be all right." Later when we all stopped for lunch beside a waterfall, stretching out on flat rocks during a brief break in the clouds, they were silent as she lay back exhausted and he fumbled with the matches, which had gotten wet. We never saw them again.

That first full day out would be a twelve-miler, not bad for rookies on their shakedown, and everything was still new and simple. From my journal: "Warnings of Army maneuvers day or night. Ranger training, choppers all day. . . . First deer spotted by Dave ahead at Hightower Gap (8 miles from Springer), white tail flashing as it bursts up a knoll. . . . Last Camel after breakfast, but then two guys in pickup lost at intersection of USFS roads 42 and 69, 'just driving around.' . . . Old boy in Red Man cap offers beer, I say no, blows smoke in my face and I say yes to a Winston. . . . Dave gets out map and shows them where they are. . . . They say bad weather coming. Keep asking us about the walk, and why, never quite understand why." About an hour later, dusk descending, we found a pleasant campsite on a ridge at 2,700 feet. David quickly set up the tent for the first time as a guard against the rain that was sure to come. We found enough dry wood for a good fire. David, who had worn his shorts and was shirtless for much of the day, slipped on his long johns while I taped patches of moleskin over hot spots I had discovered on my heels.

It was after a supper of Ramen noodles and some awful oxtail soup and Sierra cups of hot chocolate, when the first drops of rain splattered and sizzled on the campfire, that I was reminded of what had brought me out there in the first place. Here we were, me and the boy, and he was saying, "Dad?"

"Yeah."

"When was the first time you slept with a woman?"

"Why, you got plans?"

"Naw, I was just asking."

*Again I'm riding with my old man but this time I'm eighteen and I'm off on my first adventure. He'll drop me off at Cocoa, Florida, at dawn and I'll take a shot at professional baseball. The boy is leaving the nest and the father feels obliged to instruct but is having a hell of a time at it.* Gonna be a lot of little girls hanging around the ballpark, *says the old man.* Aw, I don't know. Yeah, they like to hang out with the players, all right. Probably, *I say. He clears his throat and blurts it out:* Always use a rubber, son. *That's all he ever tells me.*

"I was a late starter," I said. "It was your mama. I guess I was about twenty-four."

"Oh."

"I had this apartment, see."

"It's okay."

"I was always shy, you know? I don't know why it took so long."

"So y'all got married," David said.

"Yeah. I liked it so much I married her."

"Uh-hunh."

"Ain't no accident that in both of my novels I've got fathers desperate to get their boys laid so they'll get it out of their system.''

"Yeah, I remember Jamie and that hooker in Panama City.''

"Right, and now I got Jaybird and 'Ti-Hi,' the Indian girl.''

" 'Ti-Hi Tompkins.' I read that part.''

"Sonofabitch if it didn't backfire on Jaybird's father, though. Christ, Jaybird liked it so much he couldn't wait to marry Becky, the rich kid, so he can get it every night. See what I mean?''

"I guess.''

"I mean, the same goddam thing happened to me. I liked it, man. I was on my knees proposing to your mama within a month. Look where it got me.'' *For God's sake.* There wouldn't *be* a David Hemphill if not for those stolen hot-blooded afternoons on a Murphy bed in an $80-a-month bachelor apartment during a blistering Birmingham summer. *I love you, let's do it again, and baby makes three, tra-la.* "Well, hell. Tenting tonight. Here comes the rain.''

## 3

THAT WAS AT A PLACE CALLED HORSE GAP, ONLY 19.1 miles from Amicalola Falls, and maybe that's where the fellow from Huntsville with eighteen food boxes waiting to be mailed to him on the trail first began to have second thoughts. "Covered 10 miles this day," my own journal reads, "mostly through rain, hail and winds. Off and on with rain gear, pain in ass, lot of boring up and down, not so fun. Quick lunch, duty calls, press on." When the hail got fierce at midafternoon we mounted some steep log steps, hoping to find cover from the marble-sized hailstones stinging the backs of our hands, but when we came upon the Gooch Gap Shelter on the ridge we found a gaggle of hikers with the same idea. I took an irrational dislike to a couple of them—college kids from upstate New York, rosy-cheeked rich boys lolling around the shelter in $100 creased wool trousers, taking up the space of four hikers with their Abercrombie & Fitch gear, interviewing other hikers with tape recorders so they could earn college credits—and after a slug of water we moved on. It took us nearly three hours to cover the four miles to where the trail crosses a road.

Woody Gap is a high mountain pass (3,150 feet) on a twisting blacktopped road to nowhere, Georgia Highway 60, the sort of wayside where drivers of logging trucks stop to let their brakes cool and families in station wagons pile out to look at the scenery or use the two-hole "facility." With dark coming fast, and a long rugged uphill pull of ten miles to Blood Mountain facing us, we decided to make camp in a picnic area beside the road. It took us fifteen minutes to put up the tent in winds gusting up to forty miles an hour. David had just cranked up the stove inside the tent—sometimes you say to hell with the rule book—when a car came crunching right up to the tent and somebody blinked its lights.

A bearded man, about my age, leaned out the car window. "Probably got some wet clothes, do you?"

"You been reading my mail," I said.

"Got a washer and dryer at home. Right down the road."

"Well, I don't know, we just got set up."

"Gonna be a lot more weather. Got coffee, too."

*Well, now.* "Go on," said Dave, "I'll have some tea and take a nap. Just don't wash the cotton stuff in hot water." We threw everything we weren't wearing into one of the plastic garbage bags and I promised I wouldn't accept a hot meal and I hurled myself inside the car. The man had his wife with him. They lived in the little blinker-light town of Suches, as in "such as," a mile and a half west on 60. Jim and Ruth Ann Miner, puffing madly on Pall Mall cigarettes, said they liked to help backpackers. Said they had a sofa bed. Said they had a woodburning stove. Said they remembered when I wrote for the Atlanta papers. Said would I like a cigarette. "Desperately," I said.

Suches, unincorporated, isn't even listed in the Rand McNally. That's fine with the Miners. After several years of dealing with the hassles that go with living in the crowded suburbs of a city like Atlanta they said goodbye to all of that ("I got tired of living in the flight pattern of the DeKalb-Peachtree Airport," said Jim) and in the fall of 1983 they bailed out, this couple in their forties with a daughter in college and a son in high school, and headed for the hills. They found a plain white frame house, with a well for water and a wood stove for heat, and they found Thoreau's simplicity. Jim continued working for 3M in Norcross, on the northern fringe of Atlanta, but now there was a ninety-minute commute ("I'll see a dozen sunsets driving home every day"). Ruth Ann began teaching at the high school in Dahlonega, a twisting half-hour drive down the mountain on Highway 60. Their daughter Jennifer was a senior at Berry College in the northwest Georgia town of Rome and their seventeen-year-old son, Bruce, was a student and basketball star at the private Woody Gap School.

The move was working. "It's country, real country," Jim Miner was saying as his wife sorted our filthy clothes and cranked up the washer. "I'm from the Adirondacks and Ruth Ann's from upstate New York, so the terrain and the vegetation are familiar. Favors are so freely given here. No score is being kept. I mean, it's little things. Like the other day there was a man here who'd been out of work for seven months and he pulled some people out of a ditch and he wouldn't take any money from 'em. Neighborly, that's all. Do unto others."

The color television was creating a warm glow on the shellacked pine paneling of the front room, where the stove was the dominant furnishing, and I tried to squelch my guilt feelings about David being left alone in a dark tent billowing in the harsh wind and rain. The Miners, a chatty pair, kept feeding me Pall Malls and coffee and stories. Bruce, their son, six-two and only 140 pounds, came in out of the cold from somewhere. His father said, "One time Bruce went out to buy some milk and came home with a hiker. We ran an ad in the *Appalachian Trailway News*. We're about to become a regular stop on the AT."

Ruth Ann had the clothes in the dryer now. "The school is probably better than what the kids had in Atlanta," she said. "That's what worries a lot of people who think about doing what we did. But the Woody Gap School has 105 kids from kindergarten through high school and there's a nine-to-one student-teacher ratio. So that part's okay. But what we really like is the *flavor* of life up here. This is real Appalachia, you know. People up here still say 'hit' for 'it' and the only 'industry' in Suches is a sawmill. We don't have any doctors in the area, just some nurse practitioners, and sometimes the NPs use folk medicine with the roots and things like that. The mother of old Garth Moore, who calls himself 'the meanest man in the county,' shoots at people if they come too close to her place. And when old people have to go to the hospital in Atlanta they take their own milk jugs full of mountain spring water with them."

"It feels good here," Jim Miner said. "It's simple."

"I tried a small place once," I said. "Ruined my marriage."

"That happens," said Ruth Ann.

"Your marriage better be in good shape before you try it."

"Where was that, the 'small place'?" said Jim.

"St. Simons Island. My boy was about seven then. You move to a small place and the marriage is no good, you find out quick because you can't hide from each other. I left home when he was nine."

"So now you're trying to get to know your son."

"That's about the size of it."

They wouldn't touch that. They hadn't been there before. Instead they loaded me up with dry clothes and a mason jar of maple syrup from Ruth Ann's folks in New York and the remains of a pack of Pall Malls ("I'll bring some Camels by your tent in the morning," she said) and soon Jim and Bruce and I were in the car driving through the storm back to the tent. "If you meet any southbound hikers, tell 'em we've got a sofa bed," Jim Miner said. It was nine o'clock when I slithered into the tent, three hours after I had left, and I didn't bother to wake David. A Snickers did nicely for supper.

# 4

It had rained all during the night, the winds gusting between twenty and fifty miles an hour, and when I awoke a little after daybreak the tent was a dank blob in the fog. Rummaging through my pack, looking for a snack, I found that we were just about out of gorp and candy bars. We had a rough hike ahead of us, a persistent ten-mile climb of 1,300 feet in elevation to the fabled Blood Mountain, before we could get to our food cache at Walasi-Yi the next morning. There was a blast on a horn and when I unzipped the tent I saw Ruth Ann Miner scrambling out of a pickup truck, dashing to the tent, tossing a pack of Camels to me and sloshing back to the pickup while I fumbled for a dollar bill. "Save it, you'll need it," she shouted, roaring away in the fog. *One vice at a time*, I said, ripping open the pack and firing up the first one of the day. At least I wasn't having a Bloody Mary with it.

A voice. "Anybody in there?"

"Yo," I said. A bearded young fellow crouched at the tent.

"We've got breakfast if you want it."

"Say what?"

"Eggs, pancakes, coffee."

"Say again?"

"Across the road," he said. "I'm taking orders."

"Make it two, whatever it is."

*Father and son, communing with nature.* First a good old boy offers you a beer in the middle of the woods, then you sit by a wood stove while a stranger washes and dries your clothes, then a pack of cigarettes comes flying into your tent, and now somebody's talking hot breakfast. Thoreau would not approve. We couldn't care less.

Parked in the grass across the road, smack-dab in the middle of the AT footpath so that a hiker breaking into the clearing after his descent from Gooch Gap could have walked into it in the thick fog, was an orange-and-white Volkswagen camper with the legend THE HUNGRY HIKER painted on its sides. David and I, spoons and Sierra cups and Ruth Ann Miner's jar of New York maple syrup in the pockets of our parkas, slapped on the steamed-over windows and clambered aboard. Smells of sizzling sausage and steaming coffee. Thru-Hikers Special $3: hotcakes, syrup, two eggs, link sausage, coffee. *Cream? Sugar? Fried or scrambled?* Old hikers never forget. The year before, in 1983, both Cathy Biondi and Ron Amos (each blond and disgustingly healthy, in their twenties, she from California and he from Tennessee) had walked the entire AT. Their idea for The Hungry Hiker came naturally enough, so she spent the winter in California dehydrating produce while he was back in Tennessee setting up a mail-order business for freeze-dried hikers' food, and now with the season under way they were frantically shuttling the camper from country stores to wherever the AT crosses a navigable road. "We'll follow you all the way to Katahdin," Ron was saying while Cathy frenzied about like a short-order cook, "or as long as we can afford country-store prices and gasoline for the camper."

We emptied our Styrofoam trays quickly, making room in the camper for the Gooch Gap Shelter people now beating their mittens together and breathing steam as they queued up outside the windows, and within fifteen minutes we had dismantled the tent and shouldered our packs and slipped into the woods. The hail and the wind and flecks of snow came almost immediately as we mounted a ridge overlooking a "second-home resort," a place the developers would call "The Ranch" or something like that, and stoically leaned into the weather for the incessant climb to Blood Mountain. In the first mile we climbed 600 feet in elevation.

My feet were taking care of business, plodding along steadily over the granite boulders and the last dead leaves of winter, but as I kept my eyes on the bobbing blue-gray pack of my son just at the edge of visibility some fifty yards ahead of me, my mind was all over the place. The contrition process had begun. This had nothing to do with strapping on a backpack and getting out there to smell flowers and listen to birds ("I came to the mountains to seek the Lord. He inhabits all of Creation" and so forth and so on and please shut up). It had everything to do with the hard clear fact that I, professing to love this boy more than any person or thing in the world, had run out on him when he wasn't even ten years old. *I went to the woods because I wished to live deliberately, to front only the essential facts of life.* Here I was, virtually alone in the woods on this howling miserable day, and the essential facts of my life in regard to my only son were not pretty.

*He's only three or four years old and his mother and I are "separated," as we say, and I'm living in exile at the apartment of a friend who's out of town on business when my old man tracks me down. He goes to the bathroom and when he comes back he says, I thought your buddy Jimmy was too old to be having* girlfriends or is that his daughter's stuff? Oh that, *I say,* well, Pop, that belongs to a friend of mine and if it wasn't for her I'd be going crazy. *He says,* Try to explain that to your son.

Oh, yes, there were the women, all of them there in the name of companionship and understanding, and in some odd old-fashioned way I was always more faithful and attentive and loving to each of them, in their time, than I ever was to the one I was legally obliged to love, honor and obey. Lilly: bright, young, hot-blooded, magazine underling, capable of swallowing somebody with her love, but the sort who's always losing her keys or running out of gasoline. Maggie: could have been a debutante but opted for newspapering, sort of a pug-nosed Scarlett O'Hara, tough and bright and inquisitive and a hell of a catch if you could catch her. Nina: leggy secretary on Music Row in Nashville, best source I had while doing a book there, a giver rather than a taker, Midwestern farm girl who could take care of business (feeling labor pains, about to be an unwed mother, she calmly called the doctor and cranked the car and got herself to the hospital). And Wiregrass: wild-haired, impetuous, old Alabama money, Roaring Twenties, torn between shooting pool with roustabouts or pruning roses for a gentleman husband on Cape Cod.

During that period of my life, when against all odds I pursued the notion that it was possible to be a father and a *de facto* husband and a connoisseur of interesting women at the same time, I'd say I did okay as a father to my son. He was probably only four years old when we started going fishing together. I coached his Little League teams until his retirement, a pure case of burn-out caused by a zealous father, at the age of nine. Now and then he would go along with me on newspaper columns, seeing glimpses of the seamier life, and later when I began to free-lance magazine articles he got to hang out with Merle Haggard on his bus and sat around in a motel room while Pete Rose and some other Cincinnati Reds told baseball stories during spring training in Tampa. I bought him a collie and a bicycle and, when we moved to an island off the coast of Georgia, the basic stuff to take surf fishing. And we talked. I hadn't had much of that as a boy because *my* father, hero to me that he was as the commander of huge gleaming eighteen-wheel rigs, was gone a lot in his work and simply couldn't articulate.

(I should have known, though, that you can't guide a boy into manhood by talking about it. I wrote about that myself, in *The New York Times Magazine*, when David was only seven and I was pondering the matter of fathers and sons for the first time in a piece I called "Me and My Old Man." I wrote that there is no good reason why growing up should take so long. "Maybe one day we will become so sophisticated that we will modernize the whole system of maturing, organize it into an orderly program whereby young boys are weaned away from their childhood fantasies and patiently taught the mechanics of coping and therefore gently delivered into manhood as the grooming of young baseball players for the major leagues is done these days; you know, daily classes on Growing Up, regular weekly seminars with the old man where he speaks with candor about the times he screwed up and how it could have been avoided, and, finally, that ceremonial day of graduation into manhood. . . . Maybe there are some fathers already doing that, but I doubt it. Because it is the nature of fathers to protect the old image, to set themselves up as infallible, and the nature of sons to swallow every bit of it. So growing up must begin with the shattering discovery that one's father is not perfect, a knowledge not easily extracted or believed; and then you have to learn why he is not perfect; and, finally, you are getting somewhere when you determine how he has managed to com-

pensate for this pitiable shortcoming.'' In short, throw 'em
to the wolves.)

And didn't I reject all of them, I was thinking as I
plunged onward and upward in my reverie, choosing to
endure a flailing marriage rather than leave the boy awash
and alone in a sea of women (his mother, two sisters, his
mother's mother, two aunts)? And didn't I take care not to
embarrass his mother, to flaunt the other women, while I
dallied? Quit both Nina and Lilly, in fact, because they
both had sons the age of David and signing on with them
would mean abandoning my four-year-old for somebody
else's four-year-old? Wasn't that worth something?
*Bullshit, you just didn't get caught like many another man
has.* This wasn't contrition, it was an ass-kicking. *God,
the times she called to say she'd changed her mind and I
couldn't see the kids as long as I owed her a penny. Got
drunk and broke the phone.* Henry Gap, 3,100 feet, foot-
steps and a voice from the rear (''Passing on the right'')
as another twenty-year-old zipped past me wearing Adidas
sneakers. *That little sumbitch in Charlotte—what's his
name? the columnist? half-assed critic—he jumps this book,
Christ he must be lying in ambush for Hemphill, I'll kill
him.* Jarred Gap (3,250 feet), Gaddis Mountain, Horsebone
Gap, Turkey Stamp Mountain (3,770). *Dr. Zeb Morgan:
Paul, if you don't quit drinking right now you won't see
fifty.*

At Slaughter Gap, 3,800 feet in elevation and eight
miles out of Woody Gap, I caught up with David. Icicles
were brushed on the bushes and trees now and the brisk
gusts of wind brought threats of snow. From far down in
the valley, around Lake Winfield Scott, there came the
yowling of a dog and, curious for that time of day, the
crowing of a rooster. David had already fetched water
for us from the stream two hundred yards down the side
of the ridge, having read in the guidebook that there
would be no water on Blood Mountain, and when I

dragged into the clearing he was laid out on his pad eating peanut butter with his spoon.

"Starting to wonder why we bothered to bring toilet paper," I said, dropping my pack to the ground and lighting up.

"You, too, hunh?"

"Must be the grain diet. What do you call that?"

"Constipation," he said.

"Naw, you know what I mean. 'Roughage.' That's it."

"Yeah. And my urine's sort of yellow-green. Water tablets, I guess."

"Your mama," I said. "She used to put these things in the toilet bowl, you know, that stuff you color the water with? Made the toilet water look pretty. Well, I didn't know that so one night I stumble in drunk and take a piss and look down at the toilet. That's the first time I thought about giving up booze."

He grinned as though it had happened to him, too, and soon we were off to conquer Blood Mountain. In one mile we ascended eight hundred feet to the summit where the stone two-room enclosed shelter was embraced by ice and fog and light snow. The hiker who had zipped past me in sneakers had chased away a skunk and built a fire before racing on down the mountain for a hot shower at Vogel State Park. David was pumping up the stove for yet another dinner of rice-and-soup when the bunch came in from Gooch Gap. We had covered 12.1 miles that day, not bad in that kind of weather and this early in the trek, and so far there were only mild warnings of blisters for both of us. We slept with our water bottles and boots that night, the thermometer on one hiker's pack reading thirty-two degrees at dark and falling, and by candlelight I read from the log left in the shelter: "Seven weary men ready to head home. . . . One can see the Greatness of the Creator. Peace

of Christ be with you. Men of Universal Christian Out-
reach in Alma, Ohio.'' Mice chewed on one hiker's pigtail
that night.

# 5

THE APPALACHIAN TRAIL LEAVES ITS MARK ON EVERYBODY
it touches, they say, and this was as evident with Jeff and
Dorothy Hansen as with Cathy Biondi and Ron Amos of
The Hungry Hiker. Dorothy, an angular long-haired woman
from the scraggly flatlands of west Florida, walked the entire AT at the age of twenty-two before going on to get a
master's degree in English at the University of Florida
(where she taught under the novelist Harry Crews). Then
she began teaching at the Wolfcreek Wilderness School in
northeast Georgia and soon was married to the director, a
gentle bearish woodsman from Illinois by the name of Jeff
Hansen (his adult life had been spent at outdoor education
in places like Wyoming and Alaska), and nobody was surprised when they took over the operation of a fifty-
year-old mountain lodge right in the middle of the AT:
Walasi-Yi (Cherokee for "where the frog god lives"),
stone-and-timber, another Civilian Conservation Corps relic
from the thirties, a place where the twenty-seven-year-old
couple lived and serviced tourists and hikers and awaited
the birth of their first child in September. The only covered

portion of the entire AT is the dogtrot between the lodge and the annex where the Hansens keep house.

When we awoke at daybreak in the stone blockhouse on Blood Mountain the thermometers read twenty-eight. There had been a dusting of snow during the night but the sun shone brilliantly as we eschewed breakfast and scrambled down the rocky hill, a descent of 1,400 feet in only two miles, for the warmth of Walasi-Yi, where U.S. Highways 19 and 129 converge at Neel Gap. There we would resupply from the cardboard box we had left behind the counter on Monday morning and call home with reports to Susan and to David's mother. I felt elated at this point. "If this is all the trail's got to throw at me," I jabbered to Susan over the phone, "I'll make it all the way. I love it, I truly love it." My old pal Billy Winn, now the publisher and therefore her boss at *Goodlife*, the one who had planted the idea for the trek in my head in the first place, had wondered aloud only that morning if "maybe we shouldn't send out a search party for 'em." There had been a terrible tornado in Newberry, South Carolina, she said, and first reports said as many as a hundred had been killed. The wiring and the insulation on the house had been completed and the ashtrays were still up and the toilet lids down and, yes, it was lonesome. David's mother said the University of the South wanted a $200 reservation fee within fifteen days.

Dorothy Hansen, radiant in her pregnancy, offered to whip up some ham-and-cheese sandwiches for us while I laid out $40 for everything from a toothbrush (I had forgotten mine at home) to ten days' worth of candy bars. I also bought out Jeff Hansen's personal supply of Winston cigarettes ("I know, I know," he said, "after all of that walking you figure you owe yourself *something*"). Then David and I sat and wolfed our sandwiches on the same spot where, only four days earlier, the man from Alabama had announced that he was bored and quitting the trail.

"Now it's really begun," Jeff said.

"Many through-hikers yet?"

"Well, you can't pin 'em down on it."

"How's that?"

"You know. They're afraid to make any promises in case it gets rough and they have to quit. They'll say things like 'We'll see how it goes.' But you can see it in their eyes that they're thinking Katahdin."

"How many so far?" David said.

"Thirty-five, forty. Five or six a day now."

I said, "Do you find yourself making odds?"

"What, on which ones will make it? Nah, it's impossible."

Dorothy had a far-off smile. "It's all on the inside," she said, recollecting her own through-hike. "That's a long, long way to Katahdin. You have no idea until you try it. You forget what month it is sometimes. The physical part's hard enough, but the mental is something else. That's where you've got to be strong."

"What did it mean to you," I said, "making it all alone?"

"I knew I could do anything in the world."

"I should think so."

"But I forgot to finish the sentence," she said. "I should have added 'on my own terms.' See, what happens is, you're doing this all by yourself. You're answering to nobody else. It takes a strong will to do that, sure. But, see, when I finished I went back to college for my master's and I almost lost it. I mean, who were *they* to tell *me* I had to be somewhere at nine o'clock in the morning? I walked the AT, didn't I? The very idea, telling me what to do. The adjustment back to the real world was a very hard thing to do."

We would worry about that when we came to it. Right now we felt confident, even giddy, about our prospects. We had about forty miles of trail behind us, putting us slightly ahead of schedule when you consider a 2 P.M. start on the first day, and there were no blisters and we hadn't squabbled and we had easily endured some quirky weather. *I'll quit the ciggies under controlled circumstances, not out here*, I promised myself as David and I lugged the box and our new goodies outside to the flagstone terrace—Jeff Hansen fancied using the terrace for weekend orgies of Bluegrass music and clog dancing—and messed around for a couple of hours, shirtless in the dazzling midday sun, carefully dividing a cache of food that would sustain us for ten days and one hundred miles to the next planned stop at Wesser in North Carolina. It had been a good idea, to leave the cache at Walasi-Yi so we could travel light on the first four days, and now the forty pounds each of us carried in our packs didn't seem like too much to handle. "What we got to do," David said with some merit, "is eat big the first couple of days."

So we stepped out smartly, no discernible problems, beneath the Walasi-Yi archway and into the woods again. When the sun dropped below the ridges we decided to call it quits for the day and set up camp where the AT brushes up against a twisting new asphalt state road, the Richard B. Russell Scenic Highway, *à la* Woody Gap. While David set up the tent I foraged for dry firewood, chain-smoked Winstons, went through a pack of matches trying to start a campfire, watched the boy do it with one match, waved at the tourists and then, when he had cooked it, gorged myself on rice and mushroom soup. *Well, what the hell, I'm paying for it.*

"Let me try one of those things," he said once I had done my part by scouring the pots and utensils in a suspicious stream near the road, probably full of funny-looking things, and returned to the tent and blazing campfire. I tossed him a Winston.

"Sissy cigarettes," I said. "Camels, now, that's mainlining."

"Yeah. Slower death this way, anyways." Some Yahoos came squealing around the curve in the road and, catching sight of our fire, hurled beer cans our way. A little Friday-night fun for the locals. David said, "Who's this Richard B. Russell? The one they named the road for."

"Georgia senator. Died a few years ago."

"Liberal? Republican?"

"Your basic old-fart Southern demagogue," I said. "Built a career on bringing military bases to Georgia. Teetotaler, bachelor. There's a funny story about how one time he slapped up a memo to his staff up there in Washington. Said something like, 'For those who insist on having cocktails with their lunch, don't drink vodka. When my constituents from south Georgia come up to visit the office I'd rather they'd know you're drunk than think you're crazy.' "

"I don't get it."

"Good."

# 6

SATURDAY MEANS DAY-HIKERS—LOVEBIRDS HOLDING hands and lugging picnic baskets to their secret overlooks, bird-watchers juggling binoculars and paperback field guides as they stalk the elusive *Meleagris gallopavo* (wild turkey) in L.L. Bean's finest, grim unshaven hunters in camouflaged fatigues trying to get there first, Georgia Appalachian Trail Club volunteers marching along the trail in single file with hoes and mattocks for *their* weapons, ethereal grandparents out for a stroll with a kid and an Irish setter, Good Old Boys pissing beer onto flat rocks—and we felt downright heroic as we broke through the traffic on the morning of the last day in March, our sixth day out, already becoming veterans of the forest. A beard was sprouting now and as I scratched it I whistled the "Colonel Bogey March" from *The Bridge on the River Kwai*, Alec Guinness on a roll here, patronizing the civilians malingering along the Road to Katahdin.

David had been walking well ahead of me, as usual, and when the sun was straight overhead and I was beginning to look for the shelter where we had agreed to stop for lunch I was signaled in with the strains of "When the Saints Go Marching In" on his harmonica. It was one of those days—deer, birds, sunshine, plenty of food, good springs, the first green sprigs of spring coming at 3,000 feet—and we took our time to enjoy it. Low Gap Shelter seemed to be a relatively new one and showed few signs of heavy use, being situated between two others only twelve miles apart, so we made it our own. We stripped down to our walking shorts and our bare feet. We napped in the sun. We watched the deer and the juncos and the squirrels cavort amid the barren trees and dry brown leaves of the winter nearly past. We ate anything that struck our fancies, from Snickers to freeze-dried shrimp creole boiled in its pouch, and then we draped our sleeping bags over naked low-hanging tree limbs and watched them air out.

"Can you believe it?" I said. "I wake up this morning and the water bottle I left out of my bag was frozen. And now look. This is like summer."

"Incredible," he said.

"What's that, the Word-of-the-Month?"

"What?"

" 'Incredible.' You're always saying 'incredible.' "

"Beats saying 'wow,' " he said. "Anyways, what's really incredible is the way you pronounce protein. *'Pro*-tyun.' Where'd you get that?"

"Little residue from Harvard. *'Pro-teen'* sounds redneck."

"You been hanging around too many Yuppies," he said.

"Never saw a forty-eight-year-old Yuppie."

"Eat them *'pro*-tyuns' and drive that BMW."

"Incredible," I said, and we laughed and shoveled leaves at each other, and when we paused to watch a startled deer bolt away through the trees we saw the grandparents, the ones with the kid and the Irish setter, standing on the ridge above the shelter with serene smiles on their tired faces. We waved at them and they waved back before summoning the kid and the dog for the four-mile walk back to the parking area where they would get in their car and try to make it home before dark. In due time the boy and I gathered up our things and got back on the trail and pressed forward to the shelter where we intended to spend the night. Again David burst ahead of me and was out of sight within ten minutes.

On paper the walk between Low Gap and Rocky Knob shelters looks simple enough. The maps and the guidebooks show the distance as 6.8 miles and the profile of the trail itself promises a slow and gradual ascent of less than 1,000 feet. A lot of people at the Appalachian Trail Conference in Harpers Ferry, West Virginia, have spent a lot of time over a lot of years writing and editing and updating the detailed ten-book pocket-sized $144 set known as the Appalachian Trail Guide. The books are worth having along, for the most part, because now and then they will even throw in a little history along with distances and elevations and the locations of shelters and springs and side trails and points of interest. To wit, for the northbound hiker on the southern portion of the AT in the Smokies: "Reach Ekaneetlee Gap (3,842 ft.). (Through here, old Egwanulti Gap, passed early Cherokee route crossing mountains from valley towns to overhill towns. Primitive trail to left, brushed out in 1970, leads 5.8 mi. to Cades Cove. *Water* is found 100 yd. down Tenn. slope.) Ascend steeply from Ekaneetlee Gap for 0.3 mi. on narrow trail. Beyond, ascend gradually along open ridge through sparse timber on wide trail." All of which is fine and good and informative, if you have the time to stop and revel at every crook in the trail, but the sad fact is that there is no way any guide can warn you about the footpath itself at any given time.

I began to want my $144 back and to curse the Trail Guide as dusk approached and I found myself little more than a mile from Rocky Knob Shelter. "Continue through

thick woods passing several slides," the guidebook promised, but what I read wasn't what I was seeing. *Maybe
there was a storm, an avalanche, bad rain.* The footpath
was littered with rocks of all sizes, slippery with moss, and
I had to negotiate it one step at a time. It was level, all
right, just like the guidebook said, but an 800-foot ascent
over half a mile would be preferable to this as long as there
was sure footing. Stumbling, slipping, cursing, resting, it
took an hour for me to cover the mile to the shelter.

"I was about to come looking for you," David said.
Dark was falling fast and the temperature was headed toward freezing but he was still in his hiking shorts, sort of
showing off for the Weekend Warriors, standing around a
blazing fire with four others.

"Tomorrow *you* carry the goddam guidebook," I said.

"You lose the trail?"

"Wish I had. My knees are killing me. I got problems."

"The rocks, huh?"

"The rocks. Trail Guide didn't say anything about the
rocks."

One of the others said, "Call it the Appalachian *Trial*
Guide."

"What? Who're you?"

"John Harper, Paul. From Atlanta. Used to read your
write-ups in the paper." We shook hands. "Naw, last year
I learned pretty quick you can't count on them books. Why
I call it the 'Trial Guide.' Trial and error."

"Say you walked the AT last year?" I asked him.

"Part of it."

"How much?"

"First thirty-eight miles. Trial Guide didn't tell me I was
gonna freeze my ass off at Vogel."

The shaky knees would soon be forgotten in the company of John ("Slow Joe" in the shelter logs) Harper and
the other three hikers. The others were weekenders up from
Macon in the flatlands of middle Georgia: an affable forty-

ish bank executive named Tom; his stout wife, Linda, a
part-time baseball umpire; and a female college professor
referred to as "Dr. Beverly." In a couple of weeks Dr.
Beverly would be chaperoning twenty-two girls from Wes-
leyan College on a weekend study-hike of the north Georgia mountains and this was her way of preparing for it.
Before David and I had embarked it had been my idea to
stay away from the shelters except in the most severe
weather, but now, hanging around a roaring fire with a
convivial group after a dull day of moving alone through
the woods, I was reassessing my position. Shelter life
wasn't that bad, I found, especially when your companions
know baseball and have all sorts of wonders in their packs
that a through-hiker can't afford to lug. Steaks. Cherry tarts.
Coffee. Cokes. Cheez Balls.

"Thing I'm gonna miss the most is baseball season," I
said to Tom when David and I had finished our usual dinner of rice-and-soup and accepted a tart and coffee for dessert.

"Braves open Tuesday night against Philly," he said.

"Pascual Perez. He still in jail?"

"Probably *under* it. You know the Dominican Republic."

"Why the hell the Braves let that happen I'll never
know."

"Makes three straight winters he's gotten in trouble."

"They oughta make him stay in Atlanta, or else give
him a bodyguard. We're talking about a million-dollar
pitcher here."

So we were in agreement on the essential matters of life,
this Tom and I, and soon I felt I was back home at Manuel's Tavern laying odds on the Atlanta Braves' chances in
the National League West. Tomorrow would be the forty-
fifth birthday of Phil Niekro, the indefatigable knuckle-
baller unceremoniously released by the Braves and quickly
picked up by the Yankees, and for the sake of all middle-

aged men in America we hoped he was leading the world in everything by the All-Star break in July. I told Tom how I'd hung out with Niekro one time, for a magazine piece, and that one theory he had about baseball seemed to apply to what I was trying to do with my own life these days. "He kept talking about 'the one sixty-two,' " I said. "The baseball season, a hundred and sixty-two games. Some you win, some you lose, but it's the long haul that counts. So I'm into this for the long haul. Niekro's become the patron saint of us old farts. May he prosper."

Linda and Dr. Beverly excused themselves and walked with flashlights down the ridge to a flat space where they had pitched their gold geodesic tent. The wind was up now, spiraling hot orange embers from the fire into the black sky, and a thermometer on John Harper's pack showed the temperature at thirty degrees. Soon we were all zipped up tight in our sleeping bags, safe from the howling cold wind, aimlessly mumbling bad jokes and commentaries and observations which carried all of us back to when we were ten-year-old Cub Scouts on our first night in the woods.

"Not having any trouble with the women, are you?" Harper said.

"No," Tom said. "Am I supposed to?"

"Old boy told me they attract bears."

"That right?"

"What he said."

"Better not let my wife Linda hear you say that."

Slow Joe said, "Think it's when they're having their period. Smell attracts 'em. Old boy told me that last year."

Following the discussion, I said, "What happened last year?"

"Cold drove me off at Vogel, like I said." Harper said he was "twenty-nine going on fifty," a cabinetmaker, lived with his mother in an old neighborhood south of Atlanta near Fort McPherson, five-nine and 230 pounds, had a little trouble on the uphills but was "like a runaway bear on the downhills," scrounged all of his equipment from the house and at war-surplus stores ("Don't have much of that fancy catalogue stuff you and Dave got"), lucky to have a boss who lets him take off to walk the AT whenever he wants to ("Mama just tells everybody, 'John's gone camping' ") and he figures to keep on trying until he hikes the entire trail from Springer to Katahdin. "Sure would boost the old confidence if I could do that. Maybe you could get something in the papers if I did." The last I recall, he was saying he'd forgotten to pour some Irish whiskey into his canteen before he left home but he understood some moonshiners had set up a stand beside the trail up in Tennessee and he could wait.

# 7

SUNDAY IN AMERICA. IF THE RUSSIANS ARE SERIOUS THEY ought to do it on a Sunday morning—let the SAMs and the MIRVs and the ICBMs and the other stuff fly—because on Sunday morning America is preoccupied with celebrating itself. *This is the day we wash our cars, wash our cars, wash our cars* I sang to myself as we chirped farewell and accepted goodies from the weekenders—canned tuna, Cheez Balls, potato chips, whatever they had left—and trudged northward like true through-hikers. Sunday. April Fools' Day. Phil Niekro's forty-fifth birthday. About time to look up and down Alta Avenue, standing there in my pajamas, and be sure the coast is clear for a burst onto the lawn to grab the bulky Sunday editions of the *Atlanta Journal-Constitution* and *The New York Times*; to go inside and make the coffee and then hunker over the news of the week. *Fair to partly cloudy along the coast. Trouble in Nicaragua and Afghanistan, too. Braves lose. Divorce rate up. Obligatory men-from-Mars April Fools' Day story in college newspapers.*

Out there, though, there was no delivery of the Sunday

*Times* in a neat blue plastic bag; only some blue-black bear droppings and a soggy Appalachian Trail Data Book showing what lay between us now at Rocky Knob Shelter and the next resting place. "Absolutely beautiful day in which we made only 8.7 miles," my journal would read. "Many stops, it's so good, and both dead on our legs from climb over rocks at last shelter. Tough stretch between Rocky Knob and Montray shelters, up and down from 3,000 to 4,000 over two rugged climbs. At noon, getting up from break under trees beside a forest road, battered muddy white Fairlane comes belching and sliding to stop. . . ."

They were upon us before we knew it. David and I were talking about how even when you're walking in the woods you're still in a "Sunday mood" when the clatter began.

"Hey, cap'n, hold on there. . . . Wanta talk with y'all. . . . Just hold it right there, honey. . . ." My first thought was of James Dickey's novel *Deliverance*, where the adventurers from Atlanta are jumped (and one of them is sodomized) by rednecks in the Southern Appalachians of this very part of Georgia. The woman at the wheel of the car had no teeth left and was terminally fat. The two fellows spilling from the backseats of the wasted Fairlane Ford were quintessential Good Old Boys—scrawny unkempt punks, all baseball caps and bones and unbuttoned flannel shirts and jeans, Budweisers at noon—and we froze. David had the good sense to turn his left ear toward me. The left ear held his gold earring.

"Where hell y'all goin'?" one of them said.

"Out walking," I said.

"All that shit? I said where you goin'?"

"Maine."

"Where the fuck's Maine?"

"Long way from here."

"How far?"

David said, "We ought to get there in August."

"You hear that, Wayne? The boy here says they gon'

walk from here to August.'' They stumbled toward us and found rest against the pine trees. David and I, buying time and trying to feel it out, cinched packs. The boy wiped off his snow glasses and I made sure they saw that my right eyetooth was missing. *Just like y'all, got bad teeth, just trying to get along.* I pulled the bandanna from my forehead and took it to my face and blew my nose with a blast. It was a face-off.

"Wanna beer?" said the fellow named Wayne.

"Naw," I said, "thank you."

"How 'bout you, boy?"

"I'm all right," said David.

"Hunh." I took a good grip on my walking stick. The sun was blazing. The hag in the car broke the Appalachian quiet with a burp on the horn—*mwaaarrkkkk*—and the man who had begun the talking said, "What you doing up here?"

"I told you," I said. "Walking to Maine."

"Now who the hell would do that?"

"That's what we've been asking."

"What you eatin'?"

"Rice."

"That all?"

"Nah," I said, "we put shit on it."

"Kinda shit?"

"Mushroom soup. Other stuff."

"Goddam," he said. "Mushroom soup and rice. You hear that, Wayne? Cap'n and the boy, going to Maine on rice."

Wayne began babbling. "Where's the beef? Where's the beef?"

"What I say. Where's the beef? Where's the beef?"

I said, "I thought I wouldn't have to hear that again for five months."

"*Where's* the beef?" Wayne said. "Where's the *beef*"

"Your buddy's funny."

"Wayne's drunk, wanna know the truth. So'm I. So what?"

"Sounds like a pretty good idea to me."

"What you mean by that? You makin' fun of me and Wayne?"

"Naw, naw," I said.

"Fancy outfits. Boy in them sunglasses. Out walkin' around. Goin' to *Maine*." He raised his neck and drained the beer and then, red-eyed, nastily threw the aluminum can across the dusty road into a clump of scrawny pines. "Where do y'all shit?"

"Bushes."

"Just drop your drawers and shit?"

"That's about it."

"Hear that, Wayne?"

*Where's the beef*? rang out and echoed through the hollows at Indian Grave Gap (3,113 feet) as we crossed the road where the Fairlane sat smoldering in the dust and leaned forward to make the steady ascent through the jungle of rhododendron and laurel and galax, those calm and plushy beds of galax there since the dawn of man, to the high rocky slopes of Tray Mountain. *Where's the beef*? indeed. We were free at last of Good Old Boys and automobiles that hardly work, and civilization as we knew it, and it was quite all right when we found John (Slow Joe) Harper waiting as we glided into the shelter with the sun still hanging high. "Sponge bath from spring, wash johns, do housekeeping," I wrote in the journal. "Dave greases boots, I wash all pots after meal, burn paper, even see if can name all characters in novel, Dave shaping frame of pack, Harper telling of Britisher who already walked trail but this time has close-up lens for flowers."

David said, "Where's the beef?"

"Clayton, Georgia," I said. "Hardee's."

"Thought I'd check to see if you're paying attention."

"Maybe tomorrow," I said.

"I want a hamburger real bad."

"Me, too. Character defect."

The kid leaned forward to light the Peak I stove. He would boil water for the hot cocoa that would put us to sleep. Above his head was a hand-carved sign that said THOR HEYERDAHL WAS HERE IN SEARCH OF HIS ROOTS. At night, burrowed deep in my sleeping bag, I heard the owls and I heard the jets again making their final approach to the airport in Atlanta.

## 8

DAVID SHOOK ME AWAKE AT DAWN, THE NIKON DANgling from his neck, to tell me he had gotten some good photographs of the sunrise. "Incredible," he said, and I said I would take his word for it this time. John Harper was gone. Ahead of us, according to the "Trial Guide," was a workmanlike stretch of eleven up-anddown miles until we reached U.S. Highway 76. Nineteen miles east of that, from the picnic area where the AT crossed the highway, was Clayton, Georgia, a wide place on US 441. Home of a Hardee's. *Where's the beef?*

We reached the highway at four o'clock in the afternoon and stood beside the road for two hours, taking turns at hitching a ride, until a fellow in a bleached white Toyota pickup screeched on the two-lane blacktop and U-turned and offered a ride. He was a free-lance tree surgeon headed for Newberry, South Carolina, where the tornado had struck—"I'm Bubba, dog's Sheba"—and we piled into the back with the awesome malamute and ladders and dirty clothes and fast-food wrappers for the twisting ride through the rain and wind to Hardee's in town. "Lotta trees on the

ground and I figure somebody's gotta pick 'em up,'' Bubba
said. He joined us for dinner. Burgers, shakes, fries, cherry
tarts and let's do it again.

By nightfall we would wonder how it was going up
there in the hills with John Harper and the others, of
course, but there would be time enough for that. Soon
our $30.04 room at the Heart of Rabun Motel was a clut-
ter of smelly socks and muddy boots and crinkled wrappers. While David luxuriated in his first hot bath in a
week I called Susan at home in Atlanta with a report and
then mindlessly read the Clayton *Tribune* (for $11,000
you could have a dilapidated barn on one acre with a
stream; Rabun County High had a new basketball coach
but first they had to find his wife a job). David emerged
from the bath and immediately flopped out on the bed in
a deep sleep. And I, after draping a steaming towel over
a right knee that was beginning to ache from the walk
over the rocks to Rocky Knob Shelter, trimmed my beard
and doctored some blisters with moleskin and bought a
Coke and a pack of Camels from a machine and sat down
to write my first letter home from the trail. With Houston
and Georgetown, live from Seattle, having it out for the
college basketball championship on the color television
set.

Susan.

I'm starting this at the motel in Clayton and will
mail it from Wesser, North Carolina, along with some
film. The slides, if good, can say more than I about
what we've seen in the way of weather. What you
really should see, though, is my notes. I'll be mailing
this first notebook when it's full.

We're well, mentally and physically. I'm sitting
in the room at 11:30, David asleep, with a hot towel
across my knee. We have no strange scratches or
blisters that moleskin can't cover and our bodies

are weary but working properly. I have no doubt
that we'll make Katahdin because, unlike many of
the hikers we've seen, we're prepared. I'm amazed
at how many have come from California or the East,
thinking the AT a "super experience," but show
up wearing Nikes. (A lot of them can't spell "Katahdin" yet.) David did a hell of a job preparing.
The boy is terrific: patient, cool, tough, adult. For
the first few days I waited for an explosion—a 19-
year-old snit like the one he had over my choice of
socks—but he's been a cool combat officer, so far,
patiently leading the rookie. Not that I've been bad
at all. A little slow, yes, but I'm a damaged 48 glad
to be alive. He knows it, I think, and is showing
some surprise and pride. I'm sure he knows, from
his friends, how rare this father-and-son expedition
is.

I scribble in this book when I can—at rest stops
(10 minutes each hour) or lunch or at twilight—and
already there are eight of these pages front and back.
While I walk, to forget the sheer drudgery or hurting
and sweating and watching for rocks and snakes, I
think the wildest thoughts. Two days ago I began
trying to read the novel back to myself and listing all
of the players. Yesterday I made plans to buy a beautiful suit in the fall with 6 bow ties to go with it.
Today I saw you and me taking Martha more places
like Piedmont Park for picnics and kite-flying. And
always I think of you and *qui a racheté une génération perdue*. I'm alive. I'm doing this. I love you
and I haven't told you enough.

ME AND THE BOY sounds good, I think, and if
Macmillan will bear with me it can be an important
work. I haven't had any real surprises there, either,
except that now I'm out here gathering the things I
knew were here. I spend a lot of time at contrition—

the booze, the kids, pushing you to the limit, letting my career go on hold while I had another laugh—and I reckon this is a good place for it; where I can do it on my own time. What I'm doing here is major repairs on a once-promising machine. So. I will write about it all and hope Mr. Thoreau likes it. I'm writing for everybody who nearly blew it.

What I want when I finish is two successful books—both ways, money and critics, back-to-back—and with it the sureness and financial peace I've never had. I want to never worry about money. I want a solid old brick house in Decatur, if you still do, and such simple things as a car that works. And I want for grand windows to open up for Martha and my other three. And, most of all, for us to love each other more and more; to the extent that it almost boggles our friends. I do believe it is up to me, stumbling toward Maine with my son the mirror, and thus I walk. Simple.

Somewhere, in all of this contrition I've told you about, I got to thinking about the long letter I got before we left from the friend who got his law degree in the morning and swore in with the Marines in the afternoon. I wish I had the letter with me, but I can paraphrase that he said something like, "You're going to be the same man when you finish the trail except you're going to know yourself better in relationship to other men." And I think about the conclusions of the clinical psychologist who more or less said that foggy poets are best suited to try the AT. And then, putting those two together, I figure it out—not hard to do, with twenty-five years' experience—that in relation to other men I'm a foggy poet. That, too, is quite simple. The problem is that I'm beginning to ask myself too often these days why the hell I bother to keep on at being a writer. Sometimes, seeing a lot of my friends drop out and go TV or PR because they get tired of banging their heads against the wall while nobody listens (i.e., buys their books), I get lonesome. I feel like an Apache trapped in a box canyon with one arrow left. Maybe that's why I listen so often to Kristofferson's "The Pilgrim" and "To Beat the Devil" and to that song "Vincent."

I do run on. It's after midnight, still Clayton, and Dave has slept since his bath at 8. Laundromat was closed. I've had 5 Cokes and a dozen Camels and I can't sleep. Knee is better from the steaming towels. We'll just get up when we get up and proceed. I do want to know about the novel. Already I want it back, of course, but I must have the next advance so David and Lisa can continue college. I'm sure Sterling will advance me some of the next money the minute we finish the trail. If ever there was a time for us to say to creditors, "It's in the mail," this is it.

I've never had a fleeting thought of aborting. I'm beginning to thrive on this. I've pushed myself through pain I didn't know I could endure. This, following the crash job I did on the novel, has reminded me of patience and endurance. I feel like Father Courage himself.

There was a blue bruise on my hip bone, I noticed, where the pack had been riding for nearly eighty miles. It was well past two o'clock in the morning and David hadn't stirred in six hours. Georgetown's goons had beaten Houston's goons for the college basketball championship, I saw, and now there was an old movie on the television set. When I snapped it off there was only the buzz of the neon sign outside the door of the motel room, and light snoring from David's bed, and there was also the sound of rain.

# 9

THE DAY BROKE GLOOMY AND DANK, SHOWING LITTLE promise of getting better, and when I awoke at 6:30 I gathered up all of our dirty clothes and hustled through the rain to the laundromat across the street from the motel. David was awake when I returned, aimlessly watching the "Today Show" and trying to orient himself after a dead-heap sleep of twelve hours, and without saying a word we slipped into clean dry clothes and darted under the eaves to the motel coffee shop for what we had been dreaming of for a week: hotcakes, syrup, butter, eggs, grits, toast, juice, real coffee made in a machine.

This was Rabun County, the most northeasterly of Georgia's I59 counties, and I had fallen under its influence twenty years earlier when I first moved to Atlanta as a daily columnist for the newspapers. Rabun County was pure primitive Southern Appalachia, for better or for worse, a ragged scar fraught with chicken houses and trout streams and whiskey stills and tilting 150-year-old log cabins. Electricity didn't come to some of the hollows of Rabun Gap until the late forties; a writer named Lillian Smith wrote a

racially liberal novel entitled *Strange Fruit* in an isolated
house on the ridge overlooking this same Heart of Rabun
Motel, back in the forties, but all the Rabunites remember
about her and the novel is that she lived in the house alone
with another woman; the county is the home of "Foxfire,"
the celebrated oral-history program of books and tapes in-
spired by a young teacher named Eliot Wigginton at the
Rabun Gap-Nacoochee School; the natives were both proud
and angry that James Dickey's *Deliverance*, the novel and
the movie, was based in these parts; another time a bunch
of Good Old Boys lollygagged around a cigar-smoke room
high above Clayton, on the second floor of the Heart of
Rabun Motel, entertaining pleas from some wimpy Hollywood movie producer whose Lancia Flaminia was simmering on the concrete parking lot below (he wore a pith
helmet and a silk ascot), and when the producer tried to
explain that the only way they could promise the starring
role in *There's a Still on the Hill* to Slim Pickens was to
pay in advance there came this response from a moonshine-
millionaire who had been pondering the situation and snap-
ping a rubber band around a huge wad of hundred-dollar
bills: "If I'm gonna buy a heifer, I get to see the heifer
first."

*Winter of 1969, in a hollow of Rabun County known
as "Tate City," where William Arthur Young and
his wife live in a 170-year-old cabin featuring a one-
hole toilet astride a stream where once you could
catch trout. The Appalachian Trail runs along the
ridge above the cabin. Arthur Young is called
"Mayor of Tate City," a vague mile from the Georgia-North Carolina line, and his enthusiasm these
days is reserved for making some 'shine and playing
some fiddle and listening to the Grand Ole Opry over
a battery-operated radio hanging from a nail on the
porch. Apollo 8 has just circled the moon and we*

*have seen an astronaut walk down a ladder to take
"a giant step for mankind" on the moon. Mrs. William Arthur Young isn't buying any of it.* Lemme ask
you something, *she says.* If they was gonna put men
on the moon, how come it don't say nothing about it
in the Bible?

David was destroying a stack of hotcakes and I was
reading in the Atlanta paper about how the Braves would
open the season that night in Philadelphia against the
Phillies—Phil Niekro, the old man, would be the Yankees' opening-day pitcher—when my breakfast came. I
was tearing into it when, forkful of grits at eye level, I
spied Frank Rickman sitting at a table with a group of
men wearing Red Man Chewing Tobacco caps and oil-spattered green uniforms. *That's the way to go, Frank,* I
thought. Frank Rickman grew up in these parts and did
his share of scrambling for a living, like the rest of them
in Rabun County, but when some *real* Hollywood types
started coming around he got smart. He hired himself
out as a consultant for the filming of *Deliverance* (it was
Frank who flushed out most of the locals who played in
the movie) and caught the drift that soon people would
be "discovering" his home county. Now Frank Rickman, having sold a lot of "antique" plows and automobiles and mountain acreage in the past ten years, sat at
breakfast in the coffee shop of the Heart of Rabun Motel
in the company of men who still worked on carburetors.
His swept-back silver hair and mustache and mutton-chop
sideburns, which he tended carefully with his manicured
fingernails, gave one the idea that he had also spent some
time in the company of Burt Reynolds.

"Remember that banjo-picker from *Deliverance*?" I
asked for a coffee refill. "Inbred kid. One that sat on the
porch and played 'Dueling Banjos'?"

"Sure," David said. "Crazy kid."

"Fellow over there discovered him."

"This where they did *Deliverance*?"

"What I told you Sunday when those drunks jumped us."

"They didn't exactly *jump* us," he said.

"I notice you didn't let 'em see your earring."

"Score one for the old man."

"Well, anyway," I said, "that's not a bad way to go. Frank Rickman's got it made now. He figured out a way to make a living where he wants to live. If I get some kind of a movie deal out of the novel or something I might be giving him a call. Might become writer-in-residence of Rabun County. Five acres and a shack ought to do it."

"Let me know if you need somebody to chop firewood."

"You'll be the first to know."

The coffee shop and the motel and the laundromat and a hot breakfast and the morning's *Atlanta Constitution* and color television and talk of retirement in the mountains were a long way from the stark reality of the Appalachian Trail. Now we had to get back to it. Somewhere up there on the ridges above Clayton, army-surplus boots squishing and his mama's dented old cook-pots clattering, John (Slow Joe) Harper was lurching ahead toward Katahdin. Here we were, at the beginning of our ninth day with only seventy-eight miles behind us, paying the tab for our luxuries and inquiring about how we might hitch a ride back to the point, nineteen miles west of town, where the AT crosses U.S. 76. "If it was good weather and people was taking their boats out to [Lake] Hiawassee you wouldn't have no trouble," the woman at the desk said, "but I don't know about today." We were hanging around the lobby, pondering our next move, when a fellow in a windbreaker and a Braves cap said he had a pickup truck and for ten bucks he would take us back to the AT. He had been sitting at the table with Frank Rickman. His name was Kenneth Keener.

Within an hour we had slung our stuff in the bed of the pickup and made a run on the grocery store for provisions we hoped would take us seventy more miles to Wesser, North Carolina, and were on our way in a driving rain in Kenneth Keener's '55 Ford. He once owned a '54 Ford, he said with some pride, but "some drunk totaled it" and this '55 model was part of the restitution. "Windshield wipers ain't quite right yet, but the motor's okay so far." He was forty-eight, he said, *my age*, and he still lived in the house where he was born (on Warwoman Road, three blocks behind the Heart of Rabun Motel, "with my mama 'n' them") and most days he could be found hanging out at the Clayton fire station.

"You a fireman?"

"Sort of," he said.

"What's that mean?"

"They need help, I help 'em." Kenneth Keener was an amiable fellow, content to stay right there at the fire station in his hometown of 1,800 people, just sort of hanging around and doing what was necessary, he said. "Sometimes we go out in a helicopter looking for forest fires. About the high point in my life came when we went to Atlanta to pick up the new chopper and they let me fly it all the way back up here to Clayton. I wadn't supposed to tell anybody about that. But I tell you, that's pretty scary." The windshield wipers were doing no good at all. He leaned forward in the cab of the truck and tugged the bill of his Braves cap over his eyebrows, to tunnel his vision through the slashing rainstorm, and told a story from the days he ran an Emergency Medical Service ambulance in the mountains: "There was this little old woman and everybody knew she ran moonshine and one night she lost her car on one of these curves, right along here on 76, and when we got there she was out in

a ditch upside down. Well, we found her with our flashlights and we heard her. 'Don't worry 'bout me,' she
kept yelling, 'just hide the stuff somewhere.' We didn't
call the troopers or anybody until we'd hid the twenty-
four jugs of whiskey in the bushes and turned the car
rightside up and got her out of there. Troopers never did
find anything.''

I said, ''Frank Rickman seems to be doing okay.''

''Oh, yeah. Brought a little touch of Hollywood to Clayton.''

''William Arthur Young. You know him?''

''Hell, everybody knows Arthur. Mayor of Tate City.''

''He still up there in the hollows?''

''Nah. He and his wife, they live in a project now.''

''In Clayton?''

''Yeah. Just got too feeble to live out there alone.''

''Here we go,'' I said, ''where those picnic tables
are.'' Kenneth Keener tapped the brakes on the pickup,
turn signal blinking for nobody's advisement, and eased
onto the gravel turnaround where a sign on a four-by-
four post indicated the crossing of the AT. When I
handed him a crinkled ten-dollar bill he asked, as though
he really wanted to know, ''How come you and the boy
are doing this?'' I mumbled something about fathers-and-
sons, or challenges, or whatever. I forget. ''Send me a
postcard from up the road somewhere,'' he said, and I
promised, and I slammed the door and it was quiet again.

The rain never abated that day as we trudged upward
nearly 1,500 feet in less than nine miles. It was weather
not fit for birds and deer and squirrels and, most of all,
people. We plunged ahead, wondering if we hadn't had
our minds bent already by a glut of hamburgers and television and cushy motel beds. It was so dark when we
finally stumbled into Bly Gap, where there is only a
gnarled ancient oak in a clearing at 3,840 feet, that we

simply pitched the tent under a canopy of rhododendron and flopped asleep in the black night without a good night.

# 10

MAYBE IT'S ONLY A DREAM THAT A FATHER AND HIS SON, separated by divorce for the ten most important growing-up years of the boy's life, can abruptly pick up where they left off and resume their lives together. Too much happens to each in his own time, out of earshot of the other, and when they are suddenly reunited there is too much ground to be covered—too much background to be explained—for there to be any basis for understanding. It was too long a story, for example, for me to begin telling David just why it was that I found his mother lacking and decided to leave her. It would take him a long time, similarly, to tell me why he pulled into a shell after I ran away from home and took to fishing alone in a polluted creek near his school until dark came and he ambled on home with no good excuse. Before the doctor starts, you have to tell him where it hurts.

When I peeled my eyes open in the morning fog, wincing and cursing and reaching toward my aching knee, David was waiting for me. I guess I knew it was going to happen sooner or later.

"You shouldn't have put hot stuff on it," he said.

"Seemed like a good idea at the time."

"Hot stuff makes it swell."

"Goddam *walking* makes it swell."

"You put cold stuff on it when it's swelling up."

"Right, doctor."

"Makes the swelling go down," he said.

"You told me that."

"I thought everybody knew that."

"Don't be a smart-ass, David."

"And don't call her 'Alabama Fats,' " he said. "That's my mother."

"Christ Dave what is this? That was two years ago. You must have had a hell of a dream."

"Nightmare's more like it."

"I apologized when I said it. Jesus. Two years this summer."

"Yeah, but you're still thinking it about her."

*This is the summer of '82, when he is seventeen, and it is our first real time together since the divorce. We have been sitting side by side in the '70 Olds for nearly 5,000 miles now, from Alabama to Colorado and back, following the trail of the Arkansas River for the* Reader's Digest. *I'm drinking and he's driving through the suffocating July heat of Arkansas and Kansas and Colorado, seeing a rodeo here and catching some trout there, but on the last night of the journey we are frazzled. We're in a ratty motel room in Mississippi and I'm sloshing Scotch and opining that we all have our vices.* Take North Alabama Fats, for instance. *He snaps his head and tightens his jaw and says,* That's my mother you're talking about, *and I know that no apology will repair the damage. I'm sort of proud of him, though.*

"I don't think I'd better be touching that right now," I said. Somberly, we wiggled out of the tent and slogged through the mire in search of the springs we knew were there but had been unable to find in the foggy dark of the night before. The tent had been raised so haphazardly that nearly everything we had was soaking wet. The weather at 4,000 feet was not the sort they advertise in the outdoor-equipment ads—dank, cold, overcast, windy—and we knew better than to dwell on the comforts of the Heart of Rabun Motel down below us in Clayton. *Kenneth Keener's probably using my ten bucks to buy himself a breakfast* was my fleeting thought as David cranked up the Peak I and we silently gobbled steaming oatmeal in the drizzle. We finished eating and quickly packed everything and soon, after agreeing to meet for lunch only 3.2 miles away at the Muskrat Creek Shelter, we officially left Georgia and stepped into North Carolina.

*One state down, thirteen to go* wasn't an altogether comforting thought to me as I mounted a ridge, peering through the fog for the white blazes, and leaned forward into a climb that rose nearly 1,000 feet in the next mile. Days like that, I had learned pretty fast, are made for walking. You tighten up all of the cinches and zip up the rain gear and press forward because on days like that, to the untried eye, not even the animals are out moving around. *Thoreau, now, he'd see a teeming metropolis full of goings-on beneath all of this; but all I can see is molding leaves and slippery moss perhaps camouflaging the one round and smooth softball-sized rock that's going to break my ankle and end this adventure on the spot.* I couldn't dwell on the fact that Katahdin sat waiting for me; got all the time in the world, been there forever, 2,000 miles ahead. It was wiser to note that tomorrow, around lunchtime, we would hit the 100-mile mark on the trail. *Not bad,* I had to convince myself, *for somebody who was supposed to be dead.*

Now I had reached the ridge crest above Courthouse Bald, sweating but not hurting, time for the fierce little downhill into Sassafras Gap. It was the downhills that made the knee feel as though it would come unhinged. I was glad now that I had chosen to bring along the seven-foot walking staff. *My rod and my staff it comforts me, it keeps me from falling on my ass.* What was the apocryphal story from Vietnam about the guerrilla who ran down the Ho Chi Minh Trail for a month, trotting through the jungle, dodging 500-pound bombs and ambushes and tigers and malaria-carrying mosquitoes, lugging a fifty-pound shell all the way; finally delivering the shell with a grin; being told by the artillery commander, "Good, now go back and get another one." *Hell, it probably happened all the time if I know the Viet Cong.* And the Cherokees. What about the Cherokees? This very moment there was a relay team running through these very hills—descendants of the ones who evaded the Trail of Tears death march 150 years earlier—carrying a torch all the way to Oklahoma so the white man doesn't forget. And they didn't use American Express Cards at Blue Ridge Mountain Sports, either, in order to outfit themselves for the outing. *Outfit themselves for the outing. Got a nice ring to it.*

It occurred to me for the first time that I was asking too much of David, and of myself, on this trek. The scenario, on the face of it, was pure and simple enough; even Mom/Pop/Apple Pie/All-American as we knew those terms in the 1980s: forty-eight-year-old father and nineteen-year-old son, estranged by divorce for ten years, try to get to know each other by attempting six months' expedition of 2,142 rugged mountain miles over spine of world's longest blazed continuous backpacking trail. Everybody thought it was a hell of an idea. "You're going to get very tired," said my agent, my surrogate father, Sterling Lord, before sticking it to the publishers in New York (*You don't get the hiking*

*book unless you take the nove*l). "You want to write a book
about fathers and sons, why don't y'all just stay home and
interview each other? I wouldn't spend the night in my
backyard," said Pat Conroy, my pal, the novelist. "You
*are* going to carry guns, aren't you?" said another friend.
"It is a wise father that knows his own child," said Shakespeare. "It's got all the elements," said the book editor
we finally found: "the Appalachian Trail, fathers and sons,
people along the way, conservation, everything." The walk
was a commodity.

But now, out there actually *doing* it, the trek had become something much larger than a charming tale to be
offered for sale in bookstores across America or, God
forbid, as an entertainment on the "Tonight Show Starring Johnny Carson" (. . . *and also*, I could hear Ed
McMahon saying, *Appalachian Trail hikers Paul and
David Hemphill*!!!). It really had become Me and the
Boy. The joke was on me. It really was a hell of an
idea—a father and his son, walking and sleeping under
Nature together for half a year, struggling to reacquaint
as they struggled through the brambles, the long uphill
search for Katahdin a fine literary device for parent-
hood—but only now, as we approached the first hundred-
mile landmark, did I fully understand what I had gotten
myself into. The reading of Thoreau and the outfitting at
Blue Ridge Mountain Sports and the knee bends/push-
ups/sit-ups and all of those other preparations (talks with
other hikers, perusals of the ten-set Appalachian Trail
Guide, practicing with the Nikon, run-throughs in the
backyard with the tent and the stove and the packs and
the sleeping bags) were of the trail but not of us. It became more than a walk through the woods when my son
asked me why I had run out on his mother nearly a dec-
ade earlier.

We had gotten lost from each other. It's easy to lose
track of time and mileage when you're stumbling through

a wet forest, body aching and mind wandering and eyes aware only of fuzzy white blazes dimly seen on a tree a football field ahead atop the next ridge (*Oh, shit, not another hill*), but I was certain that I had gone beyond the shelter where we had agreed to rendezvous for lunch. *He's either farther ahead of me than usual*, I thought, *or else he really got pissed this morning.* The hiking had been fierce. "Rocks, vines, creeks, rain, fog," I would record in my journal. "I miss unmarked shelter, walk past it four miles to Deep Gap. White Chevy with Illinois tags, family picnicking in fog, wonder why, sign says only 0.8 to Standing Indian Shelter. Knee killing me now. Wait an hour for Dave, go to shelter. . . ."

As soon as I had topped the hill and spied the blessed bluish corrugated-tin roof of the Standing Indian Shelter I heard myself being paged. "Your name's Paul, right?" A rakish-looking fellow, hair turning white, feet shod with frayed house slippers, shoulders draped with an Army-surplus olive-drab blanket, came striding toward me from the log shelter.

"It used to be," I said. I winced down the path.

"What happened to your leg?"

"Broke it."

"Well, here, lemme help you."

"Naw, naw, I can make it. Sumbitch just hurts." I went ahead and slid down the rest of the footpath leading to the shelter and dropped, on the spot, beside a roaring fire sizzling with steaks. With this fellow was John Harper, Slow Joe, half-naked and hanging the rest of his odd assortment of clothes on a jury-rigged clothesline suspended between barren tree saplings beside a small angry stream. Sunlight was popping in and out through the clouds.

"How'd you know my name?" I asked the man.

"I'm Paul, too. Got two writers out here named Paul."

"That a fact."

"And both of 'em smoke Camels Regular. I can make you a deal."

"Talk," I said. I was slipping off my boots.

"Two Bic lighters, hash browns, sausage for a pack of Camels."

"Some of that steak, too?"

"A little slice of steak."

"Maybe I ain't got no Camels."

"My friend John here says you just resupplied."

It was a deal, of course. Paul Michael Fitzsimmons was his name, he said, hadn't had a smoke since he ran out more than twenty miles before at Addis Gap or somewhere in there. Word gets around pretty quick about who's on the trail, he said, and he guessed it was at Neels Gap when he heard that there was another writer named Paul who smoked Camels and was planning to walk to Maine. So the deal was consummated. When Paul Michael Fitzsimmons babbled a thumbnail biography to me—fifty-two, walked the entire AT in 1982, out now "just messing around," born in Boston but lived now in Front Royal, Virginia, where the AT exits Shenandoah National Park, used to get paid by the word for short stories in the old *Bluebook* magazine ("As a result I don't believe in Hemingway's shit about the 'iceberg theory' "), had been a "kitchen manager" for various gourmet restaurants between Florida and California but now carried four wooden hardware-store mousetraps with him on the AT "to do my part towards eradicating the little shits"—he became a friend of mine. I would follow The Irish Goat (his a.k.a.) anywhere.

"You ain't seen my kid, have you?" I said.

"Naw, but I heard about him."

"You've heard damned near everything, haven't you?"

"I get around."

"Me and the boy were supposed to meet at Muskrat Creek Shelter but I missed him. We got into a little fight. I can't find him. I'm worried."

"Well, fuck him."

"What? Holy shit, this is my kid here."

"Stories," said Paul Michael Fitzsimmons, "we're talking about stories. Nun gets on a bus in front of St. Patrick's Cathedral, goes through her purse and deposits everything she can find—buttons, pennies, paper clips, watchagot—and goes to the back of the bus and sits down next to this guy reading the *Daily News*. Bus driver ain't got time to mess with her right now because he's busy easing into the traffic on Fifth Avenue. He gets out there in the flow pretty soon and he says, 'Pardon me, Sister, but you haven't paid the right fare.' The sister is sitting there next to the guy with the *Daily News* and she's playing with her beads and reading the catechism and the bus driver he shouts this time. 'Hey, Sister,' he says, 'pay the fare or I let you off at the next stop.' Guy reading the *News* nudges the nun and says, 'Sister, I think the driver wants to speak with you.' The nun don't look up from her beads. 'Fuck 'im,' she says."

David showed up in due time. He had waited for me at the shelter but I had missed it in the rain and fog. That's all. He was glad to see me and the fire and John Harper. There was no particular fallout from the morning's snit about how to treat swollen knees and about how to speak of one's mother/ex-wife. We were just glad to be there, in fact, in the warmth of an AT shelter with a bonfire and a raconteur who carried four hardware-store mousetraps in his packs.

*Snap.*

"Got this teacher doing a pop quiz, see?" David and I and John Harper were nestled into our bags, in the mouse-infested shelter, listening to the bitter wind whistling through the trees and The Irish Goat telling his stories. *Snap.* "Makes two. Little Jap kid sitting in the front row. Teacher says what famous person said, 'Ask not what your country can do for you, but what you can do

for your country?' Jap kid says, 'John Kennedy, January
6, 1960.' Back of the room somebody says, 'Fuckin'
Japs.' Teacher runs to the back of the room and shouts,
'All right, who said that?' Little Irish kid named Sean
Michael Riggins says, 'Franklin Delano Roosevelt, De-
cember 7, 1941.' "

  *Snap*.

  "That makes three," said Paul Michael Fitzsimmons.

# 11

FITZSIMMONS WAS STILL GOING THE NEXT MORNING, holding a Sierra cup of honest-to-God percolated coffee from John Harper's apparatus, chattering away beside the smoldering campfire hardly before the bluejays and juncos could get their eyes clear. "Hiker's got to be careful, now, when he gets up there around Erwin, Tennessee," he was saying. Bits of snow and ice had collected on the barren trees and the tin roof of the shelter. Harper's pack thermometer read thirty degrees. The socks we had forgotten to take from the branches of the trees stood at attention. "Redneck City in Erwin. Good old boys get pissed off when they see you coming. Got bars all over the place. When I was up there in '82 I went into one of 'em with another hiker. We wanted a beer real bad. Goddam, that was a bad place. One old boy had passed out on the floor, right there in the sawdust, and the waitresses just stepped over him without looking. What you had there was the hikers in the booths on one side and the rednecks along the wall on the other side. Redneck Standoff. Me, I made out all right. Word spread to the other side of the place that the guy I'm walking with just got let out of prison for murder. I'd step over one of them guys passed out in the sawdust and walk over there and stick out my hand and say, 'I'm from Boston, where y'all from?' They didn't say shit.''

David had come out of his funk now, thanks to the outrageous bullshit of Paul Michael Fitzsimmons, and it looked like we had a decent day ahead of us. Today we would walk right through the hundred-mile point, hardly noticing it enough to celebrate, and the AT guidebooks promised (*promises, promises*) a high but level fifteen-mile hike to the next shelter. The supply of food and Coleman white gas looked perilously low—it could mean a stop in a day or so for supplies to carry us on to Wesser—but we had reached the point where we sort of took what came. *Que será.*

''We're gonna do a little cheating now,'' said Fitzsimmons, already stomping his frosty boots on the ground, panting steam, testing the weight of his pack.

''You? Cheat?'' I said.

''John's got to call his mama. Got a pay phone down there.''

Fitzsimmons knew the AT, all right, and how to walk it. He knew that one could take a blue-blazed trail off the AT and within two miles be making a collect call from a phone booth at the Standing Indian Campground. So they said goodbye to David and me, The Irish Goat and his mate Slow Joe, and clattered over the ridge. *Every time I leave to walk the AT, Mama just says John's gone camping*, Harper had said. David and I gathered our stuff and poured more water on the campfire and left.

This time we walked together, David only three or four strides ahead of me, and we carried on a running conversation as he loped along in his ragged khaki walking shorts and I heaved along behind him, jabbing my staff ahead of me and wincing, trying not to let him know that every step was killing me. At some point we stopped to pee and smoke and take on more water. At another I proposed taking a photograph of him fading away into the ice-shrouded trees. At still another I said I really ought to stop and wrap my knee with an Ace bandage. We were about a mile high now, in the process of doing our first fifteen-mile day, and except for the knee everything was okay.

"I think I've figured what my problem was at Sewanee," he said over his shoulder. A white double-blaze came up, signifying a switchback, and he whistled and jerked his right index finger into the air and executed a smart military column-right.

"You lost it in the road," I said.

"Well, yeah, that's the way fathers look at it."

"What happened, Dave?"

"I was enjoying the play so much that I forgot my lines."

"Meaning?"

"I got awed by the place. Sewanee ain't exactly Auburn, you know?"

"Tell me."

"All that ivy. Episcopal money. Some classes, three students. One time you told me you went to some classes that year at Harvard and they had a hundred students and a professor with a microphone. What I'm saying is, at Sewanee they'll have a half dozen kids in a class and half of those will be wearing the robe. Watch it"—he ducked through a grove of rhododendron and the icy branches snapped into my face—"and by the time I got with the program it was too late."

"Please tell me," I said, "that Kelley's name doesn't end with an 'I.' "

"It's 'Kelley' with an 'E-Y,' " he said. "Old family name."

"Good. I don't want a Barbie doll for a daughter-in-law."

"What, you don't think I'm gonna go off the deep end, do you?"

"I hope to hell not."

Trudging along ahead of me, his slightly bowed legs springing as though Katahdin were but thirty minutes ahead over the next ridge, he seemed delighted I had brought up the subject. "If I *did* go off the deep end," he said, "I could about guarantee you that Kelley and I would start a master race of our own. She's got this blond hair and blue eyes and a good long body. Me, I'm kinda skinny with the blue eyes, too, you know, like you and Pop."

"For Christ's sake, kid, take your time."

"Oh, yeah, I was just giving you a scenario."

And it was like that for hours, it seemed, just the way it was supposed to be. For a while I would lead and then, after a stop for water and peanut butter spooned from plastic containers and maybe a pee in the bushes, David would take the lead and we would amble along through the damp peaceful forest of western North Carolina in league with the deer and the squirrels and the chipmunks and the chattery birds and the other fauna whose land we were invading. We debated, as we walked, the relative merits of my JanSport pack and his Lowe Expedition. He needled me about how simple a process it was, should I hazard a try, to light a Peak I stove and maybe give a shot at boiling some water. We covered everything—how life up there must have been for the Cherokees when they were being tracked down and made to join the Trail of Tears, how we never had any stomachaches until we forsook the rice-and-oatmeal diet for Hardee's grease, what the women might be doing along about this time, whether a new Nissan front-wheel-drive had it over the basic all-American '70 Olds Cutlass—and somewhere in there we had, indeed, put one hundred miles between us and Amicalola Falls.

At midafternoon we stopped. The sun was out and we flopped out on a grassy knoll, splaying our packs out on the ground and lying back in the brown grass, and I reached into the map pocket of my pack to see exactly where we were.

## TRAIL DESCRIPTION—
## SOUTH TO NORTH

*Miles*   *Data*

9.0   Reach Carter Gap, a large level area with *campsites*. The *Carter Gap Shelter* is 50 ft. from the Trail on left. *Water* is 150 ft. downhill beside the shelter. (The A.T. leaves the Blue Ridge at the base of Ridgepole Mtn., 5,050 ft., and follows the 4,800-ft. contour around Little Ridgepole to the junction of the Nantahala range.)

11.6   Reach vista, with views of Pickens Nose and Rabun Bald.

12.8   Reach Betty's Creek Gap. Cross area by graded trail. (Woods road on left leads 0.5 mi. to USFS 67, 7 mi. S of *Standing Indian Campground*.)

13.7   Reach Mooney Gap. Cross USFS 83, a gravel road from Coweeta to Alberta Mtn. (The gap is a popular *campsite* with side trails.)

13.9   At log steps, cross culvert carrying water from *spring* above the Trail, and make sharp turn left.

14.0   Reach overlook.

14.6   Descend briefly to road.

15.0    Reach Bear Pen Gap. Descend again to road.
        About 100 ft. to right, begin the 0.3 mi.
        climb to Albert Mtn. (A 0.7-mi. detour of
        the summit trail is blue-blazed and continues
        on road. The blue-blazed Bear Pen Creek
        Trail, on left, leads 2 mi. to USFS 67.)

15.3    Reach summit of Albert Mtn. with fire tower
        and magnificent views but no water. De-
        scend along N slope on fire road.

15.5    Cross end of USFS 83 and blue-blazed de-
        tour of summit trail. Enter Big Spring Gap,
        a clearing with unmarked logging roads. (A
        trail to Little Pinnacle leads to right. There
        is a blue blaze on a large tree.)

15.8    Reach *Big Spring Shelter*. A blue-blazed
        trail on left leads 250 ft. to shelter. Water
        source is behind shelter.

"What's up?" said David.

"We're at the mercy of the 'Trial Guide' again," I said.

"How so?"

"We're maybe six miles from the next shelter. What've we got here, about two or three in the afternoon? If I can believe this fucker we can make the shelter before it gets dark."

"The problem?"

"Albert Mountain looks like Suribachi."

The walk looked simple enough for the next couple of miles. We were hovering at 4,500 feet. We had already walked a dozen miles or more, and when you have walked that far the body heat has built up so that the official thermometer temperature doesn't matter anymore, so our only concern was that there might be more in store for us than what the AT maps and guides and profiles promised. One never knows. The Appalachian Trail Conference didn't put Albert Mountain there, anyway. The Lord or Nature or whoever you choose to believe did.

Three-tenths of a mile, you say? Fire tower and magnificent views but no water, you say? What do you say, then, to a forty-eight-year-old man with a history of whiskey behind him and, say, thirty-two pounds of stuff in a pack on his back (FA Nikon, wool sweater, wet cotton T-shirts, et cetera), following in the steps, you say, of a randy nineteen-year-old boy who likes to climb sheer rock cliffs— with his *fingers*, for Christ's sake—for something to do while his father sprawls in the gravel sucking the life out of a Camel cigarette? You've got a kid who's dying to take on the fabled Albert Mountain and a grown man who ought to know better.

I never saw the likes of Albert Mountain. It looked like the Pyramids, giant granite boulders reaching upward for three city blocks, plopped right there in the middle of the forest as though somebody had dropped them there overnight as a practical joke. I don't know what the geologists have to say about it and I was in no need to ask. All I could say as we stood at the base of it and saw the white arrow blazes on the rocks pointing skyward was, "Holy shit."

"Why don't you take a rest?" said David.

"Might as well be the Berlin Wall."

"It can't be that bad."

"Don't tell me thousands of hikers have made it."

"You could take that trail around it," he said.

"That'd be chicken-shit."

"Your knee going to be okay?"

"Hell, I don't know. The going downhill's what's bad." I had thrown my pack to the ground and was taking on more water, sucking on one more cigarette, thinking about the option of taking the blue-blazed detour of 0.7 mile. There was no guarantee that the detour would be much less

imposing and, besides, that way was nearly a mile and dark
was coming fast. And I didn't want to disappoint my kid.
There was the mistake: I didn't want to disappoint my kid.
Finally I said, "Let's go."

David, unencumbered by walking stick and carrying an
alpinist's pack on his broad shoulders, began bounding up
the monster like a leopard born in those parts. It took me
some forty-five minutes to make it to the top. I would slip
on loose gravel. My acrophobia would act up on me. I
would find that the staff was too cumbersome, that the best
way to go was in a semicrawl, and I would sling the staff
up ahead of me only to catch it sliding right back. I pondered the idea of tying some rope to the pack and, after
climbing several feet, dragging it up when I found a trusty
foothold. My knee, the one I had been nursing for nearly
a week, was being twisted when I planted its foot awk-
wardly and several times I slipped and the knee slammed
full-force against the granite. I would take a smoke break
and curse and wonder, for the first time on the trek, just
what I thought I was trying to prove.

When I finally made it to the top I collapsed in a heap,
pack and all. Suddenly we were in a cloud, dark upon us,
a half mile to go until we reached the shelter. It meant little
to me at that point that we had just broken the fifteen-mile-
hike mark for the first day since we had left home. I was
a wreck.

"You can hardly see the top of the fire tower," said
David, who had gone to inspect the "magnificent view"
and now came toward me almost feeling his way through
the fog.

"Fuck the fire tower," I said.

He seemed to be smirking. "Too rough for you?"

"What?"

"Maybe you should've taken the road."

"And miss all of this fun?"

"You want to quit?" He *was* smirking, by God.

"Let me tell you something, kid." I was too tired and angry to give much of a lecture. "We've never been around each other long enough for me to give you any handy-dandy bromides to live by but by God I'll give you one as old as the hills. 'Never kick a man when he's down.' You hear?"

"I wasn't kicking you," he said.

"Anything short of calling me a folk hero, you're kicking me."

"That mountain's always been there."

"Well, fuck it. I haven't."

At the Big Spring Shelter, which we found with David's flashlight (the cold weather had finally done my batteries in), there was nothing but misery. We barely spoke. With almost the last of the gas we boiled enough water to fix the last of the rice. Mice were all but queuing up for leftovers. It promised to be the coldest night we had seen on the trail. By flickering candlelight I read the last item in the shelter log: "Fuck it. Albert Mountain just about did it. I'm not sure I can take any more. When I reach U.S. 64 I'm either going to cross it or I'm going to hitch a ride into Franklin and go home and burn my shit. I won't know until I hit the road." David and I slept on it.

# 12

WITH THE LAST OF THE GAS WE BOILED WATER FOR THE last of the oatmeal. There were patches of blue in the sky but the temperature had dropped into the twenties overnight and our boots and our water bottles were frozen. After David had made his boots reasonably pliable by working them back and forth with his mittened hands he trudged back to see what could be seen from the fire tower atop Albert Mountain. I stayed alone at the shelter to knead my knee with Ben-Gay—the knee had locked up during the night and wouldn't bend—and to figure out what we should do next.

The decision to leave the trail came easily. We had 109 miles of trail behind us but I simply couldn't walk anymore. It was going to take true grit for me to so much as negotiate the 9.1-mile downhill to U. S. Highway 64, which would take us into the little North Carolina resort town of Franklin, and we were going to have to go into town for supplies, anyway. And what was the publisher in New York saying about the novel? And how were the Braves doing? And how's about some real meat and some fresh-cooked vegetables and cornbread and milk? In Franklin they had the answers to all of those questions, and more, so the only question remaining was how long would we be there.

"Franklin's still there," David said when he returned to the shelter. It would be a cold but brilliantly clear day. He felt good.

"Glad to hear it."

"We going in?"

" 'Fraid so," I said. "A motel again. Foolish to go on."

The walk down to the highway took me more than six hours, edging sideways on the incessant nine-mile down-hill, and within half an hour we were given a ride by a kindly old gentleman farmer in a new pickup truck. He and David had to boost me into the cab. The farmer held a sack of eggs in his lap as he drove, eggs he had been collecting at his farm, and explained that he was having to rush home because his wife had called to say that their epileptic son had "darn near bit her finger off" during a seizure. I told him I knew something about seizures and he told me he knew something about "walking through the woods when I was a boy." He, too, liked the idea of a father and his son walking the AT, and when he dropped us off at the Franklin Motel he wished us luck and told me that rest was the only answer for the knee.

Soon I had Susan on the phone and at least *she* had good news to report. The editor in chief at the publishing house had called my agent, Sterling Lord, to say he thought *The Sixkiller Chronicles* was "brilliant" and had only a couple of changes to suggest.

"Say again?" I said.

"They love it."

"No, that word."

"He called it 'brilliant.' "

"I don't think I've ever been called 'brilliant' before."

David, now out of the shower and toweling off, broke into a grin and gave me the thumbs-up sign. "Changes. How dare he say changes?"

Susan said, "Take it, Hemphill, take it."

"So what's Sterling say?"

"It was interesting. He kept asking about the pressure you'd been under to write it and get on the trail. I don't think he believed it when he saw the manuscript. He told me how Joe McGinniss took a job as a columnist with the L.A. *Examiner* so it would pressure him into finishing *Going to Extremes*, the Alaska book. Anyway, Sterling's proud of you. And so am I."

"Look," I told her, "I don't know what to say about the knee right now. I mean, you could drive up here and get us in three hours or less, but I don't want to drop off unless I can't heal it myself. I've got a year's supply of Epsom salts and Ben-Gay in the room and the Braves are on TV tonight and there's a home-cooking place across the street. Let's just play it a day at a time, okay?"

"It's not easy for me, either."

"I know that, honey."

"I was finally resigned to five or six months."

"Me, too. Me, too."

I flared momentarily when she said it would be impossible to drive up to get us tomorrow, Saturday, because she had some free-lance writing to do and she had promised to baby-sit the kid of some friends while they went to a steeplechase, but that passed quickly and left me ashamed of myself. I would see how things went with the knee and we would talk in the morning, it was agreed, and I limped behind David to the restaurant for a down-home pig-out (beef tips, cooked-to-death green beans, mashed potatoes, cornbread, iced tea, cobbler) before returning to the motel to administer to the knee and watch a kid left-hander for the Braves named Ken Dayley get bombed by the Montreal Expos.

We were only twenty-eight miles short of Wesser, North Carolina, a white-water mecca for canoeists, but it might as well have been a thousand miles. Wesser is where we had intended to make this resupply, and where I had the first of my money orders waiting; but, more important, being at the end of the rugged 150-mile northbound stretch of the AT, it is where a big percentage of once-eager Georgia-to-Maine "through-hikers" stagger in and give up the dream. And we hadn't even made it to Wesser. With 118 miles and twelve hiking days behind us we found ourselves down to $47 in cash, living on American Express, cleaning and waterproofing our boots, working newspaper puzzles, watching television, eating bologna sandwiches on white bread, washing clothes and learning to live with the smell of Ben-Gay in a cramped motel in a resort town. The only upbeat development of the day came when we watched a fellow pitch a no-hitter for the Detroit Tigers on the "Game of the Week" Saturday afternoon.

David missed it. He had been reading the Atlanta papers' weekend entertainment tabloid, about what the rock stars were up to in his absence, when the Tigers' Jack Morris retired the last batter and I let out a whoop. "Sonofabitch, he did it."

"He get 'em out?" David said, still reading.

"Get 'em out? Christ, he threw a *no-hitter*."

"Pretty tough."

"Tough?" I said. "I've been in love with this game for nearly forty years and that's just the second no-hitter I've ever seen."

"That's incredible."

"Don't you want to know about the other one?"

"You threw out the last runner in it."

"I told you about it? That night in Kansas?"

"You told me," he said.

It took Susan and Martha less than two and a half hours to drive what had taken us twelve days and nights to walk.

When they walked into the motel room at noon we were ready. Martha wanted to be lied to about bears and deer and Indians, and David and I tried hard to dazzle her, but not much was said in the car on the long drive back home to Atlanta. Rain came after a hamburger stop at the same Hardee's in Clayton, and as the car sped southward we could barely make out the spiny ridges where only four and five nights earlier we had been nestled in our sleeping bags with the notion that "civilization" was worlds away.

When the car engine stopped in the driveway, everything sluggish and quiet now on a sleepy Sunday afternoon in our in-town neighborhood, we could see that spring had already come to the lowlands. The grass needed cutting and the daffodils were about to bloom. We dropped our stuff on the porch and headed straight for the bathrooms. Just before dark it occurred to me that I would need some crutches if I intended to visit my doctor first thing in the morning and it took some hustle to get outfitted in a pair at that time of day ("I told you you're too old for that," chided Ira Katz, our neighborhood pharmacist, who re-opened his place for me). We took baths. We ate hearty. We told stories. David called his mother in Birmingham but he wasn't about to call anybody else.

And finally I got around to reading that morning's Atlanta paper, which had John Harmon's long feature story about the AT ("2,100-mile Trail Hike Lures Many," read the headline), particularly the concluding paragraphs:

> While most hikers have to reckon only with themselves about finishing their goal, Atlanta writer Paul Hemphill is unique.
>
> The 48-year-old author has secured a contract with a publishing house to produce a non-fiction account of the journey with 19-year-old son David. But that's not all the pressure on Hemphill.
>
> The trek is a means toward Hemphill's more im-

portant goals—to shake away forever the effects of a drinking problem he has successfully battled for several months and to get to know the son with whom he has spent little time in recent years.

"For me, it's a reclamation," he said.

And like many who have departed northward from Springer, he added, "We're going all the way."

# 13

THERE HAD BEEN NO OCCASION FOR ME TO SEE ZEB MORgan since my seizure in the fall, when he nursed me through the first hospital stay of my life, and although on this Monday morning I struggled through the doors of his office on crutches I was anxious for the good doctor to see The New Hemphill. I had actually gained five pounds on the trail with two weeks of an essentially all-grain diet and I was sprouting a decent beard and I looked weathered in the healthy way we associate with yachtsmen or farm workers or the last of the cowboys. "Do you realize that's the first time you've come through that door sober?" he said, happy to be saying it, and I was shown down the corridor for X rays.

Soon we were sitting across from each other in the same cubicle where, some four years earlier, he had told me I had no more than five years to live if I didn't stop drinking. He hadn't bothered to bring the X rays in to show me anything. *Traction*? I was thinking. *Arthroscopic surgery like the jocks are getting these days? Maybe a Joe Namath knee brace.*

"I'd like to give it an exotic name," he said, "but all you've got is a severe sprain."

"Come on, Zeb, this thing's killing me."

"Severe sprain. That's it. Bed rest and pills."

"Just two or three days, right? We got to get back."

"Oh, it could take a week," he said.

"Come on. A *week*?"

"Or two."

"*Two* weeks? Christ, Zeb—"

"Or longer." Now he was messing with his pipe and smiling. He said he didn't hold much traffic with special knee braces; that pure and simple rest was all I needed; that it really didn't much matter what I did with Ben-Gay or hot-water or cold-water treatments; that when a knee is sprained it is sprained. He didn't hassle me about the Camels I was back to smoking. He said I was looking reasonably healthy, and he wrote a prescription for some antiarthritic pills to keep the swelling down, and he told me, "You've got to understand that your body is even older than forty-eight because of the whiskey it's seen. So do yourself a favor the next time David wants to make it to the next shelter before dark and you feel the slightest twinge in your knee. You tell David, 'Here we camp.' "

I drove on back home (an odd feeling, driving in Atlanta traffic in the heat again, after only two weeks away from it) and felt pretty good about things. "Pop the pills, get some rest, maybe Friday," I told David, just stirring awake from a twelve-hour sleep. That night, too late to change plans, Susan was hosting a modest birthday gathering at the house for Gene-Gabriel Moore, a longtime friend of mine who was now her editor at *Goodlife*, so it was unavoidable that the word would spread that the Hemphill Expedition had suffered a setback. "Even Richard Petty blows a tire now and then," I joked, sticking to stock-car-racing terminology such as "pit stop" and "grind the valves" and "get new rubber," assuring everybody that David and

I were loving every minute of it. To Bob Hannah, my AA friend, I compared walking the AT with staying sober: "one step at a time."

So began a string of days that seemed to have no end. I didn't want to go to Manuel's Tavern for lunch because they weren't looking for me until late August. I thought of sending David, under an assumed name, to the camera place with our first rolls of film. I called my agent in New York to tell him about it but advised him not to bother the publisher with it, especially since their latest expense advance for the trek was due me, because I was going to be back out there before they could respond, anyway. Days would begin with my telling David "maybe tomorrow" and end with "day *after* tomorrow." The boy, armed now with a $160 refund on his income taxes, lay low by gobbling up more rock tapes and shutting himself up in a room to listen to his music through a headset. One day he drove out to a Wendy's on the edge of the city to meet with his mother, who was in town on business, but he certainly gave no thoughts to running up to Sewanee to party with his pals at the university. We watched the weather reports closely and we wondered how Slow Joe and The Irish Goat were doing on the trail.

We didn't ask for it, of course, but the respite did come at a time when we could look back over our first twelve days and make adjustments, talk it over, spot mistakes, sort of fine-tune the science of backpacking over a very long distance. The first 118 miles had served as the shakedown, the dry run, that we had not been able to make. It was one thing to read Ed Garvey and Colin Fletcher and the other hiking experts, and to listen to the advice of everybody who had spent a night on Blood Mountain, but it was quite another matter to be suddenly let out in the woods with new equipment and a set of AT guidebooks and simply start following the white blazes to a mountain more than 2,000 miles away. So now we had seen the elephants and heard the owls—the hard way—and we had the chance to calmly make some refinements in the comforts of the house rather than in the clatter of the trail.

"The tent," I said one night when the Braves were going so poorly that I had snapped off the television set after their half of the fourth inning. "My notes show that we spent, let's see, four out of eleven nights in the tent before we got to the motel in Franklin."

"That all? Felt like I put it up a hundred times."

"Got it right here. 'One stars, four tent, five shelter, one motel.' That was the Clayton motel."

David said, "Sucker's getting heavy."

"Doesn't weigh any more than the camera stuff."

"They gonna use pictures in the book?"

"Come on, Dave, you don't walk the AT without a camera. How many times are we gonna walk the AT?"

"Well, we aren't gonna walk it *once* if I gotta carry the tent."

"If we do shelters," I said, "we can't stop when the knee hurts."

"No tent. Can't use it in the Smokies, anyways. Buy a tarp."

"A tarp? Jesus, why don't we just bivouac?"

*Calmly make some refinements*, don't you see. He was right—the tent was an older and therefore heavier model (with metal pins and bunji poles it weighed nearly six pounds), through-hikers in the seventy-mile stretch of the Smokies had to stay in shelters due to bears and heavy traffic, and a tarpaulin would do nicely in an emergency—so we bought a ten-by-ten tarp weighing less than a pound. We decided to leave some of the heavier items of clothing (one good sweater per man was sufficient) but to add more socks simply because you never have enough clean dry socks. We would carry an additional canister of white gas

for the stove because it seemed we were always having to
ration it and it was sometimes hard to find. We would
eschew hot lunches (too much white gas, too much bulky-
type food, too much time when you intend to go all the
way to Katahdin) and make up the energy with more Snickers and honey and peanut butter.

And as for the walking, presuming the knee came
around and there would be more walking to Maine, we
found we could also make improvements there. We
agreed to an earlier start each morning to ensure a ten-
mile day by the time the sun stood straight up. I bought
an elastic slip-on knee brace to use *before* a knee got
hurt. David bent the aluminum braces of his interior-
frame pack so that now, fully loaded, it was an extension
of his spine. We finally had time to figure out how the
assortment of straps and cinches played against each other
to keep the load from shifting on my exterior-frame pack.
I even decided to leave home my penny whistle, which I
hadn't tooted once (it would have caused mutiny in a
shelter) and was a pain to keep up with, remembering a
dictum another hiker had told me: "Never take anything
you can lose." And, most important adjustment of all,
we agreed to follow Dr. Zeb Morgan's advice.

"That's the hardest part, you know," I said to David
one afternoon over chili dogs at Manuel's. Nearly three
weeks had passed and I was no longer using the crutches.
Now we were packed to return to the trail at any moment
and I was taking light walks in my boots. "I can look back
and see how every time I had trouble with the knee it was
because I was pushing it."

"Yeah," he said. "I need to remember that, too."

"That's what you get for walking with an old man."

"It's all right, Dad. That's what the trek's all about."

"You know what we're gonna have to do at some point,
don't you?"

"No, what?"

"We're gonna have to make a jump if we're going to get you back in school on time."

"We'll worry about that when we get to it," he said.

On the last Sunday of April, with two weeks of hiking and three weeks of convalescence behind us, we returned to the trail. I'd finally gotten the last of my advance money for the novel (enough to enroll Lisa in her last semester at the University of Alabama). My favorite uncle, Darrell Stewart, the first to take me fishing when I was a kid and the only person in the family who could personally vouch that I really had played in a professional baseball game, had just retired from the Internal Revenue Service but now was at home in Montgomery dying of cancer. Phil Niekro was the toast of New York, leading the world in everything with the Yankees (at that age he was 4-0 with an ERA of 1.40), and the Braves were on a roll: Pascual Perez was free of drug charges in the Dominican Republic and ready to pitch; Braves pitchers had thrown two straight shutouts, and Dale Murphy on the night before we left went three-for-four with two homers and even a stolen base at the Astrodome in Houston. I watched that game on television and then plunged into a review of Gore Vidal's *Lincoln* for *Goodlife*, finishing at five o'clock in the morning, and after an hour's sleep I began packing and we left home again. We could wait on the knee no longer.

We were let out in a cold drizzle by friends (Susan and Martha came along for the ride) at Winding Stair Gap, the exact spot sixteen miles west of Franklin where we had hitched a ride with the gentleman farmer, and at two o'clock we hugged goodbye once more and ascended into the bleak woods for a reasonably easy four-mile climb up to Siler Bald Shelter. This was the first day of daylight saving time, so we had plenty of time to take it easy and readjust to being alone in the woods together. We felt awkward, as one might upon discovering he had forgotten how to swim, but we made a fire and we ate well and it was wonderful to bundle up in the sleeping bag and fall asleep watching the flames dance.

## 14

THE FIRST FULL DAY BACK ON THE TRAIL APPEARED TO BE, as I studied the maps over hot oatmeal and coffee (there was another adjustment I had made in the diet, instant coffee by the heapsful, enough to make a man stand at attention), a fair and reasonable test of the knee. We would try to make more than twelve miles to the next shelter, Cold Spring Shelter, and although the trail had a couple of fierce-looking plummets and climbs to it, peaks beginning to hit the mile-high level now, the guidebook promised fairly smooth walking with plenty of springs and campsites and logging roads. I strapped on the new knee brace as a precaution and we left the shelter just as the rain began.

It was a businesslike day, the last day of April when spring was beginning to show itself in the highlands, a day interspersed with wind and rain and hail and lightning and occasional glimpses of sunlight. On days like that you spend a lot of time putting on and taking off your rain gear and so you don't cover the miles you might have. It's also a pain in the ass. But it's the mountains, where each valley has a climate and even a personality of its own. The twittery shale-blue juncos would be flitting among bright green buds and dandelions in one gap but the next one over would be closed for the day: bleak, forbidding, only an occasional squirrel signifying life. *On with the parka and rain chaps and pack cover, off with them; on with them, off with them.* Ever mindful of the knee, I took the easy way around stumps and boulders. David, I could assume, was loping on along toward the shelter and stuffing himself with the nuts-raisins-M&Ms concoction of gorp without breaking stride. *How about, I'd walk two miles for a Camel*, I said to myself, promising not to allow myself a water-and-cigarette-and-snack break until I had covered two miles. Walk an hour (two miles, hopefully), break for ten minutes. Zeb Morgan would have been proud, I felt, except for the cigarettes. Knee okay.

David was already sprawled out in the shelter, napping in the rain, when I got there. He'd even collected some reasonably dry wood for a fire later on. It was a lovely shelter, made of heavy timbers and a bluish corrugated tin roof, situated at one end of a long grassy bald broad enough, it seemed, to hold a picnic-and-softball crowd. This was at 5,000 feet and there is no telling how many centuries have passed since the Cherokees came to clear such "balds" for summertime grazing and planting and villages. The grass was still brown but coarse and ankle deep, and around the edges of the field there were tufts of green. It occurred to me that this would have infuriated a lot of husbands out there in Suburban America, to see all of this unkempt grass growing untended, and about this time of year they would be cranking up their $5,000 rider mowers in order to leave their mark on the land.

When I wheezed and leaned my pack against the shelter David opened his eyes. "Anyone for volleyball?" he said.

"I was thinking of batting practice," I said. "Pretty place, huh?"

"Grass needs cutting, though, if you ask me."

"What I was thinking."

"How's the knee?"

"On to Katahdin, I say."

I lit a Camel, naturally, and we both lay back in the shelter to see and hear the lazy rain as it pattered and dripped from the tin roof. It became a good, quiet time for us. We changed into dry clothes and hung our wet stuff from nails in the shelter. I put on my fluffy "booties" or "muck-lucks," a gift from David two Christmases earlier which had so far been worn only on cold mornings around our drafty old house, and I noted that they were about "the favorite thing in my pack." We updated our journals. We napped. We cleaned the cleats of our boots. When the rain stopped we took a walk to explore the corners of the grassy bald and then we started a campfire and had a dinner of rice and peas-and-carrots soup. It was the signal for the mice to come out of hiding.

We were throwing more wood on the fire and spreading out our sleeping bags in the shelter, at dusk, when we heard the measured *tromp-tromp* of hikers coming up from the stream below the bald. There were two of them, in spite of the cold wearing walking shorts and yellow gaiters to protect their legs from thorns and keep water from sloshing into their boots, and they were a curious-looking pair. The one in the lead was rangy and strong and forceful, like a drill instructor, while the other was a gaunt and hollow-eyed Ichabod Crane who followed the leader in step and so closely as to be a shadow. They grunted "howdy" to us as they reached the shelter and then off-loaded their packs and parkas without a word to us.

They spoke to each other only in primitive grunts and syllables—*Chili? Leg okay? Want tea? I'll get water*—and it was very nearly dark before there was any attempt at conversation.

"Where y'all from?" I finally asked the stronger one.

"Around Atlanta," he said.

"Where 'bouts?"

"You take that last exit to Six Flags Over Georgia."

"That must be Austell," I said.

"Naw, Mableton."

"Been out long?"

"Ten days, I guess."

"You're making good time," said David.

"Just had a twenty-miler," said the leader.

Slowly their story developed. The stronger man was named Carl, the skinny hawk-faced one Mike, and they were both twenty-four years old. They had been buddies all their lives, playing ball and going to school and even holding part-time jobs together, and the parallel in their lives was continuing: they had both been devastated by their parents' divorces, they had both plunged deeply into fundamental religion and now they were grimly force-marching the Appalachian Trail to Maine in order to sort things out. I had my perception of Mableton—a rough little blue-collar enclave almost forgotten in the glitter of the new "New South" Atlanta, stuck out there in the woods west of the city amid ball-bearings plants and warehouses and bowling alleys and beer joints, a place for pickup trucks and Bible-thumpers and closet Klansmen and random drunken violence—which may have explained why Carl said that they simply lived near the "last exit to Six Flags." By their low conspiratorial tones, their general glumness, they indicated it was going to take a lot of miles of back-packing for them to find peace.

"I guess we're all out here for about the same reason," I said to Mike, the quieter one, when we were all preparing for sleep. Carl had already fallen asleep. David was studying the AT guidebook by candlelight. Mice were scurrying everywhere.

"You divorced, too?" Mike seemed to be frightened of his own voice.

"Well, that's part of it." I explained about David and me. "I'm getting over alcoholism, too."

"Oh."

"Stuff's a bitch," I said.

"You don't have to tell me about that," said Mike.

"Trouble is, you can't run from it."

"Yeah."

"I been kicking my ass every mile for everything I ever did."

Mike said, "I just don't know what to do anymore. I went to this Bible college and thought I wanted to do youth ministry, you know? Help young kids. But if I can't straighten myself out, how can I help somebody else? I mean, my parents divorced after twenty-four years. Makes me think they were staying together all that time just for my sake. I'm real close to my father but I'm still trying to forgive Mom. I don't know. Maybe I can work something out in my head out here."

Soon he, too, was asleep and both he and his buddy were snoring. It would be another cold night, not quite freezing, but for a change we could see the stars. Owls were calling from the other side of the bald, swooping down from their perches now and then to make a kill, and overhead could be heard the faint whistle of a jet plane. "If they paid a bounty for mice and The Irish Goat was here with his mousetraps, he could make a killing," David said, snuffing out the candle.

# 15

THE TWO OTHER HIKERS, MIKE AND CARL, WERE GONE without a trace when we awoke the next morning. The rain had finally broken and it was cold but clear for the twelve-mile downhill rumble into the outpost of Wesser on the white-water Nantahala River of far western North Carolina. This was the section of the country where I had created a mythical "Sixkiller Gap," the homeplace of my country singer and Appalachian farmer "Bluejay Clay" in the novel they were now poring over in New York, and during the day's walk I would occupy my mind with casting and directing and then taking bows at the gala premiere of *Sixkiller* in Atlanta ("Based Upon the Novel by PAUL HEMPHILL," rolled the credits, all of my friends in the Fox Theater standing as one, crying and applauding, I in a tuxedo bowing and kissing Susan and Martha). It kept my mind off a casual item in the AT Guide, almost an asterisk, at a point 5.6 miles from the river bridge at Wesser: "Next 2 miles consists of a precipitous descent."

David stayed with me most of the way on this stretch because it was a fairly pleasant walk, in good weather, but just as the descent became steeper and he could practically hear Wesser calling his name he bolted away with the words that maybe there was mail waiting for him from either Maggie or Kelley or maybe his mom. He would reserve bunks for us at the hostel, he said, and he remembered Dan Bruce saying they laid out a meal fit for a logger at the cafe down there on the river.

The AT Trial Guide struck again. This was no "precipitous descent," this was a parachute jump. In that two-mile section the guide talked about, the trail plummets from 3,700 feet to 1,700. This is on a sheer ridge. It is like walking *down* a tightrope. *Once again*, I thought, *I'm stuck out in the open. How do you say "here we camp" when the kid has the tarp and the stove* (I carried most of the food) *and the stopping point, in this case the hostel at Wesser, is so close?* So I tumbled forward, a flailing clatter of bony legs and swaying pack and bandaged knee, yowling every time I twisted the right knee trying to maintain my balance on the sharp rocky ridge. *Sonofabitch. Hole up for three weeks and now it's gone again after twenty-five miles.* I was only mildly cheered by the sight of daffodils and dogwood as I heard the tantalizing roar of the Nantahala, like a crowd cheering (*jeering?*) me on, and finally emerged from the woods to see David hanging around with a gaggle of canoeists in black rubber wet suits.

He broke away from them when he saw me limping along the edge of the blacktopped road. "Incredible," he said. "That's got to be a Class IV. When the water's up like that, it's as mean as the Arkansas was out there at Royal Gorge."

"Maybe you can try it tomorrow," I told him.

"Bad, huh?"

"They just gave whole new meaning to 'precipitous descent.' "

"We gonna get laid up again?"

"I don't think so. Hot meal and some rest, it'll be okay. They got room at the inn?"

"Yeah," he said. "Mike and Carl are here. There's lots of bunks. Four bucks each. Woman says we can pay tomorrow. Food smells incredible."

"Lots of *pro*-teen, I bet."

Where do these adventurers, these "outdoor enthusiasts," come from? Do they breed 'em at Aspen? Later that night, after we had picked out bunks in a rattletrap shell of a room at the hostel and chowed down on roast beef and potatoes and cornbread and green beans, I scribbled an item in my journal which would occur frequently from that point on: "Who are these people, why are they half my age, and why aren't they working?" The Nantahala Outdoor Center (NOC, or "Nock," if you're on the inside) is the merc tip of the iceberg. There's a whole subculture out there, roaming the rivers and roads and oceans and mountains of the world—canoeists, alpinists, kayakers, bicyclists, marathoners, big-game hunters, ocean racers, rock climbers, skiers, hang gliders, Scuba divers, spelunkers, surfers, dog sledders, ad infinitum—and I suppose a kindly sociologist might refer to them as so many Thoreaus-with-bucks.

Yuppiedom and the health craze of the eighties dovetailed to create them. These are not the John (Slow Joe) Harpers, affable middle-class cabinetmakers who outfit themselves at yard sales and war-surplus stores and stumble off into the woods in order to break the monotony of their dull working-class lives. These are rosy-cheeked, well-heeled, college-educated, Porsche-driving, Perrier-sipping *adventurers*. The Slow Joes like football and beer and Ernest Tubb and stock-car racing and women who can cook; these fellows are into soccer and chablis and Bluegrass music and Le Mans and women who can ski cross-country. The adventurers whose thing is backpacking will "do the AT" after graduation from high school, walk the Pacific

Crest Trail (the Rockies from Canada to Mexico) after their college undergraduate work, and start talking about a full-scale assault on the Himalayas following law school. Abercrombie & Fitch loves the adventurers.

I have trouble with that. Sons of Birmingham truck drivers weren't programmed to understand these people. We didn't own an automobile until I was ten years old (in 1946), nor a television set until I was fifteen, and what I did during my college summers was find my excitement in front of a blast furnace of a bakery oven during the graveyard shift to ensure I would be back at school in the fall. I'm a child of the Depression and World War II and a neighborhood where most of the men were out of work and begging for odd jobs, painting houses or mowing lawns, every summer when their steelworkers' unions went out on strike. "Tell you one thing," my old man would always say of Ralph Nader and the other environmentalists, "Birmingham's in trouble if there ain't no smoke. That means people are starving, son." The first "designer" product I ever bought, with money from my newspaper route, was a Louisville Slugger bat. At the age of forty-eight I drove a battered '70 Olds Cutlass because it was cheap and it worked.

At dark, standing on one leg in the lone phone booth at Wesser, I spoke with Susan. In two weeks she and her mother and the kid—three generations of women—would go to London for a week, Susan doing something on the wool industry for *Goodlife*, and the passports had finally come.

"Jesus," I said, "five-year-old kid with a passport and a ticket to London."

"Improvement of the species, Ace."

"Yeah, well, that's what's been on my mind today."

"You've said it yourself. Why, what happened?"

"I don't know, sweet. I came stumbling down the hill and there was David hanging around these kids with

Porsches and kayaks. One of 'em even had a Sewanee T-shirt on. I guess it's in my blood. I see these kids and it pisses me off.''

"You're an old fart," she said. "Admit it."

"Tell me."

"What do you want him to do, aspire to own a pickup?''

"There's something to be said for a pickup that works," I said.

"Well. You're not kidding me about the knee, are you?''

"It's okay. Really."

"I don't believe you."

"It hurts a little, but I'm keeping my eyes on it."

"What's next?''

"We got about thirty miles before we get into the Smokies," I told her. "Tomorrow we got to climb straight up to a mile-high, starting down here at the river. That won't be too bad, though, because it's the goddam downhills that kill the knee."

We rang off and I shuffled across the road to the cafe to join David in a cherry pie and glass of milk. Several other hikers were with us at a long table, comparing equipment and telling stories from the trail ("There's this guy out there, 'Festus,' migrant worker, walking back home to New York State in cowboy boots and double-knit slacks''), when a fellow named Eric, from Baltimore, came jogging up in Converse high-tops at the end of a twenty-five-mile day with his black Labrador at his heels. Eric would have to ship the dog through the Smokies, where no pets are allowed, and that seemed to be about his only problem.

When the cafe closed we fumbled through the dark to the hostel. Mike was there, separating his dirty clothes from the clean and waiting for the water to heat up again so he could take a shower, and David and I were rearranging our packs when Carl came into the room. He had been on the phone to Mableton.

"Dad says we won that bowling trophy," he said to Mike.

"Which one?"

"Two of 'em. High Game and Series."

"They have the banquet?" Mike said.

"Yeah. Dad accepted 'em for us. Said something about how we were lost in the woods and couldn't be there. Something like that. It broke 'em up." Carl held up a package that had been waiting for him at the NOC. He said, "Look at that, would you?"

"What you got?" said Mike.

"Some stuff Dad sent. Just look at that."

"What, he send canned stuff or something?"

"No. Priority Mail. Cost fifteen dollars to send it." Carl was disgusted. "Dad's girlfriend works at the post office. So she sends it Priority Mail. Fifteen dollars. That's stupid."

# 16

RAINS HAD SWOLLEN THE NANTAHALA AND SENT THE
adventurers scurrying home, so we had Wesser all to ourselves in the morning. I bought myself a pair of rain
pants and David a gray Polypro sweatshirt with the $50
money order waiting for me at NOC. It was foggy and
rainy in the bottoms, sure to be like that all day, and
since we had to cover only 6.8 miles to the next shelter
(the alternatives were to pitch the tarp in a storm somewhere in the hills or hike twenty-two miles to the only
other shelter between Wesser and the entrance to the
Smokies) we took on a massive breakfast and then a hot
lunch at the cafe before striking out around two o'clock
in the afternoon.

It was a persistent climb out of Wesser. We were joined
at the railroad tracks, which run parallel to the river, by a
scarred old bluetick hound who seemed to have nothing in
particular planned for the day. The hound, whom we nick-
named "Wesser," alternated walking with David, in the
lead, and then with me for a while. He made the cold
sloggy day interesting by now and then going berserk and

flushing out a grouse or bounding after a deer, breaking the still air with hysterical howls which reverberated through the bleak ragged hills. In the first six miles we ascended nearly 3,000 feet.

Dark was upon me when I finally caught a glint of the tin-roof shelter down the side of a ridge at 4,400 feet. David was already there, of course, well ahead of me, and it was with some relief that I saw he was all right because I had come close to panicking two or three miles back. The rain and the fog were so thick that I feared I had walked right past the shelter, as I had that day in Georgia, and when Wesser the Hound howled and circled and wouldn't quit a particularly forbidding grove of rhododendron I suffered the worst of fears: *There's one of those wild imported Russian boars in there and he jumped Dave and the kid's in there bleeding and how much good is this hickory staff going to do*? When the dog got bored and trotted away, and even led me northbound on the trail, I breathed relief and meekly followed him to the Sassafras Gap Shelter.

There were four other hikers there with David, all twenty-ish men from little North Georgia towns who were out on a four-day southbound walk to Wesser from a point in the Smokies. They were glum, didn't like the day and didn't even seem to like each other anymore, so David and I set up together in one corner of the shelter. David was flipping through the shelter log, yet another spiral composition notebook filled with poetic scribblings, when he wordlessly passed it to me and pointed to an item. It was dated some two weeks earlier and read:

> Terry's gone. Her knees and calves wouldn't take her any farther. I put her on a bus in Bryson City for Sarasota. I'll go on alone now. I've got too much invested in this thing to quit.
> Jimmy.

"You remember them?" David said.

"I think so. The ones in the yellow ponchos at Springer."

"Boy. They weren't even making five miles a day."

"At least they didn't go home for repairs," I said.

David didn't think much of the sentiments in Jimmy's note. " 'Got too much invested in this thing to quit,' " he sneered, closing the log. "What about the investment in his wife?"

We were glad to get away from that shelter fairly early the next morning, for what was going to be a rigorous hike of nearly fifteen miles to the last AT shelter before the Smoky Mountain National Park, because the four Good Old Boys from North Georgia had reminded us during the night that through-hikers don't mix with weekenders. The mice situation was as bad as we had seen but these fellows were unbearable. They must have brought along everything they could find in their closets and bureau drawers and pantries—raincoats, cast-iron skillets, blue jeans, heavy cotton athletic socks, transistor radios, even a Big Ben alarm clock and a barbecue grill—traveling that way because, well, what's an extra pound here or there when you're only going to wander through the woods for a few days? At nightfall every corner of the shelter was littered and strung with their paraphernalia, David threatening to move outside to the bushes with his sleeping bag if there were the slightest break in the rain, and they kept up a steady babble about the verities of their lives (pussy, Richard Petty, pussy, 'coon dogs, '54 Fords, pussy and pussy), like Cub Scouts afraid to go to sleep on their first night out amongst the creatures, until finally they began to snore in harmony.

The six-mile hike from the shelter to Stekoah Gap, where we would meet for lunch, appeared on the profile and in the guidebook to be fairly difficult but interesting. The closer we got to the Smokies the more often we burst upon breathtaking views of them humping in and out of the bluish haze for as far as our naked eyes could see; but the closer we got, on the other hand, the more rugged the walking became. As soon as you leave Sassafras Gap you go straight up to Cheoah Bald, a rise of some 800 feet in little more than a mile, and no sooner have you reached the summit of Cheoah than you begin to hurtle downward to a place called Locust Cove Gap and discover, exhausted, that you have just negotiated a descent of nearly 1,500 feet in exactly two miles of vigorous switchbacking and rock climbing and hacking through laurel and rhododendron.

It was somewhere along that stretch that I, feeling a bit too confident, took too long a stride while stepping down from one jutting rock to another and—*bingo*—fell on my ass. It was as though I were hook-sliding on my left buttock into second base, my right (bad) leg extended to hook the base and my left arm slamming to the ground (granite slab) for balance and my walking stick somewhere over there in the bushes. I had no balance when I went into the step and now I was akimbo on a pile of slick granite, glossy and treacherous as marble, and again I was alone and hurt. My shouts for David were answered only with echoes of my own voice. *Well, shit, this is it, end of story.*

I did the only thing I could do. I picked myself up and checked out the moving parts and found my staff and cinched my pack and looked for the next white blaze, visible maybe fifty yards ahead on a young pine that seemed to be growing out of a rock cropping, and moved on. It didn't take me an hour to cover the two remaining miles to Stekoah Gap. I felt like Alec Guinness again, bounding along gamely on the road to the River Kwai with a whistle and my staff, as I marched down a graded path to a grassy open field beside a paved road.

David sat in the high grass, his slate-gray pack pitched

over there somewhere, tossing a pine cone he had found to two blue-tick hounds, a husband and wife and two little kids standing behind their Winnebago looking on and grinning at the sight, and it was Photo Opportunity time. My boy looked like something out of an Alpo commercial. When he saw me coming he hurled the pine cone impossibly down the hill and the two hounds flashed away after it.

He smiled and his eyes disappeared, in the manner of Hemphill men, and he said, "Wesser's got a pal to walk with us now."

"Name of what?" I said. I joined him in the grass.

"I don't know. Road goes to Robbinsville. 'Robbinsville,' maybe."

"Ask me, I say they're Highwaymen. Rape, pillage, all of that."

"Nah. Just somebody's old hunting dogs."

*Minor footnote in the history of the Western world, I say, but the memory still burns hard. Sirron, the collie I bought for him when the boy wasn't seven years old, will be picked up by his new owners in the morning.* They've got a big old house out in the country in Alabama, *I tell the boy*, and he'll be a lot happier there than on the island. *We're moving to an island off the coast of Georgia where veterinarians say you should never take a dog like that. I've explained all of that, but how do you tell that to a boy whose dog is his brother? When I come home from work at dusk I find the boy with his arm draped around the collie, whose tail is flapping against the ground in the backyard, saying terrible things about me.*

I said, "Hell of a thing happened. I might have done a little chiropractry out there."

"How's that?"

"Fell on my ass and twisted my knee, and it was the same knee. But I'll be goddam if it doesn't feel better."

"Straightened it out, maybe."

"I don't know. It feels better, anyway. I ask no questions."

"If it ain't broke, don't fix it," he said.

We spent about an hour there, shoveling down peanuts and Snickers and raisins, watching the two hounds Wesser and Robbinsville gambol in the high bluegrass, taking pictures with the long lens of the view of the southern range of the Smokies we were about to attack, before moving out on the nine-mile walk at 4,000 feet into Cable Gap. The people of the Winnebago were gone in a puff of smoke toward Chattanooga. The blue-ticks chose to follow us on the trail leading into the woods.

Soon the pain returned. With it came intermittent rain. *Press on, lean into it, tough it out.* AT Guide: "Reach crest of ridge and ascend steeply. Reach the top of ridge and descend steeply to Sweetwater Gap. *Water* is 0.13 mi. to the left in gap. Pass through Sweetwater Gap and ascend steeply to rock cliffs. . . ." *Ascend, descend, rock cliffs, ascend, descend, water.* I was making a mile an hour now and by the time I reached Yellow Creek Gap, back down to about 3,000 feet in elevation, crossing a paved North Carolina state highway leading to the Alpine-ish resort of Fontana Village, it was black night and I flopped on the trail and fumbled for my flashlight. The batteries were nearly gone but I could make out quaint hand-carved lettering on a weathered post: CABLE GAP SHELTER 0.9 MI.

This shelter is so decrepit that even the mice don't bother it. It was built of hewn logs by the CCC in 1939 and outfitted with wire bunks. ("One time lightning hit one of those shelters with the wire bunks," went one of The Irish Goat's ghost stories, "and five hikers fried in their sleep.") But it was a welcome sight to see the raging campfire started by David, fully aware of his father's plight, and I was in no position to be picky when I arrived at what would pass for camp. Daddy rested.

# 17

Notes from my journal, scribbled in the half-light of dawn, between applications of Tylenol III and Ben-Gay and super-strength Maxwell House black instant coffee:

Fri 5-4

The pits. Cold wet morning, little sleep with knee. Think about holing up to rest but it's a lousy shelter and only seven miles to Fontana. . . . Even mice abandoned this place. . . . Catch up on three days' notes. . . . I CAN'T QUIT (first thought of it). For book, for Dave, for my rehabilitation. Susan says Hannah only one who asks what hike doing for me, rather than how the book going. It still strikes me, almost constantly, that I'm 48 and everybody else is 20-25. Haunted by the bad times with whiskey. Have dreams that I've pulled out of it. Novel will be hot, house in Decatur, kids successful, SAFPH and I in next 30 yrs. This pivotal means to an end. The long haul . . .

What was this, "pivotal"? Christ, every day of your life there's a "pivotal moment." How many more before I would grow up?

*I'm twenty, summer of '56, and after a twelve-hour shift in front of the ovens at Merita Bakery in Birmingham I go home to my parents' house (I'm living there in the summers until I finish college) to change into the gray wool uniform saying FLEMING TRANSFER across the chest and then my old man and I bump across town in his truck for a game against a bunch of washed-up minor leaguers representing a pipe mill. I make two errors and strike out three times and after the game I slam my Bob Dillinger glove to the ground next to Pop's truck and say,* That's it, I quit. *He says,* Just a goddam quitter, *the first time I've ever heard him cuss like that.* Eddie Stanky spent nine years in the minor leagues, *he says.* Quit, hell.

"Well?" David said.

"Next stop, the Smokies," I said.

"You okay?"

"My head's a mess and the knee ain't so hot. Other than that, it's okay."

"I got an idea there's some mail waiting at Fontana Village."

"Reason enough to blow this joint," I said, and after lolling about for a while we gathered ourselves together and sauntered through the woods for a couple of hours until we came upon an asphalt road where suddenly everything was preened and right out of *Southern Living* magazine—mown grass, orderly roadside trees, newly striped macadam roads, a golf course, sprinklers, Cadillacs holding silver-hairs gawking at us through tinted air-conditioned windshields—and we, bedraggled and bearded and sweaty hikers that we were, didn't bother to stick up our thumbs. We walked the two miles to Fontana Village, notorious among AT hikers for its inhospitality, to buy some grub.

Fontana Village is actually a neat little shopping strip, hard by the dam forming Fontana Lake at the southern boundary of the Great Smoky Mountains National Park, where a Cadillac Republican can wheel in to buy anything from *The Wall Street Journal* to some Bloody Mary mix. The connected stores (restaurant, post office, grocery, "tog shoppe," even a dry cleanery) are done up the way *Southern Living* promises: stained shag cedar, white patio chairs and tables out front on the veranda, air-conditioning, designer T-shirts; Gatlinburg Revisited, about as true to the Southern Appalachians as Opryland U.S.A. is to country music. The rub comes when a bearded foul-smelling hairy-legged backpacker stumbles upon this perfect American Express idyll, just looking for supplies, and stands in line at the grocery store ahead of a grandmother wanting only to pay for her picture postcards of cigar-store Cherokees without any fanfare. The old fellow who runs the grocery store is trapped, as a result, between two worlds.

Good thing we hailed the ranger, then, just as he was getting out of his Jeep and headed into the grocery for a pack of mints. We had to get backpacking permits to go through the park, anyway, and we figured it wouldn't prejudice our appearance in the store if we stepped in line behind a United States Forest Service ranger in his creased uniform and wraparound sunglasses and Smokey the Bear cap. Nice fellow. Given a choice, I was thinking as he went to the Jeep for his clipboard and book of regulations, he'd probably take sleeping in the woods over writing up DUI warnings.

"Through-hikers, you say."

"That's the idea," said David.

"Well," the ranger said, "you fellows know all of this

but I've got to run it past you, anyway. No dogs, no fire-arms, no campfires except in the shelters, so forth, so on."
He looked at me, standing on one leg and securing the knee brace on the other. "You okay?" he said.

"Oh, hell, yeah," I told him.

"Got some bad weather coming up."

"Tell me."

"Can't send any helicopters up there to get you."

"It ain't *that* bad," I said.

"Whatever you say." He gave us our permits, baggage tags filled out in indelible ink so they could be worn outside the pack and checked at any time ("I don't want to wake you up in the middle of the night and tell you you're in the wrong shelter"), and then we followed him into the store. The manager of the store was very nice. He had eleven boxes of Minute Rice left and we bought them all, and a lot more, the bill coming to just over $78. The food would have to last us for ten days or until we reached the little North Carolina town of Hot Springs.

We checked the post office and I called Susan (David got a top-secret letter and some colored "party beads" from Kelley; I found that an old friend, the novelist Paul Darcy Boles, had died the day before in Atlanta). We moved down the hill from the village to a pavilion and began separating the groceries—*I'll take the oatmeal, you take the rice, who wants to mix the gorp?*—and after filling the canisters with unleaded gas at the Exxon station (it was too much to ask of the old fellow at the grocery store to carry white gas for hikers' stoves) we followed the picturesque macadam road, twisting between holes of the Fontana Village golf course, stepping aside for the honking Winnebagos and Cadillacs, huffing under the load of forty-five-pound packs (the heaviest we had ever been) in search of the ultimate AT shelter: the "Fontana Hilton"

It was dusk and we stood at the dam, deep blue water on all sides of us and the smoky haze of the mountains above, not exactly sure of our whereabouts. I said, "You must've walked past it."

"What's this 'you' shit?"

"You're in the lead, pal. You got the map?"

"What map?"

"One the cop gave us."

He said, "Cop? He's a *ranger*. He's a *forest* ranger."

"Cop, ranger, what's the difference?"

"There's a *hell* of a difference."

"Shit, kid—"

"Hell of a difference."

"—it's a figure of speech. Anybody in a uniform's a cop to me. Guy at the bank in a coat and tie's a cop to me."

"*Cop*. Incredible. A *cop*. He's a *forest ranger*."

David was still ranting, not about to admit that he had missed the turnoff for the Fontana Dam Shelter, when a bearded old fellow in an orange Volkswagen van (he looked like Burl Ives and said he was waiting for his grandson to come off the trail) saw our quandary and said he would give us a lift up the road a half mile to the shelter. *A forest ranger is a hell of a lot more than a cop*, David was saying. *Stuff it, kid*, said I. The man stopped his van and he winked at me, knowingly, as he pointed to the sign saying AT SHELTER. I thanked the man and told him I hoped nothing had gone wrong for his grandson, and he said, "Ah, he'll be all right. He'll be here when he gets here. You know boys."

They call it the "Fontana Hilton" because a hiker, stumbling in from 175 miles' worth of mice-infested thirty- to fifty-year-old log lean-tos, feels like a prospector who suddenly finds himself standing in the lobby of the St. Francis Hotel in San Francisco. We're talking about an airplane hangar with a view here—split-level, A-frame, room for at least forty hikers if they like each other, several picnic tables and barbecue grills on a graveled "patio" overlooking the whole damned dam—and it was no wonder to me that when David and I finally flopped upon its lap there would be an ample young woman, standing there in the gravel, her brown hair lost in the swirl of smoke from a T-bone steak sizzling on a grill, waggling a quart bottle of Jim Beam at me and saying, "How 'bout it? Want a sip?"

"There was a time," I said, "there was a time."

Her name was Nancy and her friend's name was Keith, both from Houston, whatever the deal was, and there was another hiker there in the shadows—Don, it was, a rangy fellow who went off into the bushes to throw up now and then—and David and I just sort of dropped our packs where they landed and melted into the scene. There were stories to be told (about The Irish Goat's mousetraps and Festus' polyester suits and the very audacity of Albert Mountain) and soon David and I, me and the boy, walked down the road to the dam, where there were hot showers, and by eleven o'clock at night we were flashing our Duralites and finding our sleeping bags and snuggling in for our last night's rest before the exploration of the Smokies. The last sounds I heard, from across the way in the Fontana Hilton, where Nancy and Keith had zipped their sleeping bags together into a jury-rigged king-sized comfort (it really *does* work), were the earnest rumplings of love being made.

# 18

"KEITH'S BEEN AWFULLY SUPPORTIVE."

"He seems like a good fellow."

"He stayed at Fontana for a week while I went home for treatment."

"You go all the way to Houston?"

"Shots and stuff."

"What's wrong?"

"They don't know," she said. "They give me shots and then a shrink comes around. They talk about bone marrow and then they ask me what *I* think. They write down another fifty dollars for a half hour and they ask me what I think again. I tell 'em I don't know what I think and they say that's very interesting and do I want to come back Wednesday. It's crazy."

Nancy and I sat on a flat rock at Shuckstack, sipping water and enjoying the morning sun, while David and Keith were off exploring the fire tower a couple of hundred yards away through the brambles. The four of us, fully loaded for the seventy-mile hike through the Smokies, had ambled the climb from Fontana Dam at 1,700 feet to the perch at

Shuckstack (4,020) in a pleasant two hours. It was a hot, dry Saturday, replete with day-hikers. A couple in their seventies passed us and smiled and spoke ("Way we stay young," the woman said, "is walking up to Shuckstack every Saturday morning"). Nancy, a handsome young woman in her mid-twenties, liked that.

"I want to live forever," she said.

"Don't we all."

"I want to go to parties and I want to dance and I want to see deer and I want to sleep in the rain."

"You'll have your chances," I said.

"You wouldn't drink my Jim Beam last night."

"I can't do that anymore."

"Are you an alcoholic?"

"Probably."

"We shouldn't do it, either. Everybody we know's a drunk, I guess. You can't believe the parties in Houston. 'Let's meet for drinks,' everybody says. We can't go anywhere without that. That's probably why we're out here. I mean, give me a break."

"How's the whiskey holding out?" I said.

"Tonight we go cold turkey until Hot Springs," Nancy said.

Somewhere in Birmingham, probably deep in a drawer in the living room of the apartment where David and Lisa and Molly stay with their mother, there is a ragged black-and-white photograph of the former Susan Olive standing up in a gray 1960 Volkswagen and feeding a bear through the sunroof. This was somewhere on the twisting road between Gatlinburg and Clingman's Dome, fall of '61, and we had followed thousands of other Southern couples in picking the cool mountain air of the Great Smoky Mountains National Park for our honeymoon. We didn't know anything about the Appalachian Trail then. We couldn't care less that the Smokies were older than the Rockies by 125 million years; that the Cherokee Indian Nation fought

its last fight on those mile-high ridges in the early nineteenth century; that within the confines of the park there
are more species of plants than anyplace else in the world;
that the loggers came and tried to rape the land until FDR
came to the rescue and made it a national park. You're
interested in a different kind of rape, the more conventional
type, when you are in your twenties and in love and on
your honeymoon in a cedar-shaked A-frame overlooking
the main drag of Gatlinburg where the sad descendants of
the Cherokees ("Uncle Tomahawks") are selling war bon-
nets made in Taiwan and the great-grandsons of the Appalachian pioneers are ringing up trout-fishing-by-the-pound.
You want to screw, that's what you want to do; sort of
hang an exclamation point on what the preacher put into
motion earlier in the day in the solemn halls of a big Baptist
church in Birmingham.

*My dream is to come home at the end of the day, or*
*as soon after 5:30 as I can make it, and be greeted*
*beyond a white picket fence by you and two children.*
*One boy, one girl. (I'm writing this to Susan Olive,*
*the girl of my dreams, from Tallahassee, Florida,*
*where, soon after Gatlinburg, I've gone to take a job*
*and pave the way for our future.) What's that song—*
*"And Molly Makes Three"? We'll be happy in my*
*blue heaven. Although I prefer white. Love and kisses*
*forever.*

David and Keith came sliding down from the Shuckstack
fire tower, cameras swinging from their necks, in time to
wave at a gaggle of Girl Scouts out for a Saturday stroll.
It was going to be a hot dry day, day-hikers everywhere,
but an easy one once we had made the uphill scramble to
the 4,000-foot mesa of the Smokies. We sat on the flat
rocks and in the dust, guzzling water, and soon were joined
by the gangly fellow who had spent the night before ex-

cusing himself from the Fontana Hilton to go off and throw
up in the bushes.

"You okay?" Nancy said to him.

"I hereby proclaim Shuckstack for whoever wants it,"
he said.

"What've you got?" said Keith.

"*Giardia*. That makes twice already. Water's bad for
your health."

"You ought to put pills in the water."

"That's what my doctor tells me." His name was Don
Rorer, he said (R-O-R-E-R, only name spelled like that in
any phone book in America; he looked it up), from no
place in particular, "gonna beat this sonofabitch if it kills
me and it probably will." The first time he had been hit
with *giardia*, a violent stomach virus which most often
originates with bear feces and can't be killed by boiling
water or putting tablets in it, it was in the mountains of
north Georgia and two stretcher-bearers had to bring him
out to a hospital in Hiawassee. "I've got several doctors
now," he said.

"You going to Katahdin?" David asked Rorer.

"One way or the other. Neither rain nor sleet nor snow,
and all of that shit."

And so we were off again. Thirty miles away was Clingman's Dome, the highest point in the Smokies at 6,643
feet, but our having mounted Shuckstack at slightly above
4,000 elevation meant that now we were up there on the
shelf. Now we would be walking through the most virginal
stretch of woodlands in the eastern United States. It was
the Smokies—high and wild and lush and with a rhythm of
its own—and we were there not in a sun-roofed Volkswag-
en but wading through the laurel and the rhododendron
with packs on our backs. Rain, sleet, snow? First week of
May? Impossible.

There would be more climbing to do (we would be advised, as we stopped for a water break and flipped through

the AT Trail Guide, that not until a place called Doe Knob
at 4,520 feet would we have officially reached the crest of
the range) but that didn't matter. We found that you don't
talk very much when you're walking in the Smokies. They
are that awesome. You find yourself Up There, in the company of virgin forests and deer (protected, unafraid, going
about their business, they will all but pose for photographs)
and the first blossoms of dogwood and azalea and mountain
laurel, sometimes ankle deep in lush fields of bluet, now
and then having to step around a blue-black pile of bear
droppings to remind you that the animals are protected but
the people aren't; up there, a guest, just passing through.
You forget pretty quickly that halfway through the park
you could bum a ride in an air-conditioned car, at a paved
lot where tourists in Bermuda shorts park in order to walk
up a ramp to an observation tower on Clingman's Dome,
and be eating pizza in Gatlinburg within half an hour.

· Nancy and Keith, in love, dawdling along at their own
pace, dropped off at the first shelter, Birch Spring Shelter,
only an hour or so beyond Shuckstack, and David and I
kept striding along the footpath. Now, with spring coming
to the highlands, the footpath was trimmed in bluet and the
first bright green sprigs of the new year's grass. Juncos and
squirrels and butterflies and deer were everywhere, paying
little attention to us as we ambled through the meadows
and the abrupt clumps of rhododendron. Where was a phil-
harmonic and "Appalachian Spring"? *Aaron Copland
would have been proud*, I thought as we reached a marker
announcing Ekaneetlee Gap, which I had heard of and read
about in my perusals of the AT Guide and histories of the
Cherokee Nation, this being a hospitable crossing through
the ridge of the Smokies for centuries before Bluegrass music even had a name. Soon we were sweeping along a high
open ridge and hearing the whinnying of horses.

David got there ahead of me and had already hung his
pack in the shelter, Mollies Ridge Shelter, built-in wire

bunks on two levels, spring and latrine nearby, the "front lawn" of black loam and green grass chewed up like a rodeo ring (stamping of the horses or frenzied grubbing of the imported wild boars?), and was kibitzing with a fortyish fellow who was busy hanging saddles and blankets and bridles on wall pegs. Two steaming horses and a bright blue family-sized tent were some fifty yards behind the shelter in a grove.

"You and Mom rode a Volkswagen," David told me. "Check *this* out."

"What's happening?" I said, taking off my pack and plopping on the ledge of the shelter. I lit a Camel.

"They're on their honeymoon."

"You're kidding."

The cowboy said it was true. He and his bride were both from the horse country of Middle Tennessee, the rolling grassy balds south of Nashville, and in one day they got married and he got accepted for the graduate school in animal husbandry at the University of Tennessee and they saddled up for a honeymoon in the Smokies. I kept quiet about sore loins and being back in the saddle again—all barroom references, in fact, to the all-night plunging and groping rumored to take place during air-conditioned-motel honeymoons in the Great Smoky Mountains National Park—and asked him, instead, pointing to a sad lump in one of the lower wire bunks, "Is that her?"

"The wife? Oh, naw. Frenchman there."

"A Frenchman, you say."

"John-something. You talk French?"

*"Un petit peu."*

"What the hell's that mean?"

"Not much," I said. "Not much at all."

The cowboy left to tend to his bride and his horses, but not before he had told me what he knew about the hiker zonked in the lower wire bunk: Quebecois, maybe thirty years old, something about a car wreck, heartbroken, "fat sloppy kid ain't got no business out here on the trail,'' going to Asheville if he can find it, and you ought to ask him about the French interpreter who met him in Gatlinburg and drove him to Fontana Village and why it took them two days to get there. I couldn't wait to wake up the Frenchman after David and I had eaten our rice-and-soup.

''*Non-non-non*,'' he said.

''Okay, okay,'' I told him.

''*Qu'est-ce que?*''

''*Dormez non.*'' It sounded good at the time.

''*Qu'est-ce que?*

His name was Gene-Guy, as it turned out, and after a while, over the hooting of owls and the scratching of cicadas and the rooting of boars, we began to come to a curious sort of Quebec-Atlanta understanding of each other's native language. My ''Good Old Boy'' became Gene-Guy's ''*bon* fell*ah*'' and Gene-Guy's ''*petite jeune fille*'' turned out to mean ''pretty little thing.''

''So,'' I said, ''I *ecrivez 'Moi et Son Fils.'* ''

''You, son?''

''Yeah, we're walking together.''

''*Il est, 'Mon Fils et Moi.'* ''

''I got people that do that,'' I said. ''I'll swap you a Camel for a Gauloise.''

''Gauloise? Camel?''

''Close as you're gonna get in Asheville to Gauloise is a Camel.''

Let's see here. Gene-Guy was thirty-one, a French-Canadian from Quebec City—fat belly, rosy cheeks, chain-smoker, hiking equipment from almost everywhere—and he had been through some things lately. He had gotten kicked out by his wife two years earlier and a year after that he had almost been killed in a car wreck with a girl-friend and then he had been fired from his job as a Nautilus instructor in Quebec (''Unrepresentative,'' he said, patting his rubber-tire belly and waving a Gauloise) and now he found himself out there on the Appalachian Trail, in the midst of the Smokies, and finally he had found somebody he could latch onto.

"*La femme*," I said.

"*Oui?*"

"*Directeur.*" Stumbling, here: "*L'auto.*"

"*Ooo la-la.*"

"*Au* Fontana."

Gene-Guy fairly burst into song. He flared his hands out away from his chest, mimicking grapefruits, and then he swept his hands down his thighs. "*Interprète*," he said.

"*Voulez-vous?*" I said.

He nodded his head vigorously.

"*Du vin?*"

He did the same.

"*Couchez moi?*"

*Petit déjeuner? Du croissant? Café? Voulez-vous?* Yes-yes-yes, said Gene-Guy, before it was over trading me two Gauloises for every Camel, and I was glad David had slept through the exchange. It was raining a fury in the morning when Gene-Guy said he must leave, popping two "breakfast pills," waving goodbye and walking straight into the wind in his poncho. All but airborne.

# 19

RED SKY AT MORNING, SAILOR TAKE WARNING? You couldn't even *see* the sky at midmorning when Gene-Guy and the cowboy and his lady had broken camp. I was on my second Sierra cup of extra-strength Maxwell House, watching a family of deer finish off what the wild boars had started on the disheveled front lawn, and it came to me that maybe today I would see the horrors I had imagined less than a year earlier when I looked down on the Smokies—book contract in hand, sipping a martini, riding first-class in a Delta jet, promising that tomorrow I would get in shape—and saw Nature putting on a laser show. Hell was about to be paid.

David stirred awake in an upper wire bunk, took a look and thought better of it, and collapsed in the fetal position. After ten or fifteen minutes like that, half awake (I was on my third cup of coffee), he arched up on his elbows and said, "They've got to be kidding."

"I think they're serious," I said.

"Frenchman gone?"

"Him and the cowboy."

He unraveled himself and dropped down to the dirt floor of the shelter. I had finally chanced to try lighting the stove. Water was simmering. He opened two packs of oatmeal-and-raisins and slurped from his Sierra cup. When he was done he said, "Let me try one of those things." He motioned toward the box of Gauloise cigarettes.

"You're allowed three per day."

"That's about all I can stand."

*"Pour la patrie,"* I said.

"What's that mean?"

"I don't know. Gene-Guy said it."

"You understand what he's saying?"

"No, but it's fun trying."

These were the best times, the moments of aimless babbling, and I wondered if this was not the best way to spend time with someone you love and care for. We had a lot of catching up to do, of course, and debating the merits of détente with the Soviet Union was not on the agenda (although we did, come to think of it, hold a lively discussion about the *contra* rebels in Nicaragua). Idle commentaries about likes and dislikes and dreams and failures (mine, usually) were the stuff of our conversations as we probed and circled each other like lovers. If all went well, if we hiked the entire AT together, we would spend 150 days and nights in the company of each other. Then, too, walking 2,142 miles through the forest was not unlike what they used to say about pulling a thirteen-month hitch in Vietnam: "hours of boredom interrupted by brief moments of stark terror." We had a couple of those coming up.

Alone in the shelter at midmorning, rain pelting the tin roof now and high winds making the giant trees creak and sway, we plotted the day's trek. Maybe the guidebook *did* say that we had crested the shelf of the Smokies back there two and a half miles ago at Doe Knob, but now we were preparing to reach 5,000 feet in elevation and stay between there and more than 6,000 feet for the next fifty miles of hiking. This was a Sunday, May 6, and the day's destination was a shelter only 10.7 miles away. Now we would be getting into the big country—high grassy balds, bear country, virgin forests, the thin air, laurel and rhododendron and sugar maples, no hand-holding weekend hikers here—and it might take some time to reach Derrick Krob Shelter, even in sparkling picture-postcard weather. The AT Trail Guide and contour map and profile made no promises.

"Well," David said, the map laid out on the grungy floor of the shelter. "Meet you at the shelter?"

"With luck."

"Man. Look at that." Now he read from the pocketbook Trail Guide. " 'Turn right and enter woods. Follow along flat crest through open parklike woods, descending slightly, and enter grassy Spence Field.' Everywhere in here it's talking about meadows and virgin forests and springs. What's this Cades Cove?"

"Appalachian family, I think. Farmed up here with the Cherokees."

"Aren't there some Bluegrass songs about Cades Cove?"

"Lot of pen-and-ink sketches of it in Gatlinburg. Cabins and stuff."

The kid studied the maps some more. "It says 'splendid views' everywhere. This is incredible." He laid back and chewed some gorp. "This is the real thing, the Smokies."

"We're about to find out," I said.

The profile of that stretch of the trail looked like an X ray of a dinosaur's back—up, down, switchback left, up again, plummet, switchback right—and now there was the weather. David and I loaded up with proteins and made sure each of us had plenty of gorp and honey and Snickers reachable in our packs, in case there would not be a lunch, and soon we were off. We would meet at the shelter.

We should have walked together that day, of course, but

up that high in altitude one never knows what to project about the weather. "Chaos" will barely cover what happened to us between, say, ten o'clock in the morning and seven at night when dark had already fallen on Derrick Knob. It wasn't too bad in the beginning, walking alone (albeit with the heavy ten-day load) for the first five miles to Spence Field Shelter, high on a brownish grassy mesa at 5,000 feet, David and a half dozen other hikers, including Gene-Guy, huddled from the intermittent storms. One storm broke and David and the others left, only Gene-Guy staying behind, and then I followed. Derrick Knob was only six miles away, I figured, and I had the whole afternoon to make it before dark.

It took me five and a half hours, through three separate and distinct hail-and-lightning storms, to negotiate the six miles of trail. It was indescribable. It was Nature calling attention to itself. The thunder and lightning would crash down on me, angrily splintering the centuries-old hardwoods, blackening the sky, making a trout stream out of the footpath, crackling and echoing through the valleys below, suddenly stopping long enough for me to take pictures in bright sunshine, just as suddenly blackening again. The weather blew and crashed and bellowed, sending me on my belly in the womb of rhododendron clumps—kidding myself that the stark white flashes of lightning wouldn't find me there—before the sun would show itself again and I would whistle and walk a few hundred yards through gentle upland forest, where I didn't take note that the deer and the bear and the squirrel and the junco weren't daring to go out and play on a day like that, before the wrath would begin anew.

Dark was coming an hour early. I was on my knees, holding to a sapling, thirty-mile-an-hour gusts having put me there, halfway through an endless ascent where the trail stretched upward into the blackness. Everything I had was soaked—clothes, flashlight, food, cigarettes, probably the

$500 Nikon—and I was down to cursing trees. *If that fucking shelter ain't on top of that ridge I'll bivouac*, I swore, *and I don't even have the tarp*. There was no letup and I had no good reason to dream of one. At that point I fancied myself as nothing more or less than a man with a desire to live. So I picked myself up and I stumbled forward, grabbing at bushes and low limbs, leaning into the wind, not caring anymore about the angry flashes and sparks of lightning, telling myself that I wouldn't stop until something stopped me.

"Enter overgrown field," says the AT Trail Guide. *"Derrick Knob Shelter* on left. (Built-in wire bunks accommodate 12; *spring* and latrine nearby. Shelter is located where herder's cabin used to stand, in what was once an open field.) Keep left here. Beyond shelter, enter woods." No more woods for me today, thank you very much, for I had fumbled upon Mecca: bedraggled, sore-kneed, dripping and soaked, of despair, querulous about the crowd of people standing on the other side of the bear-cage fence giving me a standing ovation.

"My name is Moses," I said, waggling my staff, stroking my beard, hunching over, just happy to be there.

"That your dad?" came a woman's voice.

"Yeah." It was David.

". . . Moses, come to the mountaintop . . ."

"Well, hurry on in," called another woman.

". . . with one word to deliver . . ."

"Let's hear it," somebody said.

". . . bullshit."

The bear cage flew open and I fell into the shelter and the door was shut behind me. David was there, indeed, plus Don Rorer of *giardia* and another male hiker whose name I never caught and four white-haired women who called themselves "the Shelter-Belters." They were grandmothers from Connecticut, their spokesperson said, and that was their moniker because of a 151-proof rum concoction they were semifamous for mixing and serving and thoroughly enjoying at the end of each hiking day. "Last summer we went to the Big Bend National Park on the Rio Grande and we nearly killed some rattlesnakes with the Shelter-Belter one night." The woman who told me that then took David's address and promised to send him her favorite recipe for cheesecake.

Happy to be there, indeed. I draped my wet stuff wherever I could find a place on the bear cage. I heard the grandmothers say what a wonderful idea this was, father and son on the Appalachian Trail, and saw a batch of wallet-sized photographs of their grandchildren and heard their tales of summerly expeditions. David cooked up a batch of rice for me and was curiously silent, waiting for the brouhaha over my arrival to subside, and with a fire bellowing in the fireplace Rorer took the floor, as it were, with stories and observations of women ("They own or control one hundred percent of the pussy and ninety percent of the money in North America and I can prove it") and babies ("They all look like Winston Churchill with gas") and Jesus ("He told God he didn't want to go but the old man wouldn't listen") and bears. Finally, high up in the Smokies, the bear stories and rumors had begun: "Two hikers got jumped right up the trail here; came back to the shelter with rags and aluminum frames to show for their packs; all the bear wants is your Snickers; first one I see, I'm gonna knock the shit out of him and keep on walking. . . ."

And now, at full dark, flames flickering, even the Shelter-Belters softly snoring, David said, "I worried about you."

"Me, too. Believe me."

"I saw the lightning and bushwhacked back to the shelter."

"Gene-Guy there?"

"Yeah, but he wasn't about to move. Me, either, in that lightning."

"It was dumb, I guess," I said, "but I was stuck."

"Were you gonna bivouac?"

"It was a thought."

"That was crazy. You ought to know better than that."

"I know. But what can you do?"

"Anyways," David said, "I worried about you."

"I appreciate that."

"We should've stayed together." I nodded in the dark of the shelter at that. Now, maybe overcompensating for the right knee, I had screwed up the other one. I said nothing about that to the kid. I lathered up the left knee with Ben-Gay and lay back in the wire bunk and tried to sleep. Bears, huh? Somewhere in the shank of the night I dragged away to the bushes to relieve myself on a flat rock and I was startled to see the lights of Fontana Dam blazing through the fog from the valley.

# 20

IT WAS STORMING AGAIN IN THE MORNING AND NOBODY was in a mood to go anywhere, any time soon, and spirits didn't pick up until around noon when Gene-Guy suddenly appeared in front of the shelter. He had chanced it the afternoon before, between storms, but had chosen to bivouac on the exposed stretches of Thunderhead Mountain (aptly named, just where all of the storms were their nastiest, about where David and I must have passed each other headed in different directions). Now Gene-Guy stood bewildered before the bear cage, like an orphan looking for a friend, and when I prattled something in my half-French he grinned and entered the shelter to yet another standing ovation. I had found a box of Gauloises, buried deep and dry with the Nikon, and I split the cigarettes with him.

"You-all aren't leaving, are you?" Don Rorer can awaken in midsentence from a nap. We were wishing the best of luck to Gene-Guy in Asheville (he would leave the AT at the parking lot on Clingman's Dome and nose his way there). The Shelter-Belters said they might hold Rorer hostage for another day or so, however long it took to save his soul.

"We're not exactly in a hurry," David said. "It must be two o'clock."

"I wasn't kidding about the bears," said Rorer.

"Where 'bouts?" I asked.

"Pretty soon. The closer you get to Clingman's Dome the more you see of the road bears."

"Road bears."

"Bad hombres. People feed 'em out of their cars and they get to expect it. Rangers shoot 'em with darts, airlift 'em off the road, put 'em in the valleys. Next thing you know, they're back up here mugging backpackers."

"What do you do when that happens?"

"I told you. Pop 'em in the nose and keep walking."

From there we moved persistently on up the ridge to Silers Bald Shelter at a mile in elevation. The only item worth noting from there in my journal was that we shared the shelter with an inaccessible forty-ish lone hiker; was up there from Huntsville on a week's vacation, forgot to bring his Sierra cup and borrowed David's; put his wet Pivetta boots on a rock so close to the fireplace that they were baked and curled in the morning; farted all night from his wire bunk in terrifying thunderclaps, the most prodigious farter I ever even heard of. He did have some intelligence, though, about this shelter: "Yesterday morning a Mama Bear smelled the bacon and held a dozen hikers hostage for an hour. Got bored after a while and walked away. Ambushed 'em less than a mile away."

The next morning, feeling good on a crisp blue-sky morning, the blood just now coursing up from our boots to our heads after a stroll of less than a mile through the high woods from the shelter, we nearly bumped into her. David was jouncing ahead of me by five or ten paces. I had written a long letter to Molly the night before—by candlelight, between farts from Huntsville, applying Ben-Gay to my knees—and I felt pretty good about this whole thing. The footpath was smooth and easy, sweeping along a ridge at about 5,500 feet, spring blossoms coming now to the highlands, a steep drop into a ravine to the left and a sheer face of granite to the right, a small mesa known as Jenkins Knob just around the curve in the trail.

"Uh-oh," David shouted. He stopped and I nearly ran him over.

"That her?" I said.

"I'm not asking questions."

"Well, shit, kid, what do we do?"

"It's her move. She lives here, remember?"

I would let that pass. I was scared shitless. A black bear, maybe three hundred pounds, sat patiently in the middle of the footpath no more than fifty yards ahead of us. It was clear that she had done this many times before. She knew from all of her experience that we had a lot of stuff in those packs on our backs that brought her joy and she also knew that we would drop the packs and run the minute she challenged us for them. Up on the knob ahead, gamboling through the thick green grass after butterflies, were two cubs who weighed maybe forty pounds each. Mama Bear had plenty of time.

"At least we can get a picture," I said.

"You're thinking *pictures*?"

"Great for the wire services if they find us."

"Okay. Don't move." David walked backward, toward me.

"Bottom pouch of my pack," I said.

My boy's proudest moment came next. I have to tell you that. He was carefully trying to unzip the bottom compartment of my pack, trying to make no sudden moves, in search of the Nikon, when suddenly the bear reared up and growled and made a sudden charge. Both David and I just as suddenly made an aimless dash for the steep hill on our left (somewhere we had heard that if you get a bear running at hard-charge downhill he/she can't change direction at full gallop). Then, after a run of only twenty yards, she put on the brakes and again sat on her hind legs to await our next move. That's when David made a run at *her*, for Christ's sake, and she growled again and went trundling back up the footpath and up on the granite hill above us. The kid was shouting and stomping his boots and whistling and running like hell, as was I, and we didn't look back until we had run two hundred yards past the two cubs playing on the knob.

A half mile later we sat on the floor of Double Springs Gap Shelter, partaking of what was passing for lunch these days (peanut butter on some Ritz crackers we had bought at Fontana Village), watching another storm roll in. "Come on," David said, "admit it. You were scared."

"There's 'scared' and there's 'cautious.' "

"Frozen in your tracks"

"You just got to wait and see what happens next," I said.

"C'mon, Dad, where's the old spirit of adventure?"

"Did you see the teeth and the claws on that sucker?"

"It's 'Me and the Boy,' Dad."

"I wish we'd had Don Rorer with us," I said.

Onward and upward it was from there, plunging ahead in the rain and the wind on the trout-stream AT footpath, all the way to Clingman's Dome at the very cap of the Smokies. "Reach *Clingman's Dome* (6,643 ft.)," reads the guidebook. *"This is highest point on AT.* Rare mountain cranberry is abundant here. (Side trail to right leads 50 yd. to observation tower, providing splendid view above balsam fir trees)." It was here that David's mother and I, the former Susan Olive, had held hands in our honeymoon bliss and sauntered up the spiral concrete ramp nearly twenty-three years earlier to pay little attention to the massive smoky vista of wrinkled mountains spread out below us like a picture postcard. On this foggy day, though, my son and I could see nothing. We descended from the tower and walked on.

Our mileage that day would come to only 7.6—not too bad, really, considering the late start and the bear and the climb and the weather and the condition of my knees—but we decided to pack it in for the day at four o'clock in the afternoon. We were about halfway through the Smokies now, at the Mount Collins Shelter, and it appeared from the profile and the guidebook that the incessant climbing was over. Had not Don Rorer observed, for the benefit of the Shelter-Belters, that once you make it to Clingman's Dome "it's all downhill after that"?

When we steamed into the shelter the sun was shining and I began to take off my many layers of clothing, stripping down to my walking shorts and a T-shirt, while we chatted with a married couple from Indiana (she an employee at Purdue, he a television news director in LaFayette, they on a week's hiking vacation through the Smokies). Within thirty minutes it was snowing and the temperature had plunged at least twenty degrees, to the freezing mark, and just as suddenly I began to shiver and lose my bearings and find it difficult to make my hands work as I hustled back into my clothes and then tried to zip up my sleeping bag. It was then that a ranger popped in on the shelter, traveling with a "fanny pack" and a clipboard, just making his rounds to be sure all of his hikers were accounted for.

"It's my dad," I heard David say to the ranger. "We're walking together. His permit's on his pack over there."

"He okay?" the ranger said.

"Just cold and tired, I guess."

"Were y'all in the rain?"

"All the time, it seems," David said.

"You better bundle him up. Get him something hot to drink. He's about got hypothermia. That stuff can kill a fella."

The ranger, an officious young fellow in a crisp uniform,

wouldn't leave the shelter until he saw that I was bundled up and being force-fed hot tea. He learned over his walkie-talkie that the road to Clingman's Dome had just been closed due to snow and ice, and "there won't be any way in the world to get you out of here tonight." Only by drinking yourself into a stupor could you feel anything like this—shaking, slurring, seeing things, exhausted, wanting only to be left alone to curl up and sleep—and I would have the idea later that it wasn't so much that this ranger was gabby (rangering was a good life, didn't pay too much, you about had to have a Ph.D. to qualify these days, he'd just done a two-year tour in Canaveral Park in Florida) as that he wasn't about to see me go to sleep and die on him.

Much later, around ten o'clock at night, I awoke and found David nuzzled up beside me in his sleeping bag, sharing his body heat with me. He had scrounged enough semidry wood to keep a good fire going. The couple, Steve and Lisa, were burrowed in their bags and it had turned into a hard cold night.

"You okay now? You want something to eat?" David said.

"I never went through anything like that before," I told him.

"Ranger was plenty worried."

"I must've been crazy."

"He explained it. That's the way it works."

"I could use some tea," I said. "And if you could light me a cigarette I'd appreciate it."

"Sure," he said.

## 21

Now, EARLY IN MAY WITH MANY PEOPLE GETTING A JUMP on their summer vacations, the hills were alive with hikers. The Great Smoky Mountain National Park being the most-visited of any in the entire national parks system, the place would at times swirl like Daytona Beach with every imaginable type of hiker: the horse-packers, Good Old Boys traveling in packs and carrying beer coolers for a day or two, elderly couples out on day-hikes like the ones we met at Shuckstack, troops of Boy Scouts, teams of bird-watchers patiently crouching behind flat rocks at daybreak in hopes of spying one they had never seen before, teenaged lovebirds hiking with a reed picnic basket up a blue-blazed side trail to their secret place; young ones, old ones, experienced ones wearing long-haul equipment, greenhorns in discount-store sneakers, happy ones and sad ones.

And in the three-sided shelters at day's end, rustled up and secured behind the protective bear-cage screens, there was an unspoken segregation of the classes. On one side, boisterous and nibbling all manner of snacks while they borrowed salve and Band-Aids from each other and compared blisters on feet shod in wingtips only the day before, were the strollers, the short-timers, the rookies, the gawkers, the ones who had waited for forecasts of perfect weather before venturing out on a two- or three-day excursion. On the other side, subdued and grim and dirty and unshaven and rationing their rice, there were the through-hikers, the committed, the ones who scribbled their daily mileage in weathered AT guidebooks, the ones counting off the number of miles and days to go before making Katahdin, much like prisoners mark off the days before they're up for parole.

Sometimes, when curiosity had gotten the best of him, a stroller would venture conversation with a through-hiker. *So,* he would begin, *that's a pretty rough climb up from, what's the name of that shelter, hon, yeah, up from Russell Field Shelter. Huh?*

*I've seen worse.*

*Been hiking for a while, have you?*

*'bout three weeks. Running behind already.*

*How far you going with all that stuff?*

*Maine.*

*You hear that, hon? Fella's walking to Maine.*

The stroller's wife says, *My God. Where do you sleep, and things?*

*You're looking at it,* the through-hiker says.

*What made you want to do something like this?*

*It's a long story.*

And the through-hikers loved it. They felt downright heroic, in fact, just when they needed it the most. For days and weeks they had trudged forward, the truly serious among them going it alone and at their own pace, enduring the weather and the hunger and the pain and the awesome silence of the high mountain forests. The Wolves, these lonesome travelers, welcomed the chances, at night in the shelters, to be gawked at and listened to and even admired for their courage. They loved to be able to tell of the pain they had walked through and the tricks of the trade they had mastered and the reason behind their hike and the fascinating (and not-so-fascinating) people they had met and the uncommon magenta sunsets they had seen while camped alone with only the owls and other creatures of the Appalachian night to share it with. And then to tell of the grim circumstances which had brought them out there and how, if all went well and in three or four or even five months they triumphantly mounted the rocky spine of Katahdin, life would never be the same again.

But then, late at night when the Strollers had gone back to talking among themselves and reading by flashlights or even playing their transistor radios, invariably the Wolves, the through-hikers, would be left among themselves, bone-tired and already zipped tightly in their sleeping bags, speaking of things the Strollers would never appreciate, swapping rumors and intelligence picked up from a grapevine every bit as earnest and unreliable as one would find within a Marine combat unit facing imminent deployment.

*You know that couple that dragged their six-year-old kid with 'em all the way to Maine? You read that? Couple of years ago.*

*Child abuse, what I say. They ought to be arrested.*

*Think they had a story about Ryback and his brother in the Grand Canyon in the same issue. They're lost up there in a hundred feet of snow and nobody knows where they are and couldn't go get 'em if they did. Ryback's brother says, Eric, if we had some Tang we could make a hell of a snow cone.*

*Speaking of that good stuff, there's a woman up in Connecticut that sets up an ice-cream stand right on the trail.*

*Anybody seen Festus lately?*

*No, and I hope I never see the sonofabitch again.*

*Jesus. Walking the AT in cowboy boots.*

*Boots and a double-knit suit from Salvation Army.*

*What about those shelters got burned in Tennessee?*

*Punks from Erwin got 'em. Rednecks. Stay out of Erwin. Me, I'll take my Merrills any day. You can have Pivetta.*

*Grandma Gatewood. How the hell did she walk this fucker wearing sneakers and carrying a laundry sack? That's what I want to know.*

*Old woman comes up to your cabin at night, what you gonna do? Kick her out in the cold without supper?*

*That the way she did it?*

*Yeah. But still she was, what, seventy-eight?*

*You guys knock it off. Twenty-three miles tomorrow.*

And the black of night would envelop the shelters, nearly two hundred of them strung out along a ridge of the old Appalachian chain from Georgia to Maine, and on the good nights the people in them could look up and see bright sparkling stars and the red sky of the "sailor's delight" and know, finally, that it really had turned out to be worth all of the fuss after all.

# 22

THE HYPOTHERMIA SCARE WAS ONLY THAT, AS IT TURNED out, and when we awoke to a bright cold day the morning after we saw on the maps that we were exactly halfway through the Smokies. The couple from Indiana was already gone, having to hustle to meet their pickup at the nearest parking area (in hopes that the roads had been opened), leaving David and me in the shelter with the most brazen birds and squirrels we had encountered.

"Look at that, would you?" David said. "They've even chased the mice away."

"If we had any rice to spare," I told him, "I'd pull a Hemingway."

"How's that?"

"I think he wrote about it in *A Moveable Feast*. That was in Paris and he and his first wife lived above a saw-mill. They had a baby and there wasn't much money so every afternoon he'd take the baby in a stroller down to Luxembourg Gardens. That was a park, you know, with pigeons in it."

"Show the kid the pigeons, huh?"

"Boy, did he. Pigeons would come up to eat out of his hand and all of a sudden he'd grab one and smash his head against the park bench and throw him in the stroller with the baby."

"Just like that?"

"All in one motion. Took 'em home and cooked 'em for dinner."

"Hemingway did that?"

"Lot of things about Papa that isn't worth emulating," I said.

My knees were locked again and our boots were frosty. David stoked the fire and boiled some water for oatmeal and coffee and tea while I lathered Ben-Gay on the knees. When we had finished throwing down some breakfast we spent some time trying to get some of our clothing and the boots halfway dry, being maybe five days away from a laundromat in Hot Springs, and there seemed to be hope that the weather was turning clear and now we might actually be able to see some of the splendid vistas of the Smokies that we kept reading about in the guidebook.

The chance finally came during the next three days. The weather held bright and blue and cold as we hiked steadily and enjoyably through the thirty-five-mile upper stretch of the Smokies without sensing a single threat of rain. I was limping, sure, but I could forget the pain when I knew that over the next ridge there was going to be another breathless overlook. We stopped for photographs. We paused often at those overlooks for extended refueling stops (ice-cold spring water, gorp, cigarette, idle conversation). Day-trippers were everywhere on the trail, even in the middle of the week, and even the grim through-hikers were smiling and whistling. Spring was on its way to the 6,000-foot elevations.

*Noon banquet at the Ritz-Carlton in Atlanta, spring of '86, with all of Atlanta's literati there, my novel*

*is announced winner of the Townsend Prize for best
fiction by a Georgian in '85. I'm reconstituted from
walk of AT, beating whiskey, and I go to podium to
accept silver bowl.* See, *I say*, and y'all thought
Hemphill was dead. . . .

We paused at Newfound Gap for a trip to a genuine rest
room of chrome and tile and running water, then stepped
outside to speak with a horde of tourists in Winnebagoes,
waving farewell like explorers on a serious mission as we
disappeared again into the stately firs and balsams. At Ice
Water Springs Shelter there were four men from Holland,
Michigan, on their eighth annual backpacking vacation together, and a mother and her stoical medical-school son
("He's so calm, I keep hoping I can find something that'll
get him excited; but I don't suppose a surgeon is supposed
to be excitable"), and a pair of through-hikers named Mike
and James. Thirty-degree nights and puffy-clouded blue
days.

There was a long stop, on one of those perfect days, at
a spectacular granite spire called Charlies Bunion. Mike
and James and David clambered over the rocks while I,
unable to cavort because of my knees, took pictures and
contemplated matters. David joined me for lunch on a
ledge, our legs dangling, and I told him I'd about worked
out my acceptance speech for the Townsend Prize. Alice
Walker had won it the previous year for *The Color Purple*
and I hoped very much to follow her by winning with
*Sixkiller.*

"That's the one I want the most," I said. "I probably
wrote my first magazine piece for Jim Townsend when he
was at *Atlanta* magazine. Jim would have loved old Bluejay Clay in the novel. Besides, Jim killed himself with
whiskey. So this one's for him."

"You think the book's that good?" David said.

"Hell, I don't know. I have no idea."

"Who else will have novels?"

"I hope Pat Conroy does so I can beat him."

"I thought Pat was your friend."

"Of course he is. But that's got nothing to do with it."

"I don't like that," said David.

"Like what?"

"Writing a book to win a prize."

"David. It's competition. Good old-fashioned capitalistic free-enterprise American competition. I'm not worth anything if I don't want to be the best. Hemingway called it 'heavyweight champion.' "

"Hemingway again."

"Well," I said, "Conroy's a Hemingway man, too. You can bet your ass he's sitting there at home alone trying to write a world-beater. Or a Hemphill-beater, anyway. Otherwise, he'd be writing poems for himself and his family."

"I still don't like it."

"Go fishing by yourself, then."

He snapped when I said that. *So that's why he never played a team sport, even with that good body,* I thought, *not even tennis, where the competition is mano a mano.* Competition had probably put my knees in their present condition, I knew—rushing to Katahdin, going against doctor's orders, trying to beat kids half my age, refusing to say "Here we camp" because it would reek of defeatism— but I knew no other way. The real failure, as far as my generation was concerned, is in *not* trying to be the best. I was remembering a baseball coach from my teenaged years who went straight to the point: "If I'm going to be a shit-shoveler, I'm going to be the best goddam shit-shoveler the world ever saw." I grew up thinking it was basic to survival, this will to jump into the fray and let the best man win, but now I feared that my boy hadn't gotten the message. *He didn't understand about the bow tie on graduation night.*

We plummeted from 5,000 feet to 2,000 in only four

miles, a descent that looked devastating to the knees when I saw it on the profile map but was made much easier by being mostly down a broad pine-strawed old logging road, and when I pulled into the last shelter of the Smokies, Davenport Gap Shelter, David was waiting with a quart of Neapolitan ice cream he had managed to keep chilled for me. He and Mike and James had hustled to a country store a mile away and brought back a cornucopia of goodies— Mountain Dew soft drinks, an assortment of candy bars, Corn Chips, Camels—and the three were sprawled out in the shade of the shelter (the temperature was near eighty now) gorging themselves. "Small wonderful favor," I said of the ice cream David had picked up for me as I scribbled in my journal around dusk.

Of the through-hikers we had met, the ones unabashedly claiming it was Katahdin-or-Bust ("I'm GA-ME" was James's trail moniker), James and Mike were two I would have bet on. James Zdepski was a large rawboned nineteen-year-old, thick-bearded now, with a maturity about him that made me think at first that he was a Vietnam veteran; last son of a large New Jersey farm family, a high school wrestling champ, thought maybe he'd like to find the right school when this was over and become a Master Craftsman of fine furniture. Mike O'Rouarke was twenty-seven, "just say from Kansas City," a rangy ferret of a fellow who planned to find some sort of work on the land in Maine once he got there. They had met three days out of Springer when Mike's brother dropped out of the race and they discovered that they made perfectly compatible hiking partners.

We were compatible with them, too, and over the next few days we would come to enjoy them as much as anybody we had met on the trail. James was particularly interesting to me. He seemed to know as much about Voltaire and Zapata as he did beekeeping and masonry, this gentle wrestler with a high school education, and it seemed to me that David was cowed by the fact that they were the same age but he (David) had only a Mensa-level SAT score and a false start in college on *his* record.

James, for example, knew how to deal with the authorities. He was carrying the same model of JanSport backpack as I but he had had an accident. He and Mike had been chased up a tree by a black bear, and when the bear gave up and left, and they were coming down out of the tree, James's pack smashed to the ground and the aluminum frame broke. He was also carrying the special 800 customer services number of JanSport in Seattle, though, and the people at JanSport by now were wishing there were no pay phones within walking distance of the Appalachian Trail.

"What're they saying, in case I have trouble, too?" I asked.

"They promised me one in Wesser but it never showed."

"You tell 'em the whole story about the bear?"

"Well"—James, that very moment, was whittling a rhododendron branch he would tie to the frame like a splint—"it *is* broken, isn't it?"

"Yeah," said Mike, "but you forgot to tell 'em mine fell on top of it comin' out of the tree."

James said, "I told them they could fly somebody down here to look at it if they wanted to, but that I was in a hurry. So now they say they'll have a new one waiting at the Hot Springs post office. I don't even have to tell the guy my name anymore. He just says, 'Oh, it's you. It hasn't come yet?' Next time I'll tell him there's a writer with me who's going to put JanSport in his book."

Came time, then, after a meal of sorts (canned chili had also been bought at the country store), for a campfire and stories. They hadn't seen a single black face on the trail, Mike noted, and he wondered if we knew anything about that. "You know, being Southerners and all."

"Not a one," I said, "and I don't expect to."

"Why's that?"

"How'd you like to hitch into Erwin for a beer?"

"Is it still like that down here?"

"In Erwin, Tennessee, it is," I said. "Friend of mine did tell me about sharing a shelter one time with a black professor from Tuskegee Institute. I mean, this man had a Ph.D. But that's what he told my friend. He said one time he'd had to walk to an interstate to get a ride. But how about women? Y'all seen many women through-hikers? We saw one with her husband, but we saw where she had to drop off."

"There's one called 'AT Annie,' " said Mike.

"Sounds like a hooker."

"French Army used to carry whores with 'em," James said. "Cut down on VD, kept up morale."

"Naw," said Mike, "this one's okay. She can about out-hike any man out here. Got thighs like an NFL half-back and she'll pop your knuckles when you shake hands with her. Somebody said she's walking to raise money for the Special Olympics or something."

"Who's this Festus we keep hearing about?" said David.

"Better hang your stuff in a tree if he comes."

"Have y'all seen him yet?"

"Pulled into a shelter, saw him there and kept on walking."

James said, "Oh, I don't know what to believe. The best I can gather, his family was doing migrant farm work down in Florida and when it came time to go they got the car as far as Atlanta before it quit. Festus had been working on the oil rigs in Louisiana before they hooked up. Anyway, they didn't have a car and there wasn't much money left so they decided to hike all the way back home to upstate New York."

"Walk home on the AT? That don't make sense."

"It's what I hear, that's all,"James said. "That's where

the cowboy boots and polyester suit came in. Festus talked the rest of his family into hitching rides home before *all* the money was gone, and he started begging things from churches and the Salvation Army and here he is. He'll stop in a town and make some money and beg some more and then keep walking. Carries canned goods he gets from churches.''

"Yeah," said Mike, "but most of the time he's out of food. You'll be cooking something up and he'll hang around looking sad until you feel guilty about not sharing with him.''

"Festus may have a better reason than anybody to walk the AT. He's got to get home," David said, leaving us with something to ponder before the mice sent out their scouts for the evening hunt.

# 23

THE FIRST 250-MILE LEG OF THE AT HAD BEEN COM-
pleted. There was no way in the world to know how many
had tried and failed to make it from Springer Mountain and
through the Smokies—not even the through-hikers' grapevine was that good—but in the shelter logs we were reading
more and more reports like "Speedy Jake left at Gatlinburg" and "I've made a bad mistake" and "Be back next
year." The shakedown period had ended. If you didn't
know how to deal with the capricious weather or the var-
mints or the loneliness or the constant hunger and pain of
the trail by now, this was about the time you were chucking
it in. Our night at the Davenport Gap Shelter marked our
twenty-sixth night on the trail (forget the three-week convalescence at home). We were averaging about ten miles a
day hiking and only two or three times had we enjoyed the
fifteen-mile days we had planned to average after the first
two weeks. My knees, though I wouldn't admit it to David
yet, again were a mess. And ahead of us lay a mean 600-
mile stretch, between the Smokies and the Shenandoah National Park of north-central Virginia, which would take us

through the most ragged and forlorn section of the Southern Appalachians.

Right now, though, we would take it one day at a time. On everybody's mind when we awakened was Hot Springs, North Carolina, a real town with hot showers and groceries and Cokes and even a liquor store for those who wanted it. The town was only thirty-four miles away but getting there didn't appear to be easy. The trail would start at about 500 feet, zip up to some 4,200 in four miles, drop down to 2,800, level off at a give-or-take 4,000 feet for maybe nine miles, finally making a dart up to 5,000 feet before beginning a roller-coaster run down into Hot Springs at 500 feet in the valley. When I looked at the profile I thought of the legendary Warren Doyle, the one who did the entire 2,100 miles in seventy days, and wondered what he would say to my projection that it was going to take three days to make Hot Springs.

First there had to be a resupply. We eschewed breakfast and strolled a mile on a gravel road to the shambled little tin-roofed country store in the community of Mt. Sterling, home to a dozen families on the Tennessee side of the roaring Big Pigeon River, but we found slim pickings there: no sugar, no gas, no Minute Rice, but plenty of cigarettes. Cars with Tennessee license tags were all over the gravel yard, in fact, being loaded with nontaxed North Carolina cartons (I saved three dollars on a carton of Camels). "If they're in a brown bag the troopers need a warrant to check 'em and they don't want to mess with it," a customer said. We plucked what staples we could find from the forlorn shelves and, with a heavy rain suddenly coming up, loaded up with Moon Pies and ice cream and soft drinks and took them outside to have breakfast beneath the eaves of the building.

"Sorry we don't have any food to sell you boys." A fifty-ish woman in a faded cotton dress and a ragged man's cardigan and tennis shoes, old before her time, stood in the doorway. Towheaded kids in bare feet swirled around the potbellied stove while a tired man with bad teeth and little hair patiently waited for them to pick out the candy they wanted from the glass counter.

"We'll make it okay," James said. "Thank you."

"If it wadn't for the cigarettes, we'd be closed."

"Your husband seems to be doing a pretty good business with candy," I said.

"Him? That's my boy," she said.

"Oh."

"We're selling the place so he can go home to die."

"I see."

"Ain't but twenty-nine. Done rejected three of them kidneys and he don't want to try no more of 'em. Built a house over in Cosby and now we're selling the store. That's why we ain't bothering to restock the store. No reason to."

All of this was said in a flat matter-of-fact monotone. *That's the way life goes I reckon.* Everything there at Mt. Sterling was bright green and wet and cool and peaceful. Good native trout had to be in that stream for the taking. Except for a little tomato and tobacco farming, she said, the men had to drive to work to the hydroelectric plant downstream.

I said, "You must think hikers are crazy."

"My daddy used to walk ten miles before breakfast," she said.

"Maybe he had to. We don't have to. That's what I meant."

"Crazy?" she said. "Ones that's crazy are the ones that drive to Gatlinburg in air-conditioning and stay at motels. They're the one's that's crazy. They ain't really been in these mountains."

We dawdled there for nearly three hours, eating no

telling how many Moon Pies and seeing no telling how many cartons of cigarettes sold, but sluggishly walked away at noon when the rain stopped. Our supplies were low but now we figured we could make it to Hot Springs on Snickers and the little rice we had in our packs ("At least the packs are light for hiking," David said). Just ahead of us as we did a grim road-walk toward the woods again were Carl and Mike, zipping along in their bright ponchos and chaps, Mike still following the stronger Carl like a shadow. Soon we were crossing under I-40 ("Hitch a ride here and you'll wind up in Hollywood") and once again we were climbing upward in the forest.

The hike that day covered eleven miles, and when we reached the Groundhog Creek Shelter at a place called Deep Gap (it was at 2,900 feet but we had topped the 4,263-foot Snowbird Mountain to get there) it looked like a backpackers' convention was taking place. There must have been two dozen of them there, many of them people I recalled from Wesser and Fontana, and since the night was promising they had chosen to sleep under the stars in the lush green field flowing away from the shelter itself. (It was a stone five-man shelter, anyway, and it had been taken by a father and his son; the boy, sixteen, was a basketball star, and he kept swinging through the dogwood trees like an orangutan). David and I picked out a spot far away from the crowd, laid out our sleeping bags without bothering with the tarp and rationed out enough rice to stifle our hunger.

A pleasant couple strolled over from a colorful geodesic tent pitched eighty feet or so from us. Both appeared to be about thirty—he frail and bespectacled, she a wispy Earth Mother with an ethereal smile—and David recognized them from some part of the trail. They asked if they could sit and visit. They were Richard and Jeannie.

"Birmingham, right?" David said.

"Yes," she said. "And your name is—"

"David. This my dad. He's from Birmingham, too."

"Born there," I said. "Woodlawn."

And so the introductions went. Richard and Jeannie were from opposite sides of Birmingham, married now, and for some years had tried to make it with an organic farm in the country of north Alabama. Maybe something was happening around the hardscrabble yahoo country near the town of Jasper that I hadn't heard about—it was heavy on Bible-thumpers and Klansmen and bootleggers when I knew it as a kid—and I tried to picture a passive couple such as this surviving on land like that.

"It just didn't work," Richard said.

"Any trouble?" I asked him.

"Crop failure started it."

"And then the work became too much for us alone," Jeannie said.

"So here we are." Richard smiled resignedly. "We sold the farm and decided to walk from Fontana to Damascus while we talk about what we do next."

David said, "They're vegetarians, Dad."

"So are we," I said.

"No, for real. You ought to see some of the stuff she cooks."

"Better than rice and oatmeal?"

"Yeah. I mean *real* vegetarian."

Jeannie blushed. "It's nothing fancy. But it's surprising what you can do with plants you find out here in the mountains."

"You mean that really works? You're eating off the land?"

"Sure. It's everywhere."

"I'll be damned," I said. "All I'm seeing is poison ivy."

"And it's good for you."

"I got to admit," David said, "that the only time our stomachs have been messed up was after we'd pigged out on hamburgers somewhere."

"Come to the Victorian Inn in Hot Springs and I'll show you vegetarian," Jeannie said, and they were up wishing good night before we could follow up.

In the morning, with Hot Springs so close that some would try to make it before sundown, the encampment broke with the muted hustle of a caravansary dismantling and being moved on to the next town. My knees were locked up again, requiring ten to fifteen minutes of my swinging them back and forth and kneading them before I could walk, so a twenty-three-mile day was out of the question for us. It would be a hot Sunday and the profile of the AT looked promising—once we climbed 1,000 feet or so to the 4,000-foot elevation we would stay there most of the day—although there was a four-mile stretch on a hard gravel road called Max Patch and road-walking was murderous to the knees: each step sent shudders from the heels, through the knees and into the groin. My journal:

Sun 5—13

Walk 11 miles in dust and heat to Walnut Mtn. Have lunch alone, Dave well ahead, knees okay until four-mile walk on Max Patch. Pix of fathers and sons fishing together below bald, Sunday in America. Dog follows from Rube Mooneyham's trailer (added to, fire from chimney in 80-degree weather, Jeep in gravel) to George Mooneyham's long winding road to hidden cove (who are they?). . . . Three short-hikers at Walnut shelter, plus Dave, and my last 1.3 miles when left road in soaking rain. Knees locked when I sat down. James and Mike pass shelter in rain, set up on knoll, want to be together. James's JanSport dangling from back, held together by twigs and tape. . . .

David was in a snit because he still hadn't received much mail while on the trail, so the next morning he was up and out of the shelter like a shot. "See you at that Victorian Inn," he said, hustling off toward Hot Springs in a billow of dust. The road-walk on Max Patch had done its work on my knees and this time it took me nearly an hour to massage them and get myself ambulatory to the point that I could hoist my near-empty pack on my back and take on the long thirteen-mile descent into town.

It took me nine hours, in spite of a Tylenol III-inspired three-mile hour (my first) when the town was so close I could hear it. "Passing on the left," I would hear, and here would come two teenagers bursting past me, hunched over and gasping in the middle of the footpath, like stock-car drivers sling-shooting around a wreck on the third turn. To a fellow my age, walking with *his* father, I said I would pay a lot of money right now for a cab. By now I had made my final submission to nicotine: I was puffing as I walked, stubbing out my Camels on pines and shredding them and then reaching for another. When I inquired about a shortcut into Hot Springs a hiker laughed and said, "Point of no return."

I straggled into town ("Hey, mister, what's wrong with your leg?" yelled a kid from his front porch) near dusk and walked down the main drag of Hot Springs until I spied the Victorian Inn—an impressive 120-year-old airy white two-story mansion on a well-trimmed knoll encircled with stately cedars—and wearily entered. David had arrived nearly three hours ahead of me (no mail for him but two letters for me from Susan) and I hauled myself up the nineteen steps of a spiral staircase and flopped out on a huge iron bed piled with lumpy feather pillows. After that I soaked for half an hour in a claw-footed tub, puffing Camels to keep from going to sleep in the tub, and then joined eight or ten other hikers in the "music room" (somebody was playing Chopin on a baby grand in the front parlor) to await dinner.

"Elmer," came a cry from upstairs, "somebody's *smoking*."

"Where is he? I'll catch the varmint," said a large bearded man, bursting into the music room. He looked like Allen Ginsberg. *Oh, shit*, I was thinking, *arrested for possession of Camels*.

"Okay, who did it?" the man said.

I raised my hand and said, "I cannot tell a lie."

"We don't allow smoking."

"Nobody told me. I'm sorry."

"Well, it's my fault. I should've told you. I was cooking when you came in."

"Where can I smoke, then?"

"Outside. We can't do anything about it outside."

And then came dinner, with about a dozen people sitting around an impressive antique dining table laden with bowls of black beans and rice and vegetarian concoctions unidentifiable by me. The Ginsberg look-alike turned out to be Elmer Hall, a social-protest activist from the sixties who now owned the inn, and as per custom he had everyone at the table introduce himself (and herself, because Jeannie was there with Richard and had helped prepare the meal) before the clinking of silverware began. James and Mike weren't there yet, having opted to camp on a bald above town that night, but Mike and Carl of Mableton and many others we had met lately on the trail were.

After dinner I found a copy of *Mother Jones* magazine in the bathroom and took it and my Camels to the swing on the upstairs porch, figuring that qualified as "outside," and madly puffed away like a kid sneaking smokes in the barn.

# 24

WHEN ELMER HALL WAS HIKING THE APPALACHIAN TRAIL in 1976 and passed through Hot Springs, a dying town of about 1,000, then in the tenth-poorest of North Carolina's one hundred counties, he must have heard somebody playing his song. Elmer was one of those social activists from the liberal Research Triangle of Raleigh-Durham-Chapel Hill (he had once served as chaplain at Duke University) and he was out on the AT in search of himself, as it were, a sixties rebel without a cause he could sink his teeth into, and what he found was a town of great natural beauty but not much else. Interstate 40 had been built to route the Knoxville-Asheville traffic around those impossible hills of western North Carolina. Nobody had any reason to go there anymore, anyway, not since it was discovered that a backyard sauna would do the same job as natural bubbling hot springs. Kids had to be bused seventeen treacherous miles to the nearest schools. The poverty rate was more than twice the national average in spite of millions of dollars thrown at places like Hot Springs by the Appalachian Regional Commission. The only jobs in town were at a shoe factory. This was one of what the social planners called "the lost provinces" of America.

What Elmer Hall also found, if not himself, was this massive white whale of a mountain resort mansion which he dubbed "The Titanic" when he put together what little money it took to buy it in 1979 when it was boarded up and left to the bats and termites and mice and vandals. It had served many purposes in its time—escape for a rich up-East family, resort hotel, boardinghouse, even a home for the wives of high German officers doing time across town during World War II—and Elmer's dream was to re-vitalize it as his own home and, in the event tourism ever returned to Hot Springs, as a resort hotel; and, too, as a stopover for AT hikers.

David will be able to say many years from now that when we passed through Hot Springs, North Carolina, in May of 1984 he got to observe a tiny Appalachian town approaching rigor mortis. The population was down to about six hundred by then, and the shoe factory was me-thodically closing down, phasing out one department each week, until by mid-June there would not be a single in-dustry left in the town. Hot Springs itself consisted of a four-block stretch beginning with the Victorian Inn up on the hill (the main drag is U.S. Highway 25, the famed "Dixie Highway," which had taken generations of South-erners reluctantly north as far as Detroit and Flint in order to find work in the big factories of the industrial Midwest), running past an ABC (Alcoholic Beverage Commission) state-run liquor store, a motel with no sign to announce itself, a new post office, a hardware store and a small gro-cery, a convenience store, dozens of boarded-up storefronts and, on either side of the flood-prone French Broad River, the greasy-spoon Trail Cafe and the abandoned bathhouse (posted with "No Trespassing" signs) which had been the town's lifeblood from the turn of the century to the early sixties. It had truly become one of those towns where nobody, except hikers, stops on purpose.

The Trail Cafe, we found, was probably the town's community center: open six-to-six, country jukebox, hamburgers and fries and a hefty "hiker's breakfast," hangout for unemployed men and restless teenagers alike. At midmorning on our second day in town, David and James and Mike and I shared coffee over a Formica table with a couple of the local men, Larry and Warren, both about my age. Larry, who had come up to the mountains ten years earlier from West Palm Beach, Florida, for reasons of his own, was curious about what was happening these days up the hill at the Victorian Inn. He was a carpenter but he did a little preaching on the side. "Went up there one time to do a little work on the place," he said, sweeping his salt-and-pepper Merle Haggard pompadour over his bronzed forehead. "It's weird up there. I walked into the front room and there was some guy just sitting there reading a book. Next room, guy was standing on his head in one of them yogi positions. Main thing in that house, it's quiet. Spooky. Tell you the truth, I don't know what's going on up there. Elmer's got them three boys living with him, you know."

"Up there smokin' them left-handed cigarettes, you ask me," said the plump waitress behind the counter. She was making up her french fries for the day.

"You know what the big day is around here for a kid, don't you?" said Warren, Larry's pal, who is fortunate to have the best of both worlds: he can live in Hot Springs, where he was raised, but he has a good job as a troubleshooting line inspector ("Everywhere between D.C. and Atlanta") for the Southern Railway system. "Sixteenth birthday. That's when he can get his driver's license and leave. What's he gonna do if he stays—paint stripes on the highway? cut weeds for the county? get drunk? cruise up and down the main drag every night? Hell, even the bowling alley's closed."

"Take your boy there," said Larry, "where's he live?"

David said, "Birmingham."

"Godamitey. They got *a lot* of main drags in a city like that."

"But I'm in college now."

"See there?" said Warren. "You got opportunities, son. Kid here ain't got much of anything."

Sure enough. That night I stood in line at the only public telephone in town, in the gravel parking lot beside the Trail Cafe, waiting for James Zdepski to raise hell with the JanSport people in Seattle and for David to make a belated Mother's Day call before I could make *my* call to Susan in Atlanta. A ninety-three-car train passed as I waited, streaking parallel to the French Broad in the full moonlight, only one of a dozen trains which blow through Hot Springs every day without slowing down, its horns wailing and echoing through the hills like a brass section warming up in an empty concert hall. And while the bells clanged and the red lights on the barriers blinked as the train passed, the teenaged boys of Hot Springs revved the engines on their unmuffled '70 Chevys and Fords and Olds—swigging beer and smacking gum and asking where the girls were—in a tableau that would have made Walker Evans salivate.

"What's that noise?" Susan said when I finally got her.

"I could be poetic and say, 'Appalachia dying,' " I said.

"They buried Darrell today."

"Shit. I leave town and look what happens." Darrell Stewart was the favored uncle, sort of a surrogate father to me during my teenage years while my old man's job had him on the road so much of the time, and when David and I left on the trek of the AT I had been fairly certain that I would never see him again. The last time I'd called Susan I had heard about the death of Paul Boles, the novelist. And now it was looking bad for Felton Covington—J. Felton Covington III, if you please, one of the most debonair men I had ever known—the king of the publishers' sales reps, forced to retire from Simon & Schuster due to bad health well before his time, now barely hanging on in Atlanta. "Good news, I want good news."

"We're leaving for London tomorrow night," Susan said.

"I like that. Three generations of women in London."

"You going to be here when we get home?"

"We could still be right here in Hot Springs," I said.

"The knees aren't coming around?"

"I don't know, kid. I just know I can hardly climb the nineteen steps to our room at the Victorian Inn. On top of that, we've got the trots from vegetarian cooking. Black beans one night, chili the next. I'm just playing the knees a day at a time. In the meantime we're moving into this hostel the Jesuits run. Cheaper. And they got no goddam steps."

"They've got Jesuits, rednecks *and* hippies in that town?"

"You got it right," I said.

From the Victorian Inn we moved a few blocks to the barrackslike hostel operated by the order of Jesuits who moved into Hot Springs during World War II and proceeded to Catholicize people whose religious throbbings had always been reserved for rattlesnake-handlers and river-dippers and Bible-thumpers working out of revival tents. It was cheaper to flop in a wire double-decker bunk at the hostel than in a deep four-poster iron bed at the inn, and there was a long sweeping lawn where I could loll in the sun with my knees and catch up on my journal and write letters (one of them to my Aunt Vivian, widow of Uncle Darrell, the first words of my letter to her being "Ah, shit"), and to pay his rent James built a "smoking wall" for us out of random rocks he had found, and as it turned out we spent nearly a week in Hot Springs. From my journal:

Same boredom and perfect high-sky hot days. No
pack for James (his sister sends one priority from
N.J. but every morning he's on the phone PDT 800
Seattle). We eat sandwiches on patio after working,
see black racer zip across lawn, robin pulling worms,
wasps snarling, old cars, 3 guys hired to haul things
for Fr. Vincent tried 4 tires, they all went flat, before
finally get truck moving. . . . 6 contrails converge in
blue sky. . . . Clip toenails, one blister, shower. . . .
EMS goes racing off: two kids, left alone by alcoholic parents, hit by car on road out of town. People
chatter about parents . . . Rita.

It was late on Friday afternoon, on our fourth day in Hot
Springs, and I was sitting on the covered patio of the Jesuit
hostel when James came laboring and sweating up from
the far side of the priests' field beyond their trim A-frame
chapel. I had spent the afternoon "working"—editing a
flyer for an annual retreat held at the hostel each year—
while David went off with a Space Cadet twenty-one-year-
old backpacker from Brooklyn named Karen ("You from
Joisey? Yeah? What exit?" she had said to James) to discover Lover's Leap, a rock ledge overlooking the town.
James had been down in the gully with a woman named
Rita clearing kudzu for future gardens. Rita, leathery and
bronze and what is called "Appalachian-Proud," said yes
to a glass of iced tea and took a seat on a bench in the
shade and, with little prompting, launched into a soliloquy
about why Southerners stay in the hills they know against
all sensible odds.

"Me and James were down there with the scythes for
about an hour before it came out that he's from up there in
New Jersey," Rita said. She was forty-two and she wore
baggy studded khakis but she looked older and baggier.
She drew deep from a glass of iced tea I had made. "There
ain't that much difference between the farm in New Jersey

and the farm in North Carolina. It's all hard work, any way you cut it. Me, I can make it on $1,800 a year. I chop wood and I chop kudzu here for the fathers and I've got a pretty nice arrangement with this old man who's got a house over there in the hills. I take care of him and I get my rent free. That's all I've got to do, is take care of the old man. Ain't nothing 'dirty' in it. He needs the bed changed, I change the bed. Meanwhile I'm sending my boy through Mars Hill College (private, expensive, sort of a Dartmouth of the Appalachians) and I'm doing what I'm intended to do. My brother don't like what I'm doing. He wants me to move into some town and work in a department store so I can be what he calls 'respectable.' But let me tell you a story. A few months ago the postman came around to the house. I was out back chopping firewood and my boy was on the front porch, leaning back in a chair and playing his guitar, and the postman comes upon me and says, 'You ought to be ashamed of yourself, you chopping wood out here while your boy sits out front playing a guitar.' Know what I said? 'If that makes you nervous I'll move on down the hill so you can't see me. My boy's gonna play that guitar.' There you go.''

Howard Ted Moore interrupted the conversation. "Y'all *know* that the men are supposed to sleep in one room and the women in the other," he said.

"What's the problem, Ted?" Rita asked.

"Boys and girls don't sleep together, that's what I mean."

"Who said that?"

"Father Vince. The Jesuits. The rules."

"Come off it, Ted," said Rita.

My journal read further: "Howard Ted Moore. Odd jobs for Jesuits, black tank-tops, jungle fatigues, shiny boots, maybe five-two, stands in shadow of chrome growling super-bike, looks like bowling ball. Talks of 'The Colonel' (Mitch WerBell, gun supplier from Marietta, Atlanta) in hushed voice. *Soldier of Fortune* mag, gold sabres, ribbons, photos in room hostel, psychiatrist's dream. Vague talk of 'The Colonel' and missions 'in the Daytona Beach area' or 'The Keys' or 'undisclosed location.' Quandary: found Catholicism two years earlier and it screwed him up. Eight-foot chopper bike, 25, raised Hot Springs, Mama just laid off at shoe plant. . . . Fat girlfriend walks by hostel and they walk to grade-school gym for fifties 'sock hop.' Trim mustache, wavy short hair, wouldn't want him next to me in foxhole. . . .''

Saturday came. David and I had been in Hot Springs for nearly a week, lying in the sun and cutting grass and reading Louis L'Amour paperbacks and eating grease down at the Trail Cafe and listening to Howard Ted Moore finetune his chopper in the shadow of the Jesuits' A-frame chapel, and we knew the time had come to make a move. On that day there was a lot of action. James Zdepski's pack arrived at the post office and he quickly filled it and hustled up and over Lover's Leap to find his hiking pal Mike O'Rouarke. David used Karen, of Brooklyn, age twenty-one, as a front to buy himself a fifth of Jack Daniel's bourbon for his pack. Nancy and Keith finally made it out of the Smokies and so did Don Rorer, a chef by trade, who whipped up Spanish omelets for the gang on the shady patio of the Jesuit hostel.

"What's the matter, anyway?" Warren, the one who had the cushy job with Southern Railway, asked me over tea that afternoon at the Trail Cafe. He waggled a bony finger at my knees.

"They're worn out, Warren," I said.

"Got just the thing for you."

"Hadacol, right?"

"Naw, naw," he said. "Get arrested for that these days."

"Tell me, then."

"Jack Daniel's bourbon. You take some Jack and you

go down there and wallow in the hot springs for a couple of hours and I'll guarantee you what'll happen. You're either gonna get well or you won't give a damn."

## 25

Enough of this. Today we would go back out there and find out, one way or the other, what would be. When the room of the hostel had filled with morning sun I propped up in my lower bunk, both legs elevated by four lumpy feather pillows scavenged from empty bunks, and wrote Susan. It was a Sunday, the twentieth day of May.

Kid.

What I do today will be critical. Yesterday, our sixth in this place, I found a natural hot spring bubbling up through rocks on a sandy bank of the French Broad River and spent an hour lying in it like a trout fanning a bed to spawn. It helped the knee a bit. The time has come, it seems, to walk. It is about 9 A.M. and the eight hikers who came yesterday to the Jesuit Hostel, where we have become like resident care-takers, are stirring. I'm making hot coffee and rubbing the knee with Ben-Gay. Our packs are full for one week (to Erwin, TN) and we'll go on the trail by noon. I'm going to suffer fiercely through this day; I don't know how close I might be to needing surgery but the time has come to force it.

I don't have to tell you what a disaster it will be if I have to abort the trek: a payback of $5,000 to Macmillan, the end of what can be a wonderful and important book, David back to work at the Piggly-Wiggly, no money, the need to negotiate quickly with Macmillan for another book (out of a weak bargaining position), the despair of it all. What makes it worse is that I have marvelous material after only 280 miles. It's the knee. I can handle everything out here, but I can barely walk. So when we leave I will have only one thing in mind: my knee. I will take it easy, if that means doing one mile an hour, and pay attention to nobody and nothing else. This must work. If it doesn't, and I should know by the time I find a phone and call you on Thursday or so, I suspect I will pack it in and come home.

That, then, overrides everything. We've added $200 to Hot Springs' economy in a week. By working we've held the bill to $24 for four days and nights at the hostel, but we had to eat and resupply with food. David disappointed me by having to be embarrassed into doing any work at all, and he sent an air-brained 21-year-old named Karen to the ABC store to buy him a fifth of Jack Daniel's. And there must come a time when I confront him with two things which have deeply hurt and confused me in recent months: why didn't he bother to read my novel, and why didn't he even say he was proud of me when I beat whiskey? The kid is still a kid but I do think he is learning a great deal from the people he has met.

I am, obviously, still in a profound funk. There has been too much traffic with people who know no obligations or true problems or life beyond what's the best equipment. I feel very old, almost a curio, in this world of people who this winter will be hustling a way to get to Aspen. They are yet to learn that somebody's got to pay for this shit. And it's futile to bring it up. They are all out here delaying the Real World for as long as possible. They are the ones who will be in graduate school at 31, and I feel like an old fart. I need to be with you and be made to feel I'm all right. But that's for the book, if there is to be a book, and it gives you an idea of the sort of material I have.

Well. We shall see. It's times like this when I need you the most. If I can't be adored I would appreciate being understood.

Yes,
Paul

All of the other hikers were long gone by 10:30 in the morning when we took what might be our last hot showers for two weeks and settled the bill with Howard Ted Moore and cinched on our packs for the first time in nearly a week and moved out. The temperature was nearing eighty already, the blazing heat shimmering up from the surface of Bridge Street, and we walked as briskly as we could past the people strolling to their churches so we could bathe in the air-conditioning of the Trail Cafe. "Y'all just missed my hiker's breakfast," said the waitress, the one who had whispered of "left-handed cigarettes" being smoked up on the hill at the Victorian Inn, so we settled for cheeseburgers and fries and Pepsis. "Grease is grease," David said. Nobody else was in the place. He fed some quarters to the jukebox and I read the Asheville paper. The cheeseburgers came and we ate them in silence. There was nothing to talk about because he had seen me hobble and heard me curse on the six-block walk from the hostel to the cafe. He said not a word, in fact, when I paid the owner of the cafe four dollars to take us six miles up the road in his wasted bleached-white '70 Olds so I could delay the test a little longer.

At noon we sat on a grassy bank in the shade of elms beside the roller-coaster asphalt road, the fellow gone twisting back down into the valley now in a swirl of blue smoke, and we were alone with the woods again. The boy sucked on a milkweed while I cameled-up with water and had a last cigarette and, flexing the knee and tightening its bandage, read what the guidebook had to say about the five miles between us and the next shelter. We were at Tanyard Gap (2,278 feet) and would spend the night at Spring Mountain Shelter (3,300).

"Well," I said. "We aren't virgins anymore."

"How's that?"

"Missed our first blazes back there. Cheated."

"Oh, well. If we make Katahdin, we can come back for 'em."

"Damned expensive six miles if we had to come back."

"You'd have never made it over Lover's Leap, anyway," he said. "How's it look from here to the shelter?"

"Gentle ups and downs, switchbacks. Looks pretty easy from the guidebook."

"Appalachian 'Trial' Guide."

"Same ass-holes who brought us 'precipitous descent.' Let's hit it. Catch you at the shelter."

He stayed close behind me as I labored up the steep log steps leading from the roadway into the trees, laying back to break my fall in case of calamity, but when I made it to the top and was bent over to catch my breath he stepped out smartly and was gone. I wouldn't see him again for six hours.

It was a pleasant stretch of trail—smooth footpath, gently undulating dips and rises, friendly switchbacks, leafy overhangs, abundant springs and campsites, birds and squirrels and butterflies and deer saying this is a pretty good life—

and as I dragged along I figured that my twelve-year-old Molly, or even my five-year-old Martha, could negotiate the five miles to the shelter in two hours "max." But not I, not the old man, not this day, maybe never. There had been many black moments during the seven weeks since the boy and I had bounded across the bridge at Amicalola Falls. There had been the "parachute drop" into Wesser and the crawl up the rock face of Albert Mountain and the near-hypothermia and the hailstorms in the Smokies and the cold foggy disorientation at Bly Gap and the shivering sleepless nights of locked knees and Ben-Gay and Tylenol III. Somehow those horrors had always abated—a gulp of water and a Camel and a Snickers and a wry exchange about senility could work wonders—but this time that was not to be. This time the relentless physical pain was joined by something even worse: stark, utter despair. Maybe the trek was over.

It took me six hours to cover the five miles. I would walk for fifteen minutes, cursing the trees and grasping at bushes and walking backward on the gentle downhills, and then collapse in the middle of the footpath for fifteen minutes. Through it all I carried on a hallucinatory monologue. *November, December, January, February, March, April, May. Seven months. Seven months and seven days since the last drink. . . . Fucking Ken Two Trees ain't nothing but a Cherokee con artist with that "mind over matter" shit. Let him try to walk on these knees. . . . Five thousand dollars, my ass. Start adding up the time lost and the payback to Macmillan and what the book could do, if I quit it could cost me $100,000. . . . What'll David do, spend the summer carrying groceries for little old ladies? . . . Maybe I'll turn it into a novel. "Murder on the Appalachian Trail" or something. . . .* Just when I thought my life had turned around. Was I crying? *Look at that goddam squirrel, would you.* What would I tell my son?

When I finally staggered upon the shelter, which sat on

a rise right beside the trail, I found him stretched out on his foam pad idly watching a doe foraging for acorns about a hundred feet away in a grove of young oaks. We didn't speak as I plopped down on the edge of the shelter and went through the ritual of shedding the pack and taking off the boots and lighting a Camel and sipping some water and pouring the last of it over my steaming knees. By now we were so blasé about catching deer going about their business that I gave no thought to taking a photograph.

After a cigarette I said, "How long you been here?"

"Couple of hours, I guess."

"Must've climbed the fire tower."

"Yeah. Rich Mountain."

"Can you really see Mount Mitchell from there?"

"I think that was it. Skies are pretty hazy."

"So," I said, "how's the water supply?"

"Good. Real good. Probably the best spring we've seen."

"Ice-cold spring water, you say?"

"Right. Spring's about fifty yards down the hill there."

"Excellent. A bourbon and branch water will do nicely."

His back stiffened, and when he turned his head away from the deer to lock his eyes on mine I couldn't discern the look on his face. We stared at each other for a few seconds, seconds that seemed like a freeze-frame photographed for eternity, and the look went from disgust to reproachment to terror. The look said, *Am I my father's keeper?*

"Look, son," I told him, "I know. I added it up while I was walking. It's seven months and seven days exactly. If I hadn't quit I wouldn't be out here. But goddamit I'm dying and the whole world's about to go to hell. I got to make some big decisions here. I got to do some powerful thinking."

"Bourbon's not gonna help you think."

"I've never known such despair, David."

"Bourbon will make it worse"

"Ah, shit, kid, I know that. I know all of the arguments. I even made up some of 'em myself."

He was as calm and cold and unshakable as a Catholic priest saying no to birth-control pills. He gathered up his water bottles and motioned for mine, and I wordlessly slid them to him across the cruddy floor of the shelter, and then with the armload of bottles he disappeared down an embankment to the spring. The deer bolted away. Dusk was coming to the ridge. I changed into a dry sweater and put on my down vest and my "booties," propping up straight-backed against the side of the shelter, and I closed my eyes and thought of steamed rice and mushroom soup and Jack Daniel's bourbon.

Twenty minutes after he had left he came trudging back to the shelter and dropped the five full water bottles, all of them beaded and sloshy with the spring water, and when he slid one across to me he sat down and unscrewed one for himself and took a swig.

"The bourbon, please," I said.

"What bourbon?"

"Sonofabitch. You didn't."

"I did."

"Holy shit, David."

"Deer's gonna have a party tonight."

"Mother of Christ." I guzzled water instead, and drew deeply from another cigarette, and for a full five minutes we were silent. It would be dark soon and we would have to think about something to eat. The doe came back, almost up to the shelter now, and in the bottoms behind us there was the low moan of an owl as dusk crept up the ridge. Finally I said, "Something's been bugging me for a long time, kid, and I might as well bring it up now. The first time I quit drinking I wrote you to tell you because I wanted you more than anybody else in the world to be proud of me. You didn't write me back. So I wrote you again but you still didn't write back. Third time I wrote you I said something like, 'Fuck you, I'll be proud of myself on my own time.' So how come you didn't write me and say you were proud?"

"I don't write letters." He shrugged.

"No argument about that."

"I've probably written you two or three letters in my life. My generation doesn't write letters. You've said that yourself."

"Come on, Dave, that's a cop-out."

"I'm afraid to commit stuff to paper."

"That's bullshit, son. Well, how come you didn't just pick up the goddam phone and *tell* me something? Your generation do *that*?"

"I didn't do it because, well"—he turned away so I couldn't see his face—"because I was afraid I'd get like I'm about to get right now." He was trying hard not to cry openly. "Sure I was proud of what you'd done. You don't know how much. I just couldn't handle it. I'd about made up my mind that you were gonna kill yourself and I'd grow up and I'd never be able to say I ever really knew my father."

"Well." I was breaking, too. "That's a pretty noble thing you just did."

"I shouldn't have bought the stuff, anyways."

"Yeah, but pouring it out took some doing."

"I was only doing what you always told me to do. Do the right thing." He cleared his throat and wiped his eyes. He was better now. He grinned and rummaged through his pack and said, "I *can* offer you a honey-graham Granola Bar. Catch."

My notes don't show whether we ate that night. I doubt that we did. I do remember that he was tightly snuggled asleep in his bag when the fireflies came and that about two hours after full darkness cloaked our patch of the world

I was finished writing a long entry in the log someone had left at the shelter and I blew out the candle. "My son loves me" is the way I ended the entry.

## 26

THERE WASN'T MUCH LEFT FOR US TO SAY TO EACH OTHER
the next morning. My knees were a mess again and I was
going to have to go home, for either rest or arthroscopic
surgery, and we were both sort of hanging loose as I struggled along with my staff on the sweeping four-mile slope
downhill into Allen Gap where there was a blacktopped
highway. When I reached the road I saw another of those
half-abandoned gas stations, staying alive on nontaxable
cigarettes-by-the carton alone, and I saw David sitting in
front of it in the noon's shimmering heat and I shuffled
toward him in the gravel. I reached the service station and
dropped my pack and sat on one of the boulders forming
the semicircular driveway around the empty gas pumps. I
wheezed and lit a Camel.

"Got your basic Appalachian gas station," David said.

"Reckon."

"You okay?"

"Naw."

"What do you think we ought to do?"

"I don't know, kid," I said.

The woman who ran the place crunched up in the gravel in an old Ford pickup. She smiled at us and opened the door and we followed her in to buy Pepsis and ice cream and Camels, and to see whatever else she might have on her bare shelves. Now it was noon. Suddenly three station wagons pulled in, right on time, for the cigarettes. From one of the station wagons came a husky middle-aged blond woman barking directions to the two women in the back-seat—"You *vait*, you stay *heah*"—and she turned out to be German and these were her two sisters visiting from Munich and they didn't know a word of English but her brother-in-law ran a car-rental agency nineteen miles west in Greeneville, Tennessee, and we were most welcome to ride.

That, then, is how it came about that I rented a new Olds and we ran by a bank to cash my traveler's checks and we pigged out at the Pizza Hut in Greeneville and we commented on how east Tennessee turns out an inordinate percentage of high school football heroes if you want to put the size of the stadiums up against the size of the libraries. I needed at least a week at home, resting the knee, and it made sense to both of us for him to continue alone. I would catch up with him later.

At five o'clock in the afternoon we were back at the abandoned gas station, on the sticky black asphalt road we had left at noon, separating food and supplies. David now had fifty dollars in cash and two weeks' worth of food. The rental car had 1,421 miles on it—air-conditioning, radial tires, AM-FM radio, the works—and driving to Atlanta would be a joy. The only thing standing between me and a bed was maybe five hours of air-conditioned rental-automobile cruising. David had only two hours of hiking to the next shelter, two weeks' worth of food on his back and then there would be 170 miles alone to the first stop in Virginia.

"I thought maybe you'd like to try it by yourself," I said.

"It'll be different," he said. "Yeah. It'll be different."

"You got everything you need?"

"Sure."

"You'll call me collect."

"Oh, yeah, sure."

"I mean if anything"—we collapsed and slammed into each other now, sweaty bodies and hairy legs and dusty boots making a mess—"give me a call."

"I will," he said.

"It's going to be different, going alone."

"Yeah. It'll be interesting."

"I'll probably be a week, max."

"Sure," he said. "No sweat."

"You'll call me, then?"

"First phone booth."

We hugged. "It's going to be a long time before you do anything as noble as what you did yesterday," I said. I fired the rental Olds and he cinched his pack and we waved goodbye to each other. I looked in the rearview mirror and I saw my son standing alone—wiry, querulous, lost, wondering what was going to happen next—and I saw myself and my old man. I stopped for hamburgers at the Hardee's in Clayton and I was going to rush home to my neighborhood liquor store in Atlanta before I caught myself—*If this kid can stop me, why can't I?*—and I drove on home hard in a rain and rolled into the driveway at ten o'clock at night. Susan and the kid were in London and the key to the house was next door with Nancy, the carpenter, and when Nancy saw my bony legs, limping, she said, "God, Paul."

"Exactly," I said. "Just gimme the goddam key."

# 27

ZEB MORGAN, MY DOCTOR, STILL WASN'T IMPRESSED. HE
saw no need for me to go into his office and have my knees
inspected this time, in fact. "How many times have I got
to tell you that they're worn out?" he said, recommending
an antiarthritic prescription pill and leg-lifts designed to
strengthen the quadriceps. "Your knees are old, that's all,
and the whiskey made them older. Rest. And do what I
told you when David wants to keep pushing to the next
shelter. 'Here we camp.' "

For a couple of days I fumbled around the house—airing
it out, mowing the lawn, pulling dandelion weeds, popping
my Naprosyn and doing my leg-lifts, watching the Braves
on television, washing clothes, running the vacuum, piling
up in bed alone to reread *The Grapes of Wrath*—and then
Susan and the kid rolled into the driveway with many tales
of a week in London ("I knew you'd be here," Susan said,
"I *knew*"). When I told Bob Hannah of "the bourbon incident" at the shelter out of Hot Springs he begged me to
bear witness at an Alcoholics Anonymous meeting ("And
a child shall lead them," he said with fervor) but I de-

murred. On my first day home I mailed a package to David's next post office stop in Elk Park, North Carolina, a CARE package, as it were, including a fifty-dollar money order and instant pudding mix and snub-nosed candles and Minute Rice and the latest issue of *Time* magazine and even a box of Gitanes cigarettes, which cost me $1.75 at a downtown hotel.

This was true limbo. The knees weren't nearly as bad as they had been the first time. I spent a few days on crutches, pampering myself and doing the exercises and popping the Naprosyn—I was the "Soldier's Home" of the Hemingway short story—and then there was a week or so of taking tentative strolls with Martha and waggling my legs at poolside while she bounded about the "baby pool," eating a lot of ice cream and watermelon, looking at color slides I'd had developed of the first weeks on the AT, wondering where my son was at every moment of the day and night.

"Collect call for Paul from David," an operator said late one afternoon. There was a lot of crackling live air over the line. I hadn't seen him or heard from him in about ten days.

"Yes, of course," I said.

Now and then he had to shout over the rumble of eighteen-wheelers passing the roadside phone booth where the AT crosses U. S. Highway 321 in far northeastern Tennessee. This came just as I was beginning to ponder how one goes about placing an all-points bulletin on a teenaged boy walking the Appalachian Trail in the company of himself. He had done okay in the ten days since I'd had to leave him, he said, covering 130 miles in spite of some fierce near-freezing weather atop Roan Mountain (about 6,000 feet in elevation) where he had been locked in by storms and ice and snow for two lonely days and nights. From the ledgers in the shelters he had read that James, the farm boy from New Jersey, was only a day ahead of him and having fresh problems with his new JanSport; and Karen, the twenty-one-year-old from Brooklyn, was hoping that they all arrived in Damascus in time to destroy some Moosehead beer on Saturday night. The Team Hemphill banner, he assured me, was being held high. But he sounded ragged.

"The rednecks get those two shelters?" I said.

"Burned to the ground," he said.

"Where'd you sleep?"

"Used the tarp one night. Other night there was an old shack at about 5,000 feet so I just flopped out in it."

"You've got a CARE package waiting at Elk Park."

"Good. I ought to make that tomorrow."

"Got some Gitanes in it. Copy of *Time* and some other stuff."

"So," he said, "how's the knee?"

"Still forty-eight, still holding," I told him.

"No surgery or anything?"

"Shit. Zeb won't make me a hero. Pills and rest, that's all."

Over the phone there was the roar of a truck, rumbling and distant and ominous, and he had to shout. "I miss you."

"What?"

*"I said I miss you.* I didn't think I would, but I do."

"Me, too, kid. I miss the whole damned thing."

When he called again, this time it was Saturday night on the second day of June and he had made it to the hostel in Damascus, Virginia, my knees were in better shape than in a long while and I was anxious to get back on the trail with my son. I had made further refinements in the *modus operandi*, like buying a collapsible half-gallon plastic water jug to cut down on trips to springs when we reached shelters, ditching some of the redundant sweaters and T-shirts I'd been lugging, storing more batteries and sawed-off candles, buying out the neighborhood grocery of Snickers and

Minute Rice (at a better price than the strapped roadside
country stores could offer) and—most important of all—
determining that we were going to have to make a huge
"jump" of the AT if there would be any hope that we
would walk together to the summit of Katahdin on a day
in late August. I didn't tell David about that. We could
discuss that later.

There came that Sunday night, then, the first Sunday of
June, and at ten o'clock in the cramped stuffy air of downtown Atlanta we rolled up to a cab stand in front of the
Greyhound bus terminal—I in my hiking uniform of shorts
and boots and paper and thirty-five-pound pack, Susan behind the wheel of her shabby yellow Datsun 210 in her
costume of sneakers and T-shirt and jeans, the kid in her
pajamas—and I remembered all of those Sunday nights of
my youth when it came time for my old man to be delivered to his truck in a grim loading-dock area of Birmingham for the five-day Birmingham-to-Akron round trip up
and over the Appalachians with a load. There was that
piece again, the one called "Me and My Old Man," the
one in *The New York Times Magazine* which had caused
all of the trouble in the family back there when I was in
my thirties and I was still a Promising Young Man:

> During the week, when he would be on the road
> somewhere, the days at home began with the muffled
> slapping of screen doors and the dull starting of cars
> and I could look through the living-room window and
> see the same thing happening up and down the block:
> the other men, wearing drab blue factory uniforms or
> plain gray suits, carrying lunch pails or briefcases,
> going off to shuffle somebody's papers or stand in
> somebody's production line, a stolid army of beaten
> men moving out under the orders of fate to absorb
> whatever the world had to dump on them today. And
> when I saw them return in the late afternoon, their

lunch pails empty and their chalky faces more pinched than ever now, my throat would tighten and I would think, in the manner of a twelve-year-old boy, *My old man is better.* Because I could not imagine then, nor can I imagine now, how a kid could get excited about a father like one of those, a father who wasn't visible, a father who merely functioned. And because I knew that during the same day, in that nine hours between the going out and the coming back of the other men of the neighborhood, my old man had been Out There—Ohio? Kansas? California? Outwitting the Interstate Commerce Commission? Saving a life on the highway? Overtaking a Greyhound?—a mechanized Don Quixote challenging the world, spitting into its face the juice of a Dutch Masters Belvedere cigar, giving it a choice of weapons and then beating it at its own game. And, too, because I was faintly aware that a snarling four-ton Dodge pulling a sleek aluminum trailer was, unlike the portfolio of the insurance agent or the samples of the salesman, something a kid could sink his teeth into.

Then, on a Friday afternoon, my mother would be standing at the kitchen sink and suddenly say, with a slight inward smile I did not yet know, "Your daddy, he ought to be home soon." And I would go out into the front yard, and shortly a mud-spattered red behemoth would top the long hill above the house, a clattering silver warehouse dragging behind, air brakes sneezing and air horns blasting at the wide-eyed kids gamboling on the sidewalks and the stunned old ladies swinging on their porches, the excitement swelling in my bony young chest until finally there was one final burp on the horns—*for me*—before the belching engine gasped and the whole rig shuddered to rest at the curb beside the house. "How-*dee*, I'm just so proud to be *hyar*," he would yelp, *Minnie*

*Pearl at the Opry*, swinging down from the cab like a Tom Mix dismounting—sunburned face, grimy hands, squinty piercing pale blue eyes, greasy overalls and pirate boots, a half-chewed cigar jammed in the corner of the mouth—the leathery adventurer, King of the Road, home from the wars. Neighborhood kids, crowding around, daring to touch the simmering tires, while my old man digs through dirty socks and Cleveland newspapers and kitchen matches to produce a novelty-shop key to the City of Akron for me. A kiss for Mama and a hug for Sis, cowering, at the age of eight, in his presence. An hour in the vacant lot across the street, hitting mile-high pop flies until dusk over complaints from his wife ("Thirty-seven years old, acting like a *boy*"). Over supper, the stories of bad wrecks and truck stops and icy roads and outrunning the law and pulling the Appalachians at night, a born liar refining his art: "That fog was so bad I had to get out and *feel* that sign," and "They got watermelons in Texas grow so fast the bottoms wear off before they can pick 'em," and, "She had a face so ugly it wore out two bodies." And, afterward, a session at the old black upright piano in the living room, a self-taught Hoagy Carmichael: "I'd o' learned to play with the left hand, too, but before they could mail me my second lesson the Injuns shot the Pony Express." And finally to bed. Five days on the road, Birmingham to Akron and back, and he had made it home again tonight. He was my first hero and, the way things have been going lately, quite possibly the last.

So why, I am asking myself now, of all the good times we had together, why should I remember a bad one? The details are fuzzy. I must have been eighteen or so. He came in off the road, but something was wrong. There was shouting. He talked about taking

off again right after supper. My mother found a pint
of booze in his overnight bag and, with hell-fire fi-
nality, flushed the contents down the toilet. He left.
She and my sister were hysterical. "It's the son's
place to go find him and talk to him." Bewildered,
I got into the car and raced into town, to the lot
cluttered with tires and rusty engines and oil pans. I
could see him sitting all alone in a dark corner of the
cab, swigging from a pint, and when I pulled up and
parked in the gravel beside the truck we tried not to
look at each other. Blue lights laid a scary blanket
over the lot. There was the desperate choking putt-
putt-putt of a refrigerated trailer somewhere, broken
by the occasional wail of a far-off train whistle, and
after an interminable pause I heard myself say,
"They're crying."

A gurgle, a cough. "Thought I'd get started
early."

"How come you did it?"

"I don't know what you're talking about."

"Made 'em cry."

"What'd you come down here for?"

"Mama said. I don't know."

"She shouldn't o' done that."

"Well, she told me."

He tilted back his head and began draining the bottle, his Adam's apple quivering and some of the
whiskey dribbling off to the side of his face, and his
eyes looked like deep swollen ponds. I looked down
and toed the gravel with my shoe while he finished.
He sniffed and cleared his throat and then spoke in a
frightened, vulnerable voice, a voice I had never
heard come out of him before. "I'm not runnin' anywhere, son. There's a lot a boy don't know. I don't
mean to make your mother cry, but sometimes a
man's, a man's—" His voice had broken, and when

I dared look up at his face, bleached white by the pale lights on the lot, I saw that my old man, too, was crying.

She parked the car at the curb in front of the Greyhound station long after dark on Sunday night and said, "You want us to go in?"

"What the hell for?"

"You don't have to be snappy."

"Look," I said, "it's a goddam bus to Knoxville. People take it every day."

"You gonna be okay?"

"I'm tired of people asking if I'm going to be okay."

"Whatever," she said.

"Just go about your business and I'll do mine."

Martha extracted a promise that I would be nice to the bears. I wheeled out of the Datsun with my pack and bought a ticket for Chattanooga-Knoxville-Abingdon and queued up for the bus. I sat in the back so I could smoke. During the night I was entertained by a rednecked kid from Tampa who was going to win the Georgia "kickbox" championship and a belligerent Cuban who would get kicked off the bus for swigging tequila and a teenaged beauty queen who hoped her mama would be waiting for her in Chattanooga. As the bus droned on into Tennessee I sat beside a wasted black fellow, about my age, who had just spent two weeks living at the Union Mission (home for winos in downtown Atlanta) but now was going back home to his mother in Lexington, Kentucky, on the bus ticket ("She wouldn't send me no cash") she had sent.

The bus reached Abingdon, Virginia, at nine o'clock on a sultry Monday morning. I began to road-walk to Interstate 81, standing there sillily for two hours, and finally caught a ride with a fellow who drove a pickup and was on his third beer of the day. At noon he dropped me in the backyard of a sand-colored two-story house behind the

Methodist church in Damascus—THE PLACE, read a sign above the screened porch—and I heard a voice say, "Yo." It was David, in his tattered shorts, reading a ten-year-old copy of *Newsweek* (Jimmy Carter, a Georgia peanut broker, was being mentioned among the has-beens as a possible presidential candidate). Three mangy kittens swirled about his ankles.

## 28

DAMASCUS, LIKE HOT SPRINGS BEFORE IT, IS ONE OF THOSE milestone towns on the itinerary of AT through-hikers in that it is friendly and there is a comfortable place to stay and the stores stock most of the amenities. The population of the town is about 1,200, the shoe plant gives it a stable economic base (shoe plants, shoe plants, they are everywhere in the crannies of the Appalachians, moving only when workers reach pension age), there is not even a blinking caution light along the six-block main drag and there is a church of some denomination on every corner. "We could've been another Gatlinburg but we didn't want that," says Paschall Grindstaff, the postmaster and a deacon of the Methodist church that runs the hikers' hostel. The Cherokees fought off the Shawnees in the hills around Damascus and Daniel Boone did some hunting around there and the town got its name when an ex-Confederate general discovered a layer of iron ore and hastily announced that soon this Damascus would rival the other one as a steel-producing center (but the iron ore turned out to be exactly an inch deep). Lumber operations began in 1901, when the first railroad tracks came; in 1912 the county harvested more lumber than the entire state of Pennsylvania; by 1926 the timber was long gone and Mount Rogers, which majestically hovers above Damascus, was completely nude.

So much for the natural history of Damascus, Virginia. Now David and I had some business to take care of. During my second convalescence in Atlanta I had talked with George Walsh, my editor in New York, and let him know that we had two ways to go on with the walk of the AT: keep walking straight through until it became mid-August and we stopped right there, or make jumps here and there to ensure that father and son walked hand in hand to the top of Katahdin. It didn't matter very much to Walsh either way, although he leaned toward the symbolism of father-and-son-at-Katahdin.

"We can do what we want to do, really," I was saying to David on my second morning at "The Place." We were eating cold cereal and feeding the stray kittens with dry food bought at the convenience store nearby. It was going to be a blazing day.

"What kind of jump are we talking about?" he said.

"A big sumbitch," I said. "Almost four hundred miles."

"Where to?"

"To the entrance of the Shenandoah National Park."

"That's a lot."

"Yeah, I know. It's more than half of Virginia. But either we do that or we just go as far as we can and quit in time for your college."

"What do you think?"

"I kind of like the symbolism of you and me at Katahdin."

"Whatever," David said.

"At least this way," I said, "we won't have a whole bunch of little jumps in bits and pieces. I mean, if next year or the year after that we want to be able to say we've walked the whole trail we'll have this one section to walk. Keeps the bookkeeping straight, you know?''

Later that day, around dusk, we were lolling on the screened porch of the old house with two or three other hikers who had come in, doing nothing more than tease the kittens and debate over which of the town's two diners we would pick for supper, when AT Annie arrived in a cloud of dust. She was a handsome woman in her mid- to late twenties, a sturdy five feet seven inches and maybe 130 pounds, with well-turned legs that could drive a steam engine, and once she had swung her pack to the floor and vigorously pumped handshakes all the way around she said, "Anybody care for a jog?"

"A what?" said a fellow who had hiked 14.6 miles that day and only now was drying out from his shower.

"Jogging," she said. "Twenty-five-miler today and I'm pumped up, you know."

"Jesus. Jogging."

"Come on, c'mon, gotta stay in shape. Got a long way to go."

I said, "You make me very tired, you know that?"

She looked at me and saw that I had my legs propped up on the giant wire spool we were using for a coffee table, my Ben-Gay and Epsom salts and hot towels before me, and she clucked. "What happened?" she said.

"They wore out," I told her.

"You ought to know better than that."

"Whatever works, I say."

"I know acupuncture pretty well," she said. "As soon as I do some running and clean up, I'll go to work on you."

It never happened. I had my visions of this Superwoman forcing me to the ground outside in the thick grass, belly-down in the moonlight with the cicadas harping in the elms, straddling me and working my spine until—*Snap*!!!—there it was, the magical answer, *go and you are healed*, on to

Katahdin, *limp no more.* Instead, after hamburgers at some sweaty roadhouse on a hairpin curve beside a river, we all sat on the screened porch and watched the fireflies and heard a succinct biography of AT Annie (M.B.A. from Dartmouth, bailed out of Wall Street after a couple of years, doing a book for those her age who would like to drop out as she had, was being sponsored by people who would give $100,000 to the Special Olympics fund if she made it to Katahdin). And then, spread out on floors and ratty sofas and sprung mattresses all over the two-story house, we began the snoring.

Everybody else was gone the next morning, getting toward noon, when David and I walked away from "The Place" in Damascus to hitch-jump the 384 miles to central Virginia and the town of Waynesboro, where the Shenandoah National Park begins. By making this jump—and if my knees held up—we would make Katahdin together in time for him to return to the University of the South for the fall semester. We stopped by the post office to mail his signed letters of application, saying numerous farewells to Paschall Grindstaff, the friendly postmaster, and soon we were standing in the blistering heat of Interstate 81 having little luck hitching a ride to Waynesboro. Three rides in five hours covered seventy miles and found us, with the sun still burning bright-orange overhead, hanging around a Gulf station in the town of Wytheville.

There was a boy there, about David's age, wearing creased army jungle fatigues and high-shine black high-top boots, kibitzing with a deputy sheriff. When the kid noticed us, tired and sweaty and looking disoriented, he broke away from the deputy and sidled up to us and began chatting about backpacking and equipment. He was Private E-2 Clifton Dalton, eighteen, United States Army. He would make it a career, probably, he said ("I could be retired by the time I'm forty and get a college education and all the other stuff"), but for the time being he was attached to the

Emergency Medical Service in Wytheville and was living in the nearby community of Ivanhoe with his parents because his father was dying of cancer and he was the only surviving son.

"It's getting dark on us and we need a place to camp," David said.

"There's a KOA campground on the way to my house," the boy said.

"You don't mind?"

"Course not. You'd help *me*, wouldn't you?"

We threw our stuff into the back of Clifton ("It's Clifton, not Cliff") Dalton's Honda Civic and he drove ten miles to one of those clattery franchised KOA campgrounds ($12.22 for a spot to pitch a tent, no facilities for hikers, an uninviting place teeming with RVs and kids yelping around a swimming pool while their parents swilled beer and grilled steaks) and soon Clifton was making a phone call from there and telling us he had found the perfect place for us to spend the night: "Mom says how about our yard?"

Being in the company of Clifton Dalton and his family would give us another glimpse of life as it is lived in the great American outback of small towns and villages that few people have ever heard of. When we left the main roads and headed back up into the lush forbidding hills and hidden coves of southwestern Virginia, young Private Dalton serving as a tour guide, we were being given a rare and privileged look at a country no tourist ever sees: dark and green and rolling like Bavaria, small horse farms abruptly appearing at the base of high smooth balds, rushing streams full of native trout, the lazy New River (it flows north and is second-oldest in the world only to the Nile), neat white farmhouses strung out through narrow valleys, a scar up the side of a hill where teenagers have been exercising their trail bikes, a bent old man carrying a cane pole and a bucket down one of the ribbony asphalt roads, an abandoned Union

Carbide plant in the middle of the woods. And Clifton Dalton: "My dad worked in that plant for twenty-five years and that's where he got his lung disease. . . . County's about seventy-five percent agriculture and some cattle. Rich man just bought the whole town of Ivanhoe just for the timber. . . . This is my home. Everybody around here knows me and I know them." He said that as he hit the horn gently and waved to a girl his age riding a horse along the road.

When he whipped the car into a gravel drive beside a small white frame house, a pickup truck and another car already parked beneath the elms, the front yard enclosed by a three-foot chain-link fence to keep some chickens and a small nervous dog in check, we were hailed by a large woman in sneakers and a print dress who was sprawled amid a cloud of cigarette smoke on the front-porch swing. "They reroute the Appalachian Trail through Ivanhoe?" she said.

"Mama," Clifton said, "this is David and Paul. This is Wanda."

"Well, it's nice to meet y'all. Clifton's always bringing home somebody."

"Told 'em we had good camping facilities here."

"Good eats, too, if Denise ever gets home to cook it."

"Where's she at?"

"Vacation Bible School again," said Wanda.

We leaned our packs against a massive gnarled elm shading the entire front yard and joined Clifton and his mother in a glass of iced tea on the porch. Clifton's EMS beeper went off and he went into the house to get on the shortwave radio to see what was up, chuckling when he returned to his chair on the porch, explaining that a drunk had hit a deer on a back road somewhere. A truck eased along the road in front of the house, groaning in low gear, hauling a bulldozer on its flatbed trailer ("Looks like they're gonna knock down some more trees," Clifton said).

Wanda was taking some cryptic shots at Clifton's girlfriend, Jenny, an all-A student from a poor family down
the road ("Some folks are poor but proud, and some folks
got common sense," she said, failing to get a rise from her
son), when a white Vacation Bible School bus full of a
dozen calamitous children stopped in front of the house to
off-load Denise Dalton. Dark was enveloping the valleys
around Ivanhoe (pop. 600) and with it came the cicadas
and the fireflies.

"We live a decent life here; we do what we have to
do," Wanda was saying later as we all gathered around a
wide table in the kitchen covered with a red-and-white-
checkered oilcloth etched with cigarette burns, watching
sixteen-year-old Denise put together a supper of fish sticks
and frozen fries and potato salad and pork-and-beans and
white bread and iced tea. "Charlie, you met him back in
his room. He's seventy-one now. He's been sick with the
brown lung a long time and we don't know how much
longer he can hang on. He just lives back there in his
pajamas, hooked up to oxygen. Denise here, now, she's
quite a basketball player and I mean to tell you she helps
me out around the house with Charlie and all. Clifton, if
he don't do something crazy like marry Jenny, he's gonna
come out all right with the Army. Already been out to
Texas and learned EMS and next summer they might send
him to Germany for a couple of years." And she, mother
of the brood ("I have a thirty-one-year-old daughter, too,
but that's from another marriage"), turned the 6:30 A.M.-
2:30 P.M. shift at a convenience store on I-81. She is known
to the truckers as "Big Mama."

Later, after the threat of rain had brought an invitation
for David and me to bring our stuff up on the porch and
use the living room as a campsite, Wanda excused herself
and went back to the bedroom to sleep on a sofa in the
same room with her husband. It was then that Denise, a

tall and bubbly dark-haired girl with inquisitive brown eyes, began to pick away at us for news of the outside world.

"Both your wife and your daughter went to England?" she asked me. "I'd sure like to go there sometimes. Maybe if Clifton goes to Germany."

"Well, my wife's a magazine editor," I said.

"How do you get to be that?"

"Go to college. Be smart. I don't know, it just happens."

"Yeah, but y'all live in Atlanta you said."

"That's true. You've got opportunities in Atlanta."

"They've got hippies in Atlanta, don't they?" Denise said.

"Got a little bit of everything in Atlanta," I told her.

"Yeah," David said, "but not this."

"What do you mean?"

"Clean air. The country."

"Yeah, but nothing ever happens around here."

"Depends on how you look at it," David said.

The phone rang. It was Jenny, Clifton's girlfriend, calling for the second time that night. He filled her in on us ("His dad's been having a lot of trouble with his knees. . . . All the way to Maine. . . . No, he's from Birmingham, Alabama. . . . Why don't you ask him yourself?") and then he turned the phone over to David, puzzled, who got pulled into a conversation about the University of the South and the Appalachian Trail and the broadening aspects of travel, as well as I could make it out from one end of the line, and during all of that time Denise was fidgeting. David turned the phone back over to Clifton, and then Clifton hung it up after dropping his voice and cooing for a couple of minutes. It was quiet for a half minute before Denise blurted to David, "How come you've got that ring in your ear?"

David blushed and said, "It seemed like a good idea at the time."

"Don't the boys laugh at you?"

"Why would they? They all have 'em, too."

"You mean boys in Alabama wear rings in their ears?"

I said, "It's which ear that counts."

"What?" Denise said. "What's that mean?"

"If it's in the right ear, that means gay," said David.

"Well, what's the left ear mean?"

"It's an old thing from the days of the pirates," David told her. "If a sailor had made an ocean crossing he was entitled to wear a ring in his left ear. It was a sign of manhood."

"But if it's in the right ear—"

"You've got it."

"I'm almost afraid to ask you how come you're wearing beads."

"Those are party beads," David said.

"One for every party you've been to?"

"Well, not quite. They're friendship beads."

"Like an engagement ring or something? Girl-friendship beads?"

"Something like that," David said.

It became a bit too much for Denise, the Vacation Bible Schooler from the mountains, to grasp at one sitting. Soon she was off to her bedroom and Clifton to his. It was close to midnight when David and I unfurled our sleeping bags, his on the floor and mine on the short Early American sofa in the living room, and we slept soundly to the rhythmic tick-tocking of an imitation Swiss cuckoo clock resting on top of the color television set.

The next morning, awakened by roosters at dawn, we accepted a breakfast of bacon-and-eggs pushed at us by Denise and by 7:15 were being let out by Clifton at I-81. After two hours we finally took a ride of sorts—a fifteen-miler from a businessman in a new Oldsmobile ("I do a lot of hiking myself when I can") who dropped us in the little town of Dublin on the advice that our chances of thumbing would be better on old U.S. 11 than on an inter-

state—but by four o'clock we gave up and boarded a Trailways for Waynesboro. We pigged out at a pizza place there
and then walked in the dark to the fire station, where an
AT hiker knows he can get a shower and a place to pitch
his tent, and we spent that night sleeping under a full moon
with a dozen other hikers who had spread out their gear on
a twenty-by-twenty-foot patch of grass behind the station.
The music to sleep by that night was the steady rumbling
of teenaged boys in jacked-in-the-back hot rods as they
cruised up and down the main street of Waynesboro until
2:30 in the morning. The kids' cars weren't as rowdy in
Waynesboro as in Hot Springs, one of the hikers noted,
and the only thing I could figure was that the kids in
Waynesboro had more money to spend on mufflers.

## 29

Now came the Shenandoah National Park, not nearly as lofty and awesome as the Smokies but at 106 miles half again as long, and we were figuring maybe a week to make it to the northern exit at Front Royal, Virginia (home of The Irish Goat, in fact, Paul Michael Fitzsimmons of the mousetraps), as we left the fire station and had a sandwich at a "sub" shop in Waynesboro and then clumped off on a four-mile road-walk at noon (the temperature was ninety-three and rising) to the entrance of the park. The twisting road up from town to the main gate, where we would have to get briefed and tagged again by park rangers, was clogged with campers and motorbikes and air-conditioned automobiles. Skyline Drive, with dozens of scenic overlooks and several "waysides" (with restaurants, service stations, trinket shops and other amenities) and a thirty-five-mile-an-hour speed limit, makes for a popular leisurely half-day scenic cruise. The northern end of the SNP is less than an hour's drive from the District of Columbia.

Across the highway from the park entrance there was a

"welcome station" set up in a motel room by the Waynesboro Chamber of Commerce, a place with maps and pro-
motional flyers and free soft drinks and a rest room, and
while we were cooling off from the dull hot two-hour road-
walk, our loaded backpacks propped against the side of the
motel, a couple of middle-aged female hikers sidled over
to us. They were sisters who lived in different parts of the
country, one of them said, and in order to get to know each
other again they were walking the AT together.

"You doing the whole trail?" David said.

"We'll see," said the younger one. "If she'll just walk
faster."

"Now, now," said her sister. "Who wanted to quit in
Georgia?"

Theirs was no less a classic AT through-hike than ours.
They had started from Springer Mountain about the time
David and I had, but every sort of calamity had struck—
horrible weather, blisters, lame ankles, despair—and after
a couple of weeks they had gone to a pay phone and called
the headquarters of the Appalachian Trail Conference in
Harpers Ferry, West Virginia. Jean Cashin, by title the
ATC's "information specialist" but in reality the AT hikers' "mother superior," had told them that if they could
get to Harpers Ferry she would have somebody take them
to a relatively easy stretch of the trail in Pennsylvania "until you can find your legs and build some confidence." So
they did that and now they were southbound to Springer
while nearly everybody else was walking the other way.
So far, so good.

"But tell me," the older sister said, "sometimes it gets
where we can't stand the sight of each other. How's it
going for you two? Father and son, I imagine it might be
even worse."

"We've been known to keep our distance," David told
her.

"Little stuff most of the time," I said. "Like what to eat."

"Oh, yes. We've been there."

"He's always washing wool in hot water," David said.

"Yeah," I said, "and I'm bad to slurp my coffee."

"Well," said the younger of the sisters, "this thing is going to turn out one of two ways. Either we're never going to speak again or one of us is going to move and we'll live together the rest of our lives. I don't see any halfway ground."

From there it was only a six-and-a-half-mile hike to the first shelter ("hut," they are called in Virginia), "currently under construction but habitable," according to a photocopied sketch we had picked up somewhere, and it felt good to slip into the cool of the woods again after the recent days of road-walking and trying to hitch rides on shimmering pavement. The walk to the hut was smooth and undulating, most of it through private land where we either opened and closed gates or mounted stiles over barbed-wire fences, and it occurred to me that I hadn't actually walked on the AT since the day—seventeen days earlier—when I came stumbling out of the woods near Greeneville, Tennessee, to rent a car and send David on alone for 170 miles to Damascus while I went home again on the disabled list.

We reached the hut in about three hours, well before dusk, and what we saw looked like the Fontana Hilton Junior: a two-story hut for twelve, a skylight, an about-to-be-finished rock fireplace, nails for hanging stuff everywhere, a spring-box not one hundred paces away, a handsome white-painted latrine with copies of *Playboy* and *Architectural Digest*. Already there ahead of us was a woman my age named Phyllis, through-hiking alone but meeting her mother up ahead the next day on the Skyline Drive for a birthday lunch; a nurse who had lived in my neighborhood for two years during one period of her life (studying midwifery at an Atlanta hospital and at Emory University), knew exactly where my street was, and thought it was a swell idea for a father and son to walk the Appalachian Trail together. "A friend in Atlanta mailed me a clipping on the trail the other day, in fact," she said, "about a writer named Paul Hemphill doing the same thing. You know him?"

And then, hardly before David and I had determined what soup mix would go over the rice for supper, there came clattering down the embankment leading to the hut a wheelbarrow loaded with gravel and followed by a grunting red-haired Englishman. Chris Brunton, he said, and until the others showed up he was foreman of the Potomac Appalachian Trail Club crew putting the finishing touches on the new hut. This was late on a Friday afternoon and a half dozen volunteers were expected. "Been a bloody bit of work, I'll say." He was in his mid-forties, sales representative for a company dealing in car-wash equipment, and the traveling entailed in his job made it possible for him to do volunteer work like this on the AT whenever and wherever he was needed. Since work had begun on this hut eleven months ago he had been a part of everything—hauling in the heavy timbers from abandoned shelters, digging the hole for the latrine, scrounging huge rocks for the foundation, raising the beams, clearing land, creating the springbox, even enduring curious bears during the winter's snow—and it was hard for him not to speak of it as *his* hut.

"You must love it, to do all this work," David said. Phyllis, the other hiker, was already unrolling her sleeping bag in the hut. David and I sat with Brunton on the one-piece picnic table-and-benches he had also hauled down the hill.

"I do," said Brunton, who moved to Virginia in 1966 and now lived in Falls Church. "Some years ago I was out hiking with my kids and I came across some volunteers maintaining the trail. I'd always thought the trail just took care of itself, you know. So I started helping.''

"You still hike?''

"No more. It may have ended for me when I took sixteen Boy Scouts to New Mexico on a bus for a month's worth of camping.''

"Sixteen Scouts for a month?'' I said.

"Enough to cure a man of hiking,'' said Chris Brunton.

About dark another of the weekend volunteers came through the woods—a handsome forty-ish woman named Lynn Olsen, whose job was to counsel female political candidates all over the country—and she was bushed from fighting the Friday afternoon traffic out of D.C. and driving 140 miles and then walking a mile up the AT from where she had parked her car on Skyline Drive—and while she and Brunton bantered at the picnic table David and I went about the business of fetching water (in the spring-box was a fresh jug of Almaden Chablis), making supper and staking out our places in the hut. I did my leg-lift exercises and gently massaged my knees, which felt as strong now as they had in March at Springer Mountain, and when David finished reading an old *Washington Post* and blew out his candle I slipped down from the upper level of the hut and crunched across the fresh gravel to join Chris and Lynn at the picnic table.

"Have some wine?'' Brunton said.

"No, thanks,'' I said. "Seems I abused the privilege.''

"Pity.''

We sat there for nearly two hours, three educated people in their forties, and we must have touched on every subject known to man and woman except the relative merits of different makes of backpacking equipment. We talked sports. We talked England. We talked cities and race and politics and feminism (Lynn knew even more than I about the politics of my own Atlanta). It was the first time I had enjoyed a truly serious adult conversation with anyone in an AT shelter, as far as I could recall, and I was having a wonderful time. A deer came up so close that when Chris reached out and touched her nose she didn't flinch. Lynn was most impressed that I knew both Roy Blount and Joe McGinniss ("Roy's the funniest man alive and *The Selling of the President* was one of the best political books ever") and that we intended to stay with them when we got into New England. They wanted to know about my books and my work. And they especially wanted to know about our walk of the Appalachian Trail.

"*Me and the Boy* sounds like a perfect title," Lynn said.

"If there's going to *be* a book," I said. "This is *work*."

"That story about the bourbon," said Chris. "That's some kid."

"You bet he is."

"So what's the plan now?" said Lynn. "You've already made one big jump. It's June the eighth. You can't make Katahdin by the middle of August, can you?"

"No," I said. "For the time being we're going to go on through the Shenandoah. When we get to Harpers Ferry we'll have to decide. We can make a jump so we wind up walking to the top of Katahdin together, or we can walk until it's time for school to start and both of us just stop there and go home."

"What's your publisher say?"

"He doesn't much care. And there's another idea, too."

"And?"

"On August fifteenth David leaves Daddy, all alone and feeling blue, to walk the rest of it by himself," I said.

"How does Daddy feel about that?" said Lynn.

"Not so hot."

It was eleven o'clock when bouncing flashlights played through the trees and another pair of PATC volunteers came upon the clearing. They, too, had parked on Skyline Drive, but they had steaks and wine with them and the moon was full so they had thrown an impromptu dinner for themselves in a clearing of the forest. Much backslapping and hoo-hawing ensued. I excused myself and slipped through the darkness to the hut and found David—as far as I would ever know—sleeping like a rock.

# 30

ALL I ASK IN THE MORNINGS IS TO BE LEFT ALONE SO I can have my coffee and get the blood running uphill and figure out what happens next. I want no confrontations at dawn because usually there will be plenty of time for those before the sun goes down. The most discombobulated period of my life, in fact, had been the three Texas summer months I spent being kicked awake before daybreak by frenetic Air Force drill instructors during basic training. That's why, to this day, I'm an early riser. I want to get in the first licks.

Dawn was coming early now, as we moved toward the middle of June, and only the creatures of the forest were moving around the Calf Mountain Hut when I awoke to the first glints of sun flashing through the trees. I had been beaten to the punch by Phyllis, the hiker from Atlanta, who had left without a stir or a trace to make the birthday rendezvous with her mother up the way on Skyline Drive. That was fine with me. I had the morning all to myself now. I had boiled a pot full of water and was swilling a first Sierra cup of double-strength coffee and nibbling a granola bar, remembering the lively talk of the night before and feeling as good as I had felt in a long time on the trail, when the reverie was broken by the voice of David from the loft above my head.

"Was this jump George Walsh's idea?" he said. When I glanced up at him to say good morning, or something, I saw that he was fully awake and there was fire in his eyes.

"Ours," I said. "We discussed it."

"George Walsh doesn't control my life."

"Christ, Dave, we're talking about a 384-mile jump here."

"Was it his idea?"

"I told you. We agreed. We had to jump to make Katahdin and it's best for the book if we do it together."

"I don't like it, anyways. He doesn't control my life."

"Well, pal, I'll tell you what. Right now he does whether we like it or not. He controls the book and the book controls the money and the money controls whether you go to Sewanee. Therefore he controls your life right now."

So much for the serenity of the deep woods in the morning. We spoke not a word for nearly an hour as we dabbled at our oatmeal and rolled up our sleeping bags and policed the hut and visited Chris Brunton's latrine and laced our boots and applied Muskol to our arms and necks and loaded our packs and read our maps. Lynn and Chris and the late-arriving couple were beginning to gather around the picnic table for their coffee, sleepy and disheveled and agreeing on work assignments for the day, when we cinched our packs and walked away to pick up the trail. We planned a thirteen-mile hike to the Black Rock Hut.

Since the Calf Mountain Hut was new and the access trails hadn't yet been clearly established, or even blazed except for obscure plastic ribbons tied to bushes here and there, it wasn't hard to lose the way back to the AT. We were all but bushwhacking our way through the underbrush and past the spring-box when I, in the lead, finally saw a

white blaze on a tree and a familiar worn path and then
stepped out smartly. We had walked half a mile, though,
when I realized we were in a clearing we had seen the day
before while hiking up from the south. "Ah, shit, wrong
way," I said. I stopped and wheeled around and passed
David, who stood in his tracks without speaking, and
headed northbound this time. "I was about to take us back
to Waynesboro."

"Dad," I heard him say.

"Yeah."

"I *want* to go back to Waynesboro."

"What?" I stopped and faced him. "We've been there."

"And then I want to take a bus to Birmingham."

"Wait a minute, now. What's this?"

"I don't want to be with you anymore, Dad. I want to
go home."

We must have looked like gunslingers, squared off face-
to-face in the blazing sun, except that he was the one with
the fierce glower in his eyes and I was the one standing
limp and drained and beaten before the confrontation began. The confrontation was over, in fact, and I stood there
devastated by my own son. *I don't want to be with you
anymore, Dad.* Neither "despair" nor "confusion" would
cover this one. "Devastation" was close. Flies and grass-
hoppers and bees were buzzing and clicking around us as
we stood in the middle of the footpath, boring stares at
each other, unaware that we were stopped like statues laden
with forty-pound packs in a museum somewhere. "Let's
get out of the sun," I said. We walked a few feet through
high grass and dropped our packs on the ground and sat
five or six feet apart, facing each other, beneath a dogwood. We swigged from our canteens, still staring at each
other, and I lit a Camel. "Talk to me," I said.

No father should have to hear this from his only son.
What David hit me with for the next forty-five minutes or
so was total devastation—a blitzkrieg, scorched earth, take

no prisoners—and all I could do was sit agape, with a mod-
icum of self-esteem, while he flogged me mercilessly with
a litany of sins and sins perceived. This was not about my
slurping coffee and being a piss-poor example of a long-
distance backpacker and washing the woolens and the cot-
tons in hot water and having a filthy mouth and being both
an atheist and an alcoholic, although those shortcomings
certainly drew his attention. It was much, much more than
that. This was ten years' worth of fitful sleepless nights
rearing their collective head and striking like a rattlesnake
in one furious explosion at the object of its discontent. This
was a boy unleashing the demons on the father who had
cut and run, leaving him adrift at the age of ten, just when
he needed him the most.

"You used to be my hero," he said at some point. What
also amazed me was that he kept a half-smile on his face
through it all. "I can't tell you how many times I've stuck
up for you when Grandmother and Mom would start in on
you. They'd be saying terrible things about you, like 'that
sonofabitch in Atlanta,' and I'd tell 'em to shut up, that
you were my father and they were wrong. I mean, I love
you but sometimes I hate you, too, and I don't want that.
I don't want us to have a love-hate relationship like you
and Pop. The love's great, but I don't like the hate part."

"How come you hate me, then?" I said.

"I don't hate you."

"Well, for God's sake, how come you don't *like* me?"

"I just said I don't like *walking* with you," he said.

"Okay, let's have it. My skinny legs? Camels? What?"

"Your ego, for one thing."

"Ego? Christ, Dave, I'm a pussy cat."

"You don't have any self-confidence and you're hiding
it."

"Behind every pair of cowboy boots there's a pussy
cat," I said. "Don't you know that? You're damned right
I don't have any self-confidence. Helped turn me into an

alcoholic. I told you what happened to me that year at Harvard. I was the poor dumb Southerner, the truck driver's boy, didn't have any business hanging out with guys who'd gone to Yale and Harvard and worked for *The New York Times*. So what you do is put on your boots and smoke 'em. See what I mean?''

"It gets on my nerves," he said.

"Shit, I'm the one that's got to live with it. What else?''

"You won't listen to other people. Like with religion. You're just as bigoted as Grandmother is about religion.''

"I gave it forty-eight years and found it lacking.''

"And Mom," he said. "Mom loved you.''

"I loved her, too, Dave.''

"She talks about you a lot.''

"I'm sure she does.''

"No, I mean about the good times. Before you left.''

I said, "Okay. I thought I'd made it clear about the white picket fences. I wanted 'em every bit as much as she did when we got married. But we started sliding apart and I was going crazy being alone in my own house without a grown-up to talk to and there had to be another way for me to live and so I left. It wasn't pretty and maybe I cried more nights than you did but it's done.''

He said, "Sometimes I don't know whether I'm supposed to be twelve or nineteen.''

"I know, son. I don't know how to act, either.''

"It's been confusing, being with you like this.''

"Yeah. We're trying to cover too much ground in too little time. Early on I just decided I was going to treat you like an adult. That's about all we can do, is forget the nine years and take it from here.''

"This is taking me away from some people who mean a great deal to me," he said.

"Your father's not one of 'em, huh?''

"I didn't mean that.''

"I swear, Dave, you're going to be a hell of a lawyer.''

He smiled again. "It's just that you were my hero and now you aren't."

"Heroes," I said. "Heroes are fantasy. They're in the movies."

"What about you and Pop? You've written that he was your hero."

"He was, he was. But the next chance you get, you go back and keep reading 'Me and My Old Man.' Get to the part where I found him crying and gurgling whiskey in the truck one night and telling me, 'There's a lot a boy don't know. . . . I don't mean to hurt your mama, but there's a lot a boy don't know.' I've about got it memorized by now. But you go on and read the rest of it, where I say something like, 'From there we began.' He became the father I loved once I got the hero shit out of my head."

"I looked up to you," he said. He wasn't smiling anymore.

"I wish you wouldn't, Dave, I really do," I told him.

*What happened to the kid who poured the bourbon*? Stunned, having no other choice, I stood up and slipped the pack on my back and led the way back to Waynesboro. We spoke only in grunts as we walked to the nearest crossing of Skyline Drive and caught a couple of rides back to town. David walked on to the fire station, once I found that the next southbound bus wouldn't leave until four o'clock in the afternoon, and I stepped into a steaming phone booth on the sidewalk to alert Susan ("Do you think he needs professional help?" she said, and all I could say was that I was merely reporting the news as it broke). The two hiking sisters were at the station, shocked to hear of the rift ("We thought you were just kidding about arguing"), and I don't know what David said when he ran into a high school buddy from Birmingham we had been hoping to meet on the trail. When we boarded the Trailways David grabbed the shotgun seat next to the driver and I went all the way to the rear, next to the john and a whole family of rowdy little pigtailed daughters, in order to smoke and be alone. Darkness came as the bus creaked through the grimy hills of Lynchburg.

And then, with the Sunday morning sun beginning to flash off of the World's Tallest Hotel in downtown Atlanta at dawn, we tumbled wordlessly off the bus and hailed a black cabbie ("Bedrosian and the Braves done blown another one to the Dodgers las' night Ellay"). Susan came to the door in her bathrobe to let us in and she hugged us both—separately but equally—and she cooked up the kind of breakfast that wanderers dream of and then David stayed on in the kitchen for a marathon talk with her while I went to the other end of the house with Martha and tried to do the Sunday *New York Times* crossword and acrostic puzzles. In the middle of the afternoon, once he had finally cranked his slap-dash VW Squareback, David left all of the camping gear with me and went back out to the driveway and revved the engine until he was satisfied it would make the 150-mile drive to Birmingham. "Take a week," I told him, "but whatever you decide, make it stick." And he was gone.

# 31

HOME AGAIN, HOME AGAIN, BUT THIS TIME IT WAS LIKE being in a holding cell while a judge pondered sentencing. As soon as David had driven away that afternoon I called his mother in Birmingham to tell her to look for him and to please give me a report on what she thought he was thinking. The open hostility between the former Susan Olive and me had withered in time and now we were united in doing the best we could for our three children.

"That must have hurt," she was saying.

"It destroyed me," I said.

"Was there anything you did? Anything in particular?"

"I don't know. He might have been playing possum the night before when I was talking with some older people at the shelter."

"Maybe he's just homesick."

"It's a possibility."

"The last thing in the world he's going to admit is that he's homesick," she said.

"That's true," I said. "But look. Be gentle with him. Let him talk. And let me know what you think's on his mind. This is going to be a disaster if we have to quit the trail. It's not just the book and the money involved. It's me, too. He's killing me.''

And at dusk, after I had tried to take a nap, my second Susan and I sat in the darkened den of the house trying to plumb every corner of the nineteen-year-old mind. Her reading from the two-hour talk they'd had at the kitchen table that morning after breakfast (all of my kids had always seemed to be able to open up to her from the day they met Daddy's future wife) was that David and I had tried to do too much too soon. ''You talk about 'the one sixty-two' all the time, the long baseball season, but this is like cramming it all into a one-week series,'' she said. ''He's confused. He always wanted to walk the Appalachian Trail and he always wanted to get to know you better and now he's doing it and he's saying, 'Is that all there is?' I think he feels like he's being used, too, and I even think the title of the book bothers him. He's 'the boy.' All you can do is let him have some rope and take his time. I think he's going to go back with you but I wouldn't bet on it.''

Finally, around bedtime, I took my copy of *The Good Old Boys* and opened to the piece, ''Me and My Old Man,'' and read until I found the part I had told David he should reread when he got back home. And there it was, clear as day, what I had written nearly a dozen years earlier when I really didn't know what I was talking about when it came to fathers and sons:

> . . . I had seen him running scared, and it brought me to the first vague stirrings that life was not going to be easy or even fun; that life could be a bitch not above kicking you in the groin if you so much as winked at her; that there would be a young boy looking up at me, wanting answers, and about all I might be able to give him in the way of solid advice would

be to suggest he go into a clinch when they started working on the head. Here we had been working on the theory that he was unbeaten and untied, the last of the indomitable heroes, and now I knew differently and he knew I knew differently. From there, we began.

It was limbo, in the purest definition of the word, and when I would unavoidably bump into friends and they would ask what it was this time I could only mumble something to the effect that this time it was David who needed a break from the trail. I was devastated, given to sitting alone and staring at the walls for long periods. On Father's Day, when I still hadn't heard from David for a week, I called my old man—fathers and sons were on my mind now more than ever before and with that call I intended to begin the healing process with Pop—but Mama said he was "sleeping in the basement" (her euphemism, now, for his being passed out on the cot) and when she shook him awake and he came to the phone about all I could say was that riding over the Appalachians in a truck sure beat walking. I played and replayed "Texas Girl at the Funeral of Her Father" and played and replayed the color slides we had so far of our trek. I watched the Braves on television. I ate watermelon and ice cream. I did my leg-lifts and took my Naprosyn. I rearranged my pack and greased my boots. I cut the grass, cooked meals, read in the papers about the rape of a female through-hiker in north Georgia back in May when we were in the Smokies ("I wouldn't walk that trail without a weapon, and I'd carry more ammunition than food," a sheriff told John Harmon of the *Atlanta Constitution*), learned that finally the *Reader's Digest* would run the piece about David and me tracking the Arkansas River two summers earlier. The copy-edited manuscript of my novel arrived and I learned that at Macmillan they hyphenate "ass-hole."

I would hear scattered reports, mainly from his mother, about how and what David was doing. One night he had called Maggie Thompson, the tough sisterly girlfriend who was in summer school at Sewanee, and she had given him an ass-kicking and told him he should be ashamed of himself. He was going to movies and drinking beer with a pal from high school, about the closest thing he had to a friend in Birmingham, and tinkering with his VW. On the weekend of Father's Day he drove over to Tuscaloosa to hang out and spend the night with Lisa, his older sister, who was about to finish at the University of Alabama (I waited by the phone much of that Sunday, wanting the blissful irony that he would call that day to say he was ready to return to the AT, but knew that he never had called me on Father's Day), and Lisa said only that he seemed melancholy and didn't talk much about me and the trail. "He did say that if y'all got to that mountain in Maine where it ends," said Lisa, "it would be on Mom's birthday and the day I finish college." Somewhere in there I had coffee in an Atlanta diner with David's closest adviser in the dean's office at Sewanee, a fellow who happened to be in town on business, and when I asked him to tell me about the psyche of a nineteen-year-old boy he could only shrug and say, "It's supposed to be my career, but I still don't know."

Finally, on the eighth day, the phone rang and I snatched it on the first ring. *Collect to Paul from David in Birmingham.* We were tentative, circling each other, at times acting as though nothing more had happened than that we had both taken separate well-earned respites from the trail and now we were working out the logistics of our return.

"I just need a couple of days to clear up some things," he said.

"You're sure?"

"Oh, yeah, I kinda miss it."

"No turning back?"

"Let's just pick up at Waynesboro and keep on going."

"Okay," I said. "I'll tell Dan Bruce. You remember Dan, the little fellow we kept running into at the backpacking stores? One that weighs everything with baby scales?"

"Oh, yeah, how's he doing?"

"I think he'll go with us for a few days."

"Incredible. That sounds great."

"He can ride with us to Waynesboro, walk some of the Shenandoah and then bring the car back to Atlanta. Save us a little money."

"Hey, great," David said.

Hey, great.

# 32

THIS TIME DAVID LEFT HIS CAR AT THE APARTMENT IN Birmingham and took the three-hour Greyhound to Atlanta. When he swung off the bus at three o'clock on a Thursday afternoon, exactly eleven days to the hour since I had seen him drive away from my house, he wore the same familiar hiking outfit—tattered khaki shorts, gray polypro long-sleeved shirt, blue bandanna around his neck, feet shod in two pair of socks and now-scarred brown boots—but he seemed to have a different aura about him this time. The smile wasn't a boyish grin anymore, I thought as Dan Bruce and I greeted him and led him to the '70 Olds double-parked outside the depot, and in its place was the rollicking look of a lad who has gone off to sea and come back home a man. There was almost a swagger about him as he tossed his blue-gray pack into the trunk of the car and took the keys from me and bantered with us as he deftly slipped onto the interstate and stomped it for Damascus. I liked what I was seeing. I figured maybe *he* had lost some sleep, too.

He powered the old car to Damascus, some 350 miles

of interstate, in less than six hours. By dark the three of us were ensconced at a tight booth in the Douglas Inn, the boisterous beer joint-cafe beside the river near the Methodist hostel, shouting above the jousting of Good Old Boys and trout fishermen and the yowling of Willie Nelson on the jukebox. Out of deference to me, I suppose, they drank coffee instead of beer. There was no talk about what had happened between David and me previously. We were there to have a good time.

"Dan," I said, "I still can't get it straight about what you do for a living. Are you a preacher, or not?"

"Not in the truest sense of the word," Dan Bruce said.

"But you're trying to sell Jews on Jesus."

"There *was* a Jesus, you know."

"Yeah, but that's beside the point."

"David, I think your dad really means it about his atheism."

"Yeah"—David grinned—"he's a bigot, all right."

"But look," I said, "isn't that preaching, going around spreading the word about this Jesus fellow to people who don't believe in him? And what the hell do you care for, anyway?"

"It's my ministry," he said.

"Ah-hah. A preacher. There's the buzz word, 'ministry.' "

"No," Bruce said, "what I do is look out after elderly Jewish people and while I'm at it I try to show them that they and the Christians aren't so far apart after all, that Jesus was Jewish. I'm a mediator."

Well, yes. *Mediator.* Both Dan and I had good reasons of our own for his going along for a few days in the Shenandoah—I saw it as a less expensive way of getting David and me back on the AT and Dan wanted to explore that part of the trail before the through-hike he planned for the following year—but it went unspoken between us that maybe David and I needed a third party along for a while.

We'd been bumping into Dan Bruce in the backpacking
outfitters' stores of Atlanta ever since before Christmas,
when we first began to equip ourselves for the trek, and
we both enjoyed his company. He was an energetic elf in
his early forties—at five feet six inches and 140 pounds,
short and firm of limb, with a low center of gravity, he had
the ideal hiker's physique—and he was probably as peri-
patetic a man as David had ever met. He had a degree in
physics from Georgia Tech and had done time at a semi-
nary in Chattanooga. He read the philosophers and Louis
L'Amour. Once he made $70,000 in a period of six months
on an electronic football game of his invention and then
turned right around and spent a full year, out of his per-
sonal curiosity, sleeping on the floor with a family of hippies during Atlanta's modest social revolution of the
mid-sixties ("It lasted until they found out I had a car and a
checking account"). He had never been married and now
he was living with his aging mother on a farm twenty miles
east of Atlanta, about to close out his "ministry," looking
for some kind of part-time job so he could begin his final
training and preparation for a long-planned solo walk of
the AT in 1985. He was the sort to buy a pair of baby
scales at a yard sale and weigh his hiking baggage right
down to the ounce; the type who planned to average not
"about fifteen miles a day" on the trail but precisely 14.85.

We stayed that night at the hostel, where there were two
other grim and beaten hikers pondering whether they would
continue their through-hikes or quit while they were near
an interstate, and in the morning before we left Dan scribbled a note for Paschall Grindstaff (postmaster and overseer
of the hostel) recommending that "loving homes be found"
for the three kittens because they were "growing up like
wildcats." Then we piled into the car and barreled to
Waynesboro and parked beside the Howard Johnson's motel near the entrance to the Shenandoah National Park and
made the 6.5-mile hike through private land to the Calf

Mountain Shelter. It had been exactly two weeks since David and I had checked into there—the night of my animated late-night rapport with Chris Brunton and Lynn Olsen and the two late-arriving PATC volunteers—and now the finishing touches had been applied to the shelter and the massive stone fireplace. We had it all to ourselves.

Walking the Shenandoah is a snap compared to the Smokies. The mountains are smoother and more tame here, lacking the wild grandeur we found at 6,000-plus feet around Clingman's Dome, and it seems that you are forever waiting for cars to pass before crossing Skyline Drive. It is nothing to have to shoo a deer off the trail so you can keep on hiking. The Shenandoah is made for families who want to stroll through the woods for a couple of miles, without any provisions except an Instamatic, before returning to the car and driving on ahead for lunch at an air-conditioned restaurant at one of the wayside stations. With David and Dan walking together, as I had hoped, I kept a discreet distance behind them as we easily cruised thirteen miles to the next shelter at Blackrock Gap. When I pulled into the shelter only five minutes behind them, looking good and barely sweating, David seemed startled that I was only five minutes behind their pace. "Anybody care for a jog?" I said.

On the next day, as though Dan had planned it that way, he and I walked together on a fourteen-miler to Pinefield Hut and it was David who tarried over breakfast and lagged behind. I couldn't wait to hear what they had talked about the day before, walking together for six leisurely hours, and as it turned out there was plenty.

"I don't think you have to worry about Dave anymore," Bruce said. We had called a snack break at a Skyline Drive overlook where there was a spectacular view of the Shenandoah Valley looking toward West Virginia. Golden hawks caught the thermals rising up from the floor of the valley and soared for several minutes without having to move their wings. The elevation was only about 3,000 feet and the Skyline Drive gawkers in their air-conditioned cars were out in force on this hot muggy Sunday.

"Tell me it was just a case of homesickness," I said.

"You could call it that, I guess, but that's too simplistic."

"Always is when you're dealing with a nineteen-year-old."

"That's what you have to understand," Dan said. "That's a very bright, very sensitive son you've got there."

"Tell me."

"I told him that I'm in my eighth year of celibacy and it about blew his mind."

"You? Celibate? Why?"

He said, "I've had enough chasing women. It's a discipline for the trail, too. But when I told David that he couldn't understand. This new morality is giving him trouble, you know? He goes off to college and there's all those women and he's still sort of old-fashioned about sex."

"Yeah, but what's that got to do with his turning on me?"

"It's just a part of the pattern. He wants everything to go perfectly. He had a vision of a perfect through-hike of the AT and first one thing went wrong, then another. There's probably been too much 'Daddy' for him to swallow in such a short time and then I don't think he was too keen on walking by himself for two weeks to Damascus and now there's the jumps y'all are having to make. It got to be too much for him to handle."

"So he struck out at me," I said.

"Right. And he doesn't feel so hot about it, either."

A deer came right up to the road, long enough for a tourist to snap a picture, before prancing back down the slope into the woods. "You think he's okay now, you say."

"He brought along a paperback of *Hamlet* this time."

"So? I noticed that."

"He's thinking reality now," Dan said. "First things first, one step at a time, take care of business, all of that. I think he did a lot of growing up when he went home. Gave him a break when he needed it."

We spent that evening at Pinefield Hut, an idyllic shelter set on a knoll amid dogwood and elms and pines with a gurgling stream meandering around its base, and it was another of those starry picturebook nights of deer practically feeding from our hands and owls sweeping through the coves after field mice and no signs whatsoever that the capital of the most powerful nation in the world lay little more than fifty miles to the east. Our companions in the shelter were a sixty-ish couple named Eff and Jay who maintained a stretch of the AT near their home in central Virginia and told of recently discovering two young Appalachian families actually living in one of the AT shelters: they were from upper West Virginia, had a total of three children, and when Eff and Jay happened upon them they saw the two fathers stumbling down the hill blind-drunk from a foray to Pittsburgh to collect their unemployment checks. That was all right, to hear stories like that from Eff and Jay, but then we learned that they were born-again religious zealots who signed the shelter logs with ⟨PTL⟩ and they drove even Dan Bruce to the point of madness with their fervor. They were laying out rice for the mice and seemed on the verge of speaking in tongues when I fell asleep.

Dan would be leaving us after three nights and four days of testing the Shenandoah. Eff and Jay left at daybreak ("Beware of people who say, 'I can't explain it, I just can't explain it,' because that usually means they really haven't been born again," said Dan) and we dallied over breakfast. I felt up to trying a twenty-mile cruise to the next wayside park, my knees and my spirits as fit as they had been in a long while, and since Dan had only a ten-miler to the point

where he could hitch rides back to my car and then to
Atlanta—and David knew he could always catch up with
the old man—I said goodbye to Dan Bruce and left him
and David chatting as I swept away into the woods on a
happy solo hike to the Lewis Mountain Campground. The
walking was smooth and easy, deer were everywhere, the
protective covering of trees fully leafed for the summer
kept it cool, springs were anywhere you wanted them to
be, and for a while I had the feeling that I could walk to
Canada.

The campstore had closed when I came smoking into
Lewis Mountain Campground late in the afternoon, my first
twenty-miler behind me in a wisp of dust, but a silver-
haired woman opened the door long enough for me to buy
some stuff—Camels, a beer for Dave and a Coke for me,
cans of chili and beef stew—and I had finished with my
shopping and was in the phone booth outside the store talking with Susan on this Sunday evening ("I think now we're
going to just start enjoying ourselves like we were supposed to") when I saw a teenaged girl standing outside the
booth holding a sliced quarter of watermelon and pointing
to it. *Roughing it again on the ol' AT*, I thought, hanging
up the phone and following the girl across the campground
road to one of the rental cabins. A couple from Philadelphia was spending a week there with their two daughters—he was Reid, a restoration architect for the federal
government, on a working vacation—and I joined them at
a picnic table for watermelon and chitchat.

Soon, as it was getting along toward dark, I hailed David
as he came trudging up to the campstore (he had walked
with Dan Bruce to Dan's hitching place and then, running
so late, himself hitched a ride to the campground) and we
ate them out of watermelon. We walked down to a camping
area and picked a spot to rig up the tarpaulin, for rain and
wind were coming up that night, and we sloppily tore open
the cans of chili and Dinty Moore's Beef Stew and had

ourselves a semicivilized supper in the grass while kids chased fireflies and parents in Bermuda shorts sat on cabin porches sipping martinis.

"Dan ought to be back at the hostel in Damascus about now," David said as we finished some canned peaches and ice cream I had bought at the store and topped it with hot black coffee. The stars were still out but we could smell the rain coming.

"Y'all had a pretty good talk," I said.

"Yeah. I like him. He's a catholic fellow."

I laughed. "Can you imagine him living with hippies?"

"Sure. I think he'd fit right in anywhere."

"Probably right. I'd bet on him next year when he walks the AT."

"Me, too. Sometimes he'll drive you crazy being so picky. But it probably pays off when you're trying to walk two thousand miles alone."

"Probably," I said.

There had, indeed, been a remarkable turnaround and I wasn't about to disturb it. *Here we had been working on the theory that he was unbeaten and untied, the last of the indomitable heroes, and now I knew differently and he knew I knew differently. From there, we began. . . .* So far we had actually backpacked together for exactly 341.9 miles on the Appalachian Trail. It had taken years.

# 33

"WOULD YOU RUN THAT BY ME ONE MORE TIME?" I WAS standing in the phone booth at the campstore the next morning, my knees hurting again from the twenty-mile hike of the day before, returning a call to a *Reader's Digest* editor in D.C. who wanted to make her final edits on the piece about the Arkansas River. It had been two years since David and I had driven 5,000 miles together in order for me to do the piece and I could hardly remember the trip.

"I said we always read the quotes back to those who're quoted."

"What the hell do you do that for?" I shouted.

"For accuracy," she said.

"My ass. You're letting 'em clean up their act."

"The woman at the Chamber of Commerce in Salida was horrified."

"About what?"

"You quoted that sign saying, let's see here, saying, 'In Case of Flash Flood Climb to Safety.' "

"So? What it said. Even had a stick figure climbing a hill."

"But she says the river's not dangerous," the editor said.

"Holy Christ," I said. "Why didn't you just hire her to write the piece?"

Arguing with her was impossible. The only reason I had agreed to write for the *Reader's Digest* was that they paid $3,500 and I was broke at the time. Now I was finding out, firsthand, why the *literati* and other discerning readers ridiculed the *Digest* and the people who read it (including President Ronald Reagan). The editors there had taken 7,500 pretty good words I had written and now they had beaten and kneaded them into an unrecognizable 2,500-word glob of putty and I was swearing that my next collection of my journalism—and I had saved the original manuscript of the Arkansas River piece and scores of others—would consist of all of the originals and be entitled *The Way I Wrote 'Em* or *First Draft* with a long and vitriolic exposé about editors such as this *Digest* word processor from D.C. The irony was that finally, after a lifetime of writing for people like the *Atlantic* and *The New York Times Magazine*, by appearing in the *Reader's Digest* I would be acknowledged by my parents and my sister and my host of aunts and uncles and cousins and the rest as The Writer in the Family.

She wanted to talk to David, too, to double-check *his* quotes, and when that was done we headed for the woods where there were no telephones. It was ten o'clock in the morning before we got away from the clatter of the wayside. We were getting sloppy now—just ambling along, canned food in our packs, senses not exactly attuned to nature, I smoking as I walked and stubbing out Camels on pine trees—probably attributable to the ease of the footpath in the Shenandoah and the knowledge that our dream of being heroic Georgia-to-Maine through-hikers lay sprawled in the dust somewhere back there in North Carolina. Day-hikers were everywhere and so was the sound of traffic on Skyline Drive. We joined the vacationers for a sandwich and iced tea at the restaurant in the Big Meadows complex, where I bought nearly forty dollars worth of groceries and snacks with my American Express Card, and as we left we were hailed by the couple and their two daughters, whom we had met the night before at the first of the waysides ("Hi, Paul," shouted their four-year-old Louisa, startling me at first, sounding just like my Martha).

There was a semblance of the way it was supposed to be that night when, after an easy twelve-mile walk, we stopped at the Rock Spring Hut. A half dozen backpackers of different ilk were there, including a PATC "field patrol" volunteer named Denny Shaffer (a dapper fellow, maybe forty, former through-hiker, just checking out conditions on the trail) and an energetic young college student named Shawn Carson, whom David remembered from his solo walk between Hot Springs and Damascus ("You must be 'Dad' "). Cranking up the Peak I stove, spreading out the sleeping bags, fetching water from a spring, eating rice from a Sierra cup (with beef stew for a topping this time), cleaning the boots, sharing gossip from the trail; for a while it was like the good times/bad times of what seemed like months past.

*That woman that got raped on the trail in Georgia? I ran into her after that and told her I was surprised she was still hiking. Know what she said? It happens, it happens. Still going to Katahdin.*

*Eggs are hell to carry, but I promised myself an omelet every morning.*

*Somebody told me, though, that Festus has a college education.*

*Shenandoah's like a vacation compared to the Georgia part.*

*You're lucky, Dave. I hardly saw my dad after the divorce. One time he did take me hunting. We sat and listened to the woods and that was about the size of it.*

*You know The Irish Goat? Went home to Front Royal*

*and now they say he's moved his typewriter and books into*
*Manassas Gap Shelter. Got a regular office set up there.*
*Says he misses his friends.*

And the food bags were strung up in the trees and the
fireflies and the deer came, and from a cabin down the
slope only fifty yards away came the sweet sounds of
somebody fiddling "Cripple Creek" and all of the old Appalachian tunes (a young fellow courting his bride on their
honeymoon), and everything was okay. Just okay. As I lay
there under the fine starry Virginia sky, listening to the
fiddler and watching a doe forage for leftovers only twenty
feet away, I tried to figure out what wasn't right. My belly
was full and my knees were at least ambulatory and there
was a calm about David that I had never seen, certainly
not since our return to the trail only six days before, and
we were capable now of putting fifteen or more miles a
day behind us. But the adrenaline was gone, whatever the
reasons, and I had the queasy feeling that our affair with
the Appalachian Trail was settling into a placid stultifying
rut like marriages that last too long.

The next day, after another lunch in an air-conditioned
wayside restaurant (it was trout amandine this time, for me,
and a BLT and beer in a glass for David) and another
leisurely walk of nearly a dozen miles, we decided to overnight at a shelter called Byrd's Nest #3 (for Governor Harry
F. Byrd of Virginia, instrumental in establishing the SNP
during the twenties). Nobody else was there when we arrived around four o'clock. We napped and took some pictures and washed out some clothes at the rock fountain
featuring piped-in spring water and we agreed that things
were becoming a bit too civilized.

"I never thought I'd be missing the hail-and-lightning
storms like we saw in the Smokies," I said after a two-
cigarette visit to the latrine down the slope behind the concrete-floored shelter. David lay atop one of the two picnic

tables, down to his shorts while the other clothes dried, taking his sun.

"Man," he said, "that seems like years ago."

"And Albert Mountain. Let's not forget Albert Mountain."

" 'Precipitous descents.' As in Wesser. You *miss* that?" he said.

"Sort of. At least I felt like I was hiking the AT."

"Yeah."

I'd been doing some scribbling on a blank page in the spiral notebook I used for a journal, adding up the days and nights and mileage we had covered since Susan had let us out at Amicalola Falls on the last Monday in March. I was embarrassed. "Boy," I said, "Grandma Gatewood would spin in her grave."

"What you got?"

"If nothing had happened to the knees or anything else"—I glanced up at him, now sitting on the edge of the table, but he didn't blink—"if we'd been able to do ten miles a day during the first two weeks and then fifteen a day after that, we'd be, lemme see, we would have walked about 1,340 miles of the trail. Christ, we'd be eating steaks with Sterling Lord and George Walsh at Bear Mountain State Park in New York right now. And in a couple of days we'd be in Connecticut."

"Things happen," David said.

"Yeah, but this is disgraceful."

"How many miles do we have?"

"Okay, let's see." I double-checked the figures. "This makes the ninety-fourth day since Amicalola. Our figures are different because you did 170 miles in fourteen days by yourself while I went home."

"What've I got?"

"You got about 535 miles in about fifty-one days of walking."

"Man," he said, shaking his head. "Eleven miles a day."

"Me," I said, "365 miles, maybe thirty-seven days. Can you believe it? I've spent fifty-seven out of ninety-four days convalescing. As it were."

"Well, when we walk we do okay. We've had some fifteen-milers."

"Yeah, and every goddam one of 'em put me in bed."

"Okay now, aren't you?" said David.

"Ah. I shouldn't have tried the twenty-miler Monday. But they're okay, I guess, if I just keep going like we've been going lately. Thing is, though, we've got to make the one more huge jump to make Katahdin in time for you to get back to school. I mean one hell of a jump, like to the Whites."

"Whatever you say."

"Shit," I said. "I was gonna be a hero."

"Yeah, well, we've already been over that," he said, and he smiled.

# 34

Since we had agreed that the final decision on when and where to make our last giant leap would be made at Harpers Ferry, West Virginia, headquarters for the Appalachian Trail Conference, and Harpers Ferry was still eighty miles north of us by the AT, we decided to hitchhike our way for the next thirty miles to Front Royal, Virginia, where we needed to resupply with food and white gas and to check out the post office. We paused for nearly an hour at a splendid overlook called Marys Rock, where David literally tried his hands at scaling the bald granite outcrop and I took some pictures and we gawked at three golden hawks soaring on the thermals coming up from the hot floor of the Shenandoah Valley, and then sauntered the two more miles down the trail for breakfast at the Panorama wayside and soon were standing in the shimmering heat of noon trying to hitch a ride to Luray and then on to Front Royal.

It was a toss-up about what was harder on the knees, clumping down treacherous rocky descents on the trail or digging the heels into macadam roads, but both of mine began to ache again as we walked along U.S. 211 toward

Luray trying to hail a ride on the umpromising roadway. I asked David to do the thumbing, as usual, on the theory that the sight of a handsome teenager was more appealing than that of a gray-bearded spider with wrapped knees and a seven-foot staff, and after being ogled by station-wagon-loads of vacationing families we finally piled into the bed of a woman's pickup. Ten minutes later she let us out at the intersection of 211 with U.S. 340, northbound to Front Royal, and we stood for nearly an hour in the broiling sun beside a decrepit old baseball park with a wooden grandstand and insufficient lights hanging from crooked creosote telephone poles.

I can't see an old ballpark like that without placing myself in a dirty gray uniform, crouched low at the second-base position, waiting for a ground ball to come skittering my way through the churned and furrowed brown dirt of the infield; then racing in, the runner plowing down the line to first base, grabbing the ball with my Bob Dillinger glove and neatly making the quick underhanded flip to nail the runner by a blink, the crowd murmuring and the umpire's right hand going up with the "out" sign. I wandered away from the road, leaving the hitching chores to David, and found a loose slat in the fence behind third base so I could take a closer look at the park. How many times had I fought off bad hops, sometimes successfully and sometimes not, at places like this?

*It is the spring of '54 in the sultry little Florida Panhandle town of Graceville, smallest town in professional baseball, and I'm the only second baseman in town with opening night less than a week away. The night before, in an exhibition game, I have struck out all four times but turned the pivot on two double plays with my Mexican shortstop and I'm not worried.* Hey, roomie, drop your bat and get your glove, you don't want to overexpose yourself, *says the* *catcher, Tommy Doherty, my roommate at the old hotel, and after the morning workout Tommy and I go up to the crusty old manager of this Class D hodgepodge to get my $2.50 meal money for the day.* Either of y'all got change for a five? *says old Cat Milner, the manager, and when Tommy says we'd take the five and split it he says,* I'm sorry, but I gotta let the kid go. *Within an hour I'm out on the road, crying and hitching a ride away from the first dream I ever had.*

There was little traffic between Luray and Front Royal this time of day and I found David sitting on a large rock beside the road sign when I swept through the high weeds to rejoin him.

"Is that a Class D park?" he said as I plopped beside him.

"Nah," I said, "they don't even have Class D anymore. It's probably for American Legion ball or maybe they've got an amateur league in town. I bet that park's fifty years old, though. Probably *was* Class D one time."

"Looks a little like the one in Graceville."

"That's right, you saw it once. The time *Life* took pictures."

"I always liked that piece," he said.

"Yeah, me, too. That and 'Me and My Old Man.' Both of 'em hurt."

"You still wish you'd played pro ball, Dad?"

"How can I tell you," I said. "I'd have a Pulitzer behind me if I wanted to write half as much as I wanted to play baseball. That was the first thing I ever really wanted to do. I reckon I could say I wasted a lot of time fielding ground balls and trying to learn how to hit and bumming around the country trying to prove I could play. But I won't say that."

"Still hurts, though, huh?"

"Yeah, it sure does, Dave, but in a positive kind of way."

"How so?"

"Aw, you know, at least I tried. Way I'm starting to feel about this trek now. At least I'm not gonna be sitting around when I'm sixty-five saying, 'Damn, I wish I'd tried to walk that Appalachian Trail before my body wore out.' Failing isn't nearly as bad as not having tried."

"I guess we've gotta look at it like that now," David said.

"Suppose so."

After more than an hour we finally got a ride to Front Royal, in a ragged pickup truck, with a fellow in his late thirties who seemed to mirror his surroundings. My journal: "Scraggly country, more like WV than VA, ride with Raymond Jones. Vietnam vet, 3 small kids, drives 60 miles every day to work as steel fabricator 3-to-midnite, left Alexandria 'tired of D.C. traffic,' still has nightmares Nam. '2 buddies shot by sniper on night watch, I got the sniper and his 3 buddies,' 1969. Jones like this country: unkempt, sweaty, hard, but friendly. . . ." Front Royal, we would see when he let us out there, sounds pretty but is not. It choked in its own dust and engine smoke as we beat the pavement once more to the post office to collect a money order from Susan and to mail back the AT guidebooks we wouldn't be needing anymore (Central & Southern Virginia, Pennsylvania, Massachusetts-Connecticut), and then hiked to the big Safeway supermarket across the street. First we bought supplies and then we went back outside to a pay phone, where I talked to Susan and David talked to his younger sister Molly about mailing us our heavy winter stuff ahead to Hanover, New Hampshire, so we could walk the treacherous White Mountains en route to Katahdin in a week or so. That was the new plan: to get ourselves to Hanover, the home of Dartmouth College, and walk the 440 miles to the northern end of the AT and some kind of glory.

By sundown we had hitched and walked and then
hacked our way through muddy streams and rhododendron ''slicks'' (the name, I had just heard somewhere,
they use in Appalachia for those dark forbidding clumps
so thick that bears can lay ambushes from them) until we
reached a grubby shelter at Manassas Gap. This was the
shelter where Paul Michael Fitzsimmons of Front Royal
(I had been tempted to look him up in the phone book
while we made calls from the Safeway in town but I was
afraid an irate wife/lover/creditor/parent/child might be
stirred) was alleged to be keeping house. There was some
evidence of that in the form of a pile of cheap paperback
novels and a note in the shelter log, signed by The Irish
Goat, saying he hoped the amenities were agreeable and
he should be back momentarily with some ''gen'' (Hemingway's pet term for ''intelligence'') about conditions
of the trail in Pennsylvania. There were no mousetraps,
sadly, but there were fascinating back-to-back entries in
the shelter log.

Dated June 24, four days earlier, there was this in neat
feminine Palmer Method ballpoint scroll:

This is my first time into the wilderness. It is exciting
and refreshing. Roger has been to Manassas Gap before. I was expecting only the two of us for the evening. Being so naive, I was definitely shocked when
the Long Distance Long Hair showed up. . . . I'm
glad we brought our gourmet food to be shared. It
was an experience just listening to the fantastic stories. Roger and I will be returning to civilization now,
but wish you all lots of luck and days of enjoyment.
We have an abundance of fresh fruits and vegetables.
Knowing these are rarities on the trail, we leave some
behind for your enjoyment. They are hanging inside
the shelter ready for consumption.

                                             (Signed) D.C. Deb

And then there was the next entry in the log, dated two days later, the net bag of D.C. Deb's fruits and vegetables hanging limp and empty, this one in a penciled scrawled third-grade print:

Well, Toots (Deborah), you like the woods? Exciting? Refreshing? HA!! Good cover on Time Magazine in here (Why Pain Hurts), very *apprapo* for hikers and shit, but anyway, hope you and Rogerdear have a good time in good ole civilization; ME, I'm staying in the WOODS cause I HATES EVERYBODY and I DON'T likes NOBODY. ONLY things I care about is my BOTTLE an' my WOMAN!!!
                                                   (Signed) Sid Friendly

It would be a while before the Yuppies and the Good Old Boys ever agreed on so much as a negotiating site, I was thinking, so in the meantime David and I located the nearest spring and staked out our sleeping spaces in the ratty shelter and remembered The Irish Goat ("And then the nun said, *'Fuck* 'im,' " David said, howling, repeating The Goat's story about the nun-on-the-bus, told back there on a freezing night at campfire eons ago at the base of Standing Indian Mountain on the Georgia-North Carolina ridges). There were forty miles to go to Harpers Ferry, the confluence of the Potomac and the Shenandoah, historical not only for "John Brown's Body" but also for where Paul and David Hemphill decided what would happen next.

The first of our shelter companions to show up, long before dusk began to throw long shadows over the rhododendron, was Shawn Carson. I wasn't sure I had met a through-hiker so far that I would bet on to make it to Katahdin—already I had heard of too many of the "racers" having burned out on some anonymous 6,000-foot hillside and hunkering in the long grass for two days before somebody, anybody, could come to their rescue—but in Shawn

Carson I saw one who had, as they say, all it takes: taut
body like that of Dan Bruce (maybe five-nine, maybe one-
fifty, low butt, heavy thighs, curved back, short choppy
steps), Southern farm boy, deep religious faith (he, too,
like the rambling old couple from central Virginia, signed
his name in the logs with a ⟨PTL⟩ symbol of the
born-again Christians), averaging twenty-five-mile days on
the trail, working three jobs while going to college, had to
be back on the campus by August 28 in order to complete
his degree at East Carolina University on the flat dull plain
of coastal North Carolina. One of his three jobs was to
play drums in what he called a "contemporary gospel"
band.

"Do y'all know anything about the Re-Lo?" Shawn
Carson said. He had hung up his pack and gone for water
and taken off his limber Nikes and now he sat at the picnic
bench in front of the shelter, carved with decades' worth
of initials, with David and me.

"It takes you off that road-walk is all we know," said
David.

"You know if they've cut it yet?" Shawn Carson said.

"No idea," I said. "We just follow the blazes."

"Well," Shawn said, "that's what I'm trying to do. I
want to be honest about the Trail. I haven't missed a white
blaze yet. But now I don't know where the white blazes
are. I thought you might know."

"No idea," I said.

"I just don't want to cheat."

*Kid may be the hope of America even if he does idolize
Ronald Reagan*, I thought, but then here came another one
as dusk enveloped the shelter of The Irish Goat. This one
called himself "The Vermont Special," nineteen-year-old
by the name of Mike, and did he have a story to tell.
"Vermont," this gaunt curly-haired long-distance runner
who had been so cowed by stories of the rural South that
he had refused to venture into towns like Erwin and Hot

Springs on the way up from Springer, had only the night before sat on the ground for a concert by the Grateful Dead, the last of the psychedelic rock bands from the sixties. He had pitched his tent in the grass behind the Ramada Inn in Alexandria after the concert, and hitched in one ride back to the AT, hardly losing a stride on his march northward.

"And then I got word at the post office in Minden, right down the trail, that I've been accepted for Johnson College," he was telling David as he dropped his pack and unshucked his boots.

"Where's that?" said David.

"Up in Vermont close to Hanover. Close to Canada."

"You trying for Katahdin?"

"Nah. I could, probably, but I'll stop at Hanover so I can go home and get ready for college."

I said, "Everything seems to be falling in place for you. You get the tickets for the Grateful Dead and then you get rides. And now you've got college acceptance."

"Yeah," said The Vermont Special, "I can't believe it. Last night I'm sleeping next to the Dempsey Dumpster behind the Ramada and tonight I'm in Manassas Gap. Didn't miss a lick. How 'bout that?"

# 35

IT DOESN'T MEAN MUCH NOW, IN THE OVERALL CONTEXT of the history of the world, but the next morning I got the shit scared out of me while I was brushing my teeth. I've got slides to prove it. Shawn Carson—"The Runner" is how he signed himself in the logs with the ⟨ PTL ⟩ sign—was long gone, having bolted through the bushes in his Nikes on another of his twenty-five-mile daily bursts leaving David and The Vermont Special and my Nikon as witnesses. I had scrubbed my teeth well, paying particular attention to the crevice where once there was a right eye-tooth, and it was when I bent over to spit out the Close-Up toothpaste that I saw the three-foot copperhead coiled maybe a foot away from my sandals on the rocks. "Aaahhhhh," I yelled, spilling backward across the picnic table where Vermont was scrambling eggs and David was picking at his toes, eliciting little more than curiosity as I fumbled for the camera and checked my ankles for the telltale fang marks.

"They're lazy in the morning like humans," Vermont said.

"Holy shit," I said, "I damned near stepped on him."

"Probably ate mice all night," David said. "Sluggish now."

"Sluggish?" I was out of control. "A foot away, max. Maybe eight inches. Look at that sonofabitch."

"Come on, Dad. If he bites you, you just sit down and get sick for a while. That's what you said."

"Yeah, but shit. That's what the *books* say."

"Calm down, Dad." David found a stick and played with the snake for a few minutes. I had found the Nikon and set it on zoom and was firing away, catching the way the dew and the morning sun created a menacing flash from the copperhead's striped scaly body, when suddenly it tired of David's play and simply flipped over the edge of the stone wall and disappeared into the thick bushes below.

Vermont moved on and David and I waited until noon for The Irish Goat to show up, curious to hear about what happened after he and John (Slow Joe) Harper left us in Georgia two months earlier so John could call his mama in Atlanta from the pay phone at Standing Indian Campground, but we understood that The Goat marched to his own drummer and so we hitched up and moved out ourselves. For lunch we stopped at a roadside joint called Paris Mountain Restaurant, hard-by U.S. 50 with a collage of pickups and sleek Camaros hunkered down in the gravel drive, listening to Hank Williams Jr. sing "A Country Boy Can Survive" and shoveling down a heap of pork chops and pinto beans and apple dumplings ahead of a quart of presweetened iced tea, before lurching through the scraggly pines in a thunderstorm and setting up the tarp in the middle of the AT footpath and sharing accommodations with Vermont during a heavy all-night storm.

At this point the only thing we wanted was to make Harpers Ferry. We had seen enough of hell and high water to be nonchalant about it. We would take whatever the AT gave us—original white-blazed road-walk, the fresh-hoed

Re-Lo, whatever—in order to reach the American Youth Hostel above the confluence of the Potomac and Shenandoah *(John Brown's body lies a-moulding in the grave)* so we could determine precisely how we would make the final assault on Katahdin. And so we trudged on.

Sat 6-30

9 miserable hours on Re-Lo of trail, cover 14 miles. AT rocky, plowed, new, poor blazes, up-and-down, no rewards. Muggy, rain, we and some other hikers lost. . . . At 7 P.M. on 601, backyard of Tony Carbone (had been signs inviting hikers). Computer man, 42, D.C., works at home, empathy for "all the tired hikers" some years back, so he opened up his place in '72. . . . Dozen Boy Scouts from Baltimore on shakedown for next week's trip to two-weeker in Colorado. They had left Hwy. 7 at 7 A.M., took wrong turn and wound up where started. Rain, Scouts everywhere, we tarp in backyard, water from faucet. D.C. 50 miles east. . . . Tony Carbone giving Scouts guided tour of computer panel. . . .

Sunday broke across Tony Carbone's lush green backyard. The Boy Scouts had broken camp, as it were, and headed back to Baltimore and their final adjustments before boarding the plane to Colorado Springs and then the bus that would take them to the organized wilds of the Rockies. David and I slopped around in the mire and filled up with water from the faucet next to the house and hunkered over the AT maps and guidebooks. About eighteen miles of trail remained between us and the hostel near Harpers Ferry—broken neatly into three six-mile sections—and it looked okay. I'd heard that story before, of course, and I was leery when the AT "Trial" Guide cautioned of "precipitous descents" and all of that, but still I had faith. What else could I believe in?

Thru rain, over slippery rocks, increments of three
6-milers to Shenandoah-Potomac and Harpers Ferry.
*Did the knees in.* Stopped at country roadside store
with last 6-miler to do, AT "Trial" Guide showed it
flat and easy, but did it mile-an-hour. Another "precipitous descent" and then endless walk across bridge
to AYH hostel Knoxville MD. . . .

It was there, on the final six-mile hike over slippery
round mossy rocks into Harpers Ferry late on that Sunday
afternoon, the first day of July, with the promise of a hot-
shower hostel and a chance to visit with Jean Cashin at the
Mother-Church offices of the Appalachian Trail Conference, that I finally asked too much of my knees. The view
was stunning as I followed David by one hundred yards
across the river bridge, leaning on the concrete rail and
both cursing the sweaty traffic and pondering what history
had transpired down there on those very shoals, but by the
time we had threshed through the brambles and climbed a
stony hill to the frame building housing the AYH hostel I
was a shambles. I paid up at the front desk ($5.25 per man
per night), found that the washer and dryer were broken
again, tossed my stuff on a barrackslike double-decker cot,
got a busy signal when I tried to call Susan in Atlanta from
the pay phone in the big front room, took a shower and
then wound up sitting in the grass in the backyard—fireflies, cicadas, bikers fine-tuning their machines, David
himself showering—with Shawn Carson.

"David seems to be cowed by you," I said to Shawn.
Since I had come across Shawn at the shelter in the Shenandoah and further observed him going about his business, a
young man possessed with making it to Katahdin on his
own Spartan terms, at Manassas Gap Shelter, I had thought
of him often.

"Oh," he said, "David's gonna be okay."

"Y'all must have met when he was walking by himself."

"I think you're right. It was around Roan Mountain."

"I'd gone home with my knees."

"Right. I remember now. It was at Watauga, getting up there toward Damascus, and I was walking with Will then. He's this older man. Anyway, we came on Dave and I remember it now that you ask. He seemed confused. Will and I couldn't explain it. I mean, he knew everything about equipment and hiking but he wasn't there. You know?"

"Well," I said, "a hell of a lot had happened to him right before that."

"We figured."

"In two weeks the kid had gone from saving my life"— I told Shawn of the bourbon incident—"to turning on me. It was pretty devastating to me. God knows what was going on in *his* mind."

Shawn said, "He talked about 'Dad' a lot. The book and all."

"That may be the problem right there," I said. "I think maybe he figures he's being used."

"I don't know anything about that. All I know is, I'm just about halfway to Katahdin and I haven't missed a blaze yet."

"By yourself," I said.

"By myself," he said. "Me and the Lord."

# 36

THE DISJOINTED OLD HOUSE IN KNOXVILLE, MARYLAND, which was a stop in the franchised American Youth Hostel chain—Spartan bunks and showers and a pay phone and proximity to a restaurant and laundry facilities if they worked—was awash with Adventurers. It was the week of the Fourth of July in America and the bikers and canoeists and hikers were out in force. In charge of it all was a multigenerational family (a bronze muscled fellow of thirty who stormed about in a black rubber diving suit, a dazed young woman in a bikini who maybe propositioned me and maybe she didn't one night while "Bonanza" played on the TV set, a haggard mama who kept feeding them all out of cans in the makeshift kitchen, a bitter stepfather who had his vodka cleverly stashed) giving the hostel a personality of its own.

It was tempting for me to arrange that David and I take the Metroliner to D.C. for the Fourth. I had many friends there, including the now-happily-married Maggie of my philandering days (of my ladies of that time she had been the one, and I still cared for her in her new life, and I was

curious about how David might take to her), and I could
think of no better way for a nineteen-year-old to spend July
the Fourth than wandering around D.C., sitting on the grass
in front of the Washington obelisk and ogling Abe in his
chambers and listening to the Beach Boys with thousands
of others while Reagan's America applauded itself. We
could take the train, was my thinking, and Maggie or
Wayne or Jon or Jim or Joe—most of them dear old friends
from my Atlanta newspapering days—would meet us with
glee at the train station and we would have a good old-
fashioned American ball.

That didn't make much sense, though, given the fact that
my knees were raw hamburger and the last thing I needed
was to do all of the walking required of D.C. on the Fourth.
What I needed was to rest the knees and make plans to
jump to Hanover, New Hampshire, so we could do the last
440 miles to Katahdin together by the time David had to
be back home for college in late August. It was time to
take care of business, again, and I began by talking to my
agent, Sterling Lord, about having dinner with him and my
editor (George Walsh of Macmillan) in Manhattan on
Thursday the fifth, and checking schedules for the Metroliner to New York and then a bus from there to Hanover
on the sixth, and seeing when the three fifty-dollar money
orders from Susan might arrive at the post office in Harpers
Ferry.

"Kid," I said to David when he slumped out of his bunk
Monday morning, en route to the john, "it's about here
that Pop used to go a little crazy."

"What?" he said. Somebody was revving a motorbike
outside.

"Mason-Dixon line's maybe a hundred miles north."

"So?"

"It'd be three in the morning and he'd hit his horns and
say, 'Thought I'd wake up the Yankees and let 'em know
we're here.' "

"Funny. Definitely funny." He slouched away.

The fellow in the wet-suit told me that in the hostel's past the building had served as a schoolhouse and a brothel and a church and a saloon/dance hall, and I said I wasn't surprised, and after tearing out an interview of Roy Blount in the *Baltimore Sun* (he had a new book out, *What Men Don't Tell Women*) and mailing it to him in Massachusetts with a note saying we wouldn't be passing that way after all, I walked to the road down the hill and took the three-mile walk to Harpers Ferry and the obligatory meeting with Jean Cashin of the Appalachian Trail Conference.

To say that the ATC is housed in an historic building on a quiet creaky-clean street in Harpers Ferry is redundant because everything is that way there. Harpers Ferry isn't so much a town as it is a museum, a quirky little clump of shiny little two-story edifices done up in pastel tones, given to the memory of John Brown's rebellion a century ago in the form of picture postcards and establishments beginning with the name of "Ye Olde." The ATC, the place to which thousands of hikers and would-be hikers have addressed urgent letters over the years, is headquartered in a two-story stone building right up the street from the post office—dedicated July Fourth, naturally, 1892, at various times a temperance hall and a men's poker-and-drinking club and an antique "shoppe" and a garage where you could get your brakes fixed—and it is behind a perfectly modern desk beyond the front door that one finds Jean Cashin, every hiker's mother, seated.

She was in her fifties, I guessed, and on this steamy July morning she wore her silver hair in a short crop and moved about in a gay pink blouse. This was the woman who, through her "Up Front" column in the bimonthly *Appalachian Trailway News* magazine, had become the grandmotherly saint of the trail. To wit, from the May/June 1984 issue:

One of the 1983 Trail Tots, Steve Queen has a reminder for hikers looking for shelter in the Elk Park, N.C., area. The owner of the supermarket in Elk Park allows overnight use of the loft in his barn behind the market. And, prices are good at the market, Steve adds, so it is a good side trip. It is 2.4 miles east of the A.T. (South-North).

Further comments from Steve include: "Hiking Maine in boots is insane; light-weight hiking shoes give ample support. The Maine maps get the prize, and the profiles are the best of any . . . even the relocations are good! Bravo for MATC!"

And so it goes with the *Appalachian Trailway News*. It is loaded with exclamation points because so are the hikers and Jean Cashin. "The K-2 team of 1983, Kathy Stachowski and Kathi Weiss, write that they are ready to return to the A.T. in Maine and will finish this year. Go K-2!!!" Pump it up, walk the trail, send money for relocations away from Tony Carbone's backyard, lobby Congress, tips-for-the-gourmet-hiker, a word about The Hungry Hiker; your basic subculture newsletter, the *Appalachian Trailway News*, all of it made possible by this woman who, only twelve years earlier, had been "working for the mentally handicapped" up the road in Frederick, Maryland.

"It's like an extended family," she was saying. Over in the corner, boots off, massaging his ankles, a bearded hiker sat on the gray carpet next to a glassed counter proffering everything from matched sets of the AT Trail guidebooks to coffee mugs saying "AT: GA-ME" with a line snaking up the seaboard of North America.

"I feel like I know you already, and we just met," I said.

"I'd hoped to meet your son," she said.

"He's tired."

"By the time they get here, *everybody's* tired."

Jean Cashin knows just about everything there is to be known about the Appalachian Trail. "Ed Garvey says he's going to walk it again in 1990 when he's pushing seventy. . . . Warren Doyle [the one who did the trail in seventy days] is about the most complete man I've ever known. He did the trail like that and now he runs a folk-life center for poor Appalachian kids in West Virginia. He's what the trail's about. . . . William O. Douglas, the Supreme Court Justice, walked the trail on his honeymoon but wouldn't accept a plaque for it. . . . Somewhere out there, there's a kid named Georgia Maine who was conceived on the AT. . . . A lot of marriages take place up in Connecticut at this place called 'Cathedral of the Pines.' Couples figure if they like each other after walking that far together on the AT they can endure anything. . . . Every day of the year I get five letters from people who say they want to walk the AT. . . ."

I said, "Well, I feel like crap. My knees are gone and we've been hitching rides all over the place and me and the boy were going to do this right."

"You shouldn't feel like that."

"But I do."

"You tried, didn't you?"

"See, past tense."

"Let me give you some figures." Jean Cashin opened a drawer of her desk and produced a shamble of papers. "Here we go. Between 1936 and 1969 there would be three or four people who'd go all the way on the trail. All of a sudden in 1970 ten did it. The total then was fifty-five who'd walked the trail all the way. But then it got to be 1979 and look at this: 121 people did it that year. The job market was down. People had time on their hands and figured if they didn't do it now they never would. So in 1980 there were 156 and in '81 you had 137 and in '82 there were 111. It's been declining a little bit ever since. Last year ninety-four people wrote me and said they'd made it. But do you have any idea how many people *tried*?"

"Tell me it's up in the millions," I said.

"The thousands, anyway."

"How many? How many each year say they're going to do it?"

"Oh," she said, "nobody knows that. They lie."

"Give me a guess. Make my day."

"Maybe one out of ten. One out of ten who say they're going to walk from Springer to Katahdin actually make it."

"From what I've seen," I said, "it's more like one out of a hundred."

"Either way," said Jean Cashin, "you've joined the club."

Most assuredly it was to make me feel better—to harbor no ill feelings toward the trail, as it were, for that was her job—but the ATC's "information specialist" then sallied off into a routine about the brotherhood of AT hikers. It was convincing. "When I came to work here there were only 5,000 paid members of the ATC but now we've got 20,000. That's a pretty good circulation for this little newsletter. What it shows is that there are a lot of armchair hikers out there, people who care about the trees if you want to get poetic about it, and a lot more standing behind them who wish they had done what you and your son are doing." She told a story about a retired Navy admiral who had walked the AT alone and, a couple of years later, dropped in on this same ATC headquarters building for a visit. "You see that sign at the foot of the stairs that says 'Private'?" she said. "He walked into here, full of himself, like he was the only person in the world who had ever walked the trail by himself, and when he started to walk upstairs past the 'Private' sign I went after him and said, 'Don't you see the sign? You can't go up there. Even admirals can't go up there.' Well, he stomped out of here like an angry little boy. I didn't see him again until a convention two years later. Apparently he'd had time to think about the trail and what it had meant to him because he came up to me and hugged me and laughed about the 'Private' sign and told me, 'I'm just one of the boys now. Rank doesn't mean anything, does it?' So you see, the trail is an equalizer.''

The knees had frozen up on me, sitting there for an hour or so in the air-conditioning, and when I stepped outside in the blazing sun I had to swing my legs back and forth to limber them up for a walk down the hill to the Harpers Ferry post office. The money orders still hadn't arrived from Atlanta *(Catch-22:* "It was a good idea to send 'em Express Mail over the holiday," said a blank-eyed clerk, "but the problem is there ain't no Express service to Harpers Ferry"). I visited for a couple of hours with a delightful old woman named Clara Cassidy, who writes columns for small-town newspapers and turns them into books *(Off My Rocker* and *Up in Years)* and so far that season had invited forty-seven AT hikers to pitch camp in the backyard of her two-story Cape Cod only four blocks up the hill from the ATC headquarters ("I've had a lot of macaroni-and-cheese dinners so far this summer"), and then I drifted back to bum a ride with Jean Cashin to the hostel across the rivers.

When I got there I found David splayed out, sweating in his sleep, on one of the cots in the musty bunk room of the hostel. Over his face was the "Style" section of that morning's *Washington Post*, with its stories and pictures and maps about what would transpire in D.C. on the Fourth. There had been a call for me from Sterling Lord in New York, I was advised by the snarling stepfather of the clan, and when I got Sterling on the line we agreed on a rather bizarre plan for our meeting—me, David, my agent, my editor—on the Appalachian Trail. We would all have dinner together on Thursday, the day after the Fourth, at the Marigold restaurant in the upper East Sixties of Manhattan. Packs, bandages, ointment, appetites and all.

And then I wandered into the sweeping backyard of the hostel, the size of three volleyball courts, and I struck up a conversation with someone I really shouldn't have been meeting at a time like that. His name was Frank Kemp, a fellow David's age, and he had pitched his tent in the yard in order to pay a dollar rather than $5.25 for a night's sleep. He was from Atlanta, he said, and we had met on the trail back there toward the end of March.

"There were some deer running down into a cove," he said.

"Yeah," I said. "You said, 'Sandy Springs Express, passing on the right,' or something like that."

"Probably."

"You were fat then. I remember thinking you were fat. And bald."

"I've lost fifty pounds since then," he said. "I'd shaved my head, too."

"What for? Shaved."

"Oh, you know, sort of a milestone."

"Lost fifty pounds, you say."

"Needed to," he said.

"What kind of miles you been doing?"

"I think it comes out to about nine miles a day."

"Been stopping here and there, I guess."

"Sort of," he said. Frank Kemp wore more bandages than I. "Got hurt."

"Hurt."

"Knees would wear out. I'd hole up in a shelter 'til they got better."

# 37

ON THE FOURTH OF JULY WE NAPPED ATOP SOILED SHEETS and reread the Baltimore and Washington papers and took sustenance at Cindy Dee's restaurant down the hill from the hostel in the sweaty company of truckers and vacationing families of six—eggs and hash browns here, a hamburger there—with the painful knowledge that only an hour's ride east of us there were hundreds of thousands of Americans strolling the streets and the commons of the nation's capital in celebration of whatever. *That would be something for David to talk about*, I thought, but as I pondered the two of us sitting on the sloping lawn of the Washington Monument that night, listening to the Beach Boys croon of California, I sat on a musty sofa in the hostel and massaged my knees. I wasn't sure I would ever walk again like a normal person.

We got a ride the next day from Paul, stepfather to the clan at the hostel, into Harpers Ferry. First stop was the post office (the money orders had arrived by slow mail) and then there was the bank (to cash them) and, finally, the quaint railroad depot. It would be the Metroliner for us, through Washington and on to Penn Station in New York, next stop on the Appalachian Trail.

Sterling Lord had been my literary agent for about fifteen years, ever since I quit the newspaper-column business and decided to go full-time free lance on the eve of publication of my first book, and he had proven to be a man of great patience and belief in me over those tumultuous years. He had, after all, been Jack Kerouac's agent, had he not? My sporadic failures and successes and outrages must have seemed like human lapses after the experiences with Kerouac. Sterling had been a New York literary agent for at least thirty years, after reupping in the Army after World War II just so he could win the French Amateur Tennis Open (which he did), and in his time on Madison Avenue he had seen nearly everything there is to see about the fragility of writers. He had represented Kerouac and a boggling stable of others—Jimmy Breslin, Joe McGinniss, Marshall Frady, Dan Jenkins, Larry L. King, Dick Schaap, the list seems endless—and to a man we would refer to him as a surrogate father, a calming influence, Our Man in New York. (One night he got a call from a frenetic Larry King, drunk in Texas after midnight, miffed over dragging negotiations regarding his *Best Little Whorehouse in Texas*; after Sterling let King ramble for a while he finally said, "Larry, how can a relationship go bad when the two principals involved have the names of King and Lord?" King slammed the phone on him in a West Texas blather.)

So I suppose we took the time and money and trouble to go through Manhattan because I wanted to see Uncle Sterling. I wanted him to meet David, too, and I wanted both him and George Walsh, then the editor in chief at Macmillan, to see and hear that our walk of the AT had not been a frivolous walk in the woods; to show them my limp, to tell them our stories, to let them see this loping bright-eyed boy and his reclamated father on the job; to make certain that they understood there was a story to be told about what we had been through, even if we never even got a glimpse of Katahdin. David and I could have packed it in at Harpers Ferry, saving a lot of time and trouble and money, but now was a time to take care of business.

The Metroliner reached Penn Station at five o'clock, close to quitting time in the skyscrapers of Manhattan, and I made a quick call to Sterling Lord's office to say we would be there as fast as a cab could deliver us. A thing about New York is, nobody sees anything the slightest bit unusual about two backpackers in full regalia—boots, shorts, obscene T-shirts, bandannas around their foreheads, loaded backpacks—hailing a cab and then strolling up Madison Avenue at rush hour. Sterling came up behind us as we were knocking on the door to his office, he having been down the hall at the men's room in the old Getty Building, and about all he said was, "I told you you were going to be tired." In the office David wandered along the shelves sagging with thousands of books written by the Breslins and McGinnisses and even the Hemphills while I reserved a room for us that night at a decrepit old hotel I knew of, and soon the three of us were walking up Madison Avenue to a restaurant/bar known as the Marigold.

George Walsh was there, a suntanned fifty-ish fellow in a seersucker suit and paisley tie, and we joined him. When drinks were ordered, Sterling, who now lived in a high-rise apartment directly across the street and referred to the Marigold as "my neighborhood restaurant," startled the waitress by ordering iced tea "out of deference to my client." Even there, in an Upper East Side Manhattan restaurant, nobody blinked at two beaten hikers who had come in out of the rain. At least we had stashed our packs with the guard in the Getty Building.

"So," said George Walsh, who had expressed surprise toward the beginning of our trek back in April that I could return a call he had made through Susan within a day or two from a phone booth on the AT, "who would have thought it would come to this?"

"You can tell the owner that the Marigold has just become an official rest stop on the Appalachian Trail," I said.

"Sorry it couldn't have been at Bear Mountain like we planned."

"Me, too. But you can't hardly get there from Harpers Ferry."

"This ought to add something different to the book, anyway."

I said, "I'm a little pissed off that nobody's impressed."

"By now," Sterling said, "New Yorkers have seen everything."

David, a bit cowed and uneasy on his first abrupt trip to New York City, pitched in. "The cab driver asked where we'd been and when we told him all he said was, 'So, dey got 'ny beahs out theah o' what?' "

"Well?"

"What, bears? Oh, yeah, we had a bear, all right."

David and I were off and running then, as we gave our orders for dinner, trying to impress the hell out of my agent and editor. They learned about the bear in the Smokies and the hail-and-lightning storms and my brush with hypothermia and the bourbon incident, and about David's turning on me and wanting to quit the trail, and about our diet and my knees and the mice in the shelters and the characters we had met both on and off the trail. We told them of The Hungry Hiker couple and the town of Hot Springs in its death throes and Jim and Ruth Ann Miner of the washer and dryer in north Georgia and the overnight with the family tucked away in the Bavarian woods of southwestern Virginia and the drunk rednecks yelling "Where's the beef?" that leery Sunday in *Deliverance* country; and then of the characters: Shawn Carson, The Irish Goat, Dan Bruce, Festus, the Shelter-Belters, Grandma Gatewood,

Don Rorer (*giardia* three times), James and his failing JanSport pack, Elmer Hall at the Victorian Inn and all of the rest. George Walsh, in fact, remembered AT Annie when she was younger and he spent an evening at her parents' country mansion (they were both Ph.D.s, and he would never forget that during a séance-like dinner the mother said she felt "it coming on again" and promptly began to reach for the sterling-silver setting and going into a trance and bending them with one hand, one at a time).

"It sounds like more than you bargained for," Walsh said.

"Yeah," I told him. "I remember what David said nearly four months ago when we were all packed and ready to leave the night before. He said, 'Dad, do you understand what we're about to do?' I said, 'Not really, son, but I say let's get on with it.' How little did I know."

"David looks in pretty good shape."

"Yeah, but shit. He could probably *run* the White Mountains."

"That's next? You're going to jump to the Whites?"

"If I can mount the steps to the bus that's what we'll do," I said.

We were wished Godspeed by Sterling Lord and George Walsh, they cringing as I hobbled back to the table from the rest room, and then David and I walked the six blocks or so past Sterling's building to collect our packs and then check into the old Blackstone Hotel on Fifty-eighth between Madison and Park avenues. David was still daunted by New York and chose to lie in bed and watch television until he took a steaming bath in a claw-footed tub and then flopped out in a dead-heap sleep. I called Susan to give her a report on the dinner with Sterling and George, trying my best to be upbeat about the condition of my knees, and then I worked on the knees and gathered up various IRS receipts I had stuffed in odd crannies of my pack and stuffed them in a Blackstone envelope with only the pithiest of notes to her:

> I'm very tired and we must get on with it. Many miles to go. The 440 to Katahdin will be spectacular and the longest single stretch of all.
> I suppose this bizarre sidestep was worth it. We laid it on 'em. David has matured greatly since he learned about heroes.

The bill at the hotel came to $92.50, summer rates, and there was no hot water for a bath until ten o'clock in the morning, and my only thought was that a truly committed through-hiker could walk through the woods for nearly a month on that kind of money. With an American Express Card on me, I would worry about that later. By noon we had walked to Sterling Lord's bank to cash a $500 advance he had given me, which seemed enough for us to finish the AT in the month it would take, and we took a cab to the Port Authority to join the masses waiting for buses to get them as far away from the city's heat and clamor of mid-July as possible. By 2:30 in the afternoon, along with a gaggle of plump giggly fifteen-year-old girls being dispatched to the New England "fat camps" you see advertised in the back of *The New York Times Magazine* every Sunday, we boarded a bus that would take nearly seven hours to reach Hanover, New Hampshire, home of Dartmouth College.

At a rest break somewhere in southern Vermont—bits of New York and Connecticut and the eastern edge of Massachusetts' Berkshires behind us now, the fat-campers having gotten off to change buses or be met by shuttle vans, a relentless rain rushing dusk to the country we had seen only on picture postcards—we went inside the bleak diner for sandwiches and soft drinks and whatever else the automats had to offer. David and I hadn't spoken during the four or five hours out of New York. I had sat in the back so I could smoke and gawk at the countryside (I'm one who'll always request window seats on planes, a consummate tourist, notebook and camera ready at all times) while David had sprawled out up front near the driver reading about Mick Jagger in *Rolling Stone.* He hadn't even bothered to look up for a glance at Yankee Stadium or the bowels of Harlem when we pulled out of New York.

"Well," I said, "this isn't exactly like seeing Vermont."

"I never saw so many white houses and church steeples," he said.

"So you *have* been paying attention."

"Oh, sure, a little. The rain's so thick you can't see much."

"Wonder what's happening on the ridges of the Greens?"

"Wonder who's *up* there, myself."

"We've jumped so far ahead, I guess, there's nobody we know. I mean, when we get to Hanover we'll be about where we'd planned to be if there'd been no breakdowns."

"I hadn't thought about that," he said.

At nine o'clock sharp the bus driver cranked opened the door and announced Hanover. It was a Friday night and there was a fine mist of rain and Dartmouth summer-school students were everywhere—lolling on the steps and defiantly using the white rocking chairs on the veranda of the elegant old hotel directly across the rain-slick street from the expansive lush-green Dartmouth Common—and when I asked a coed with startling long blond hair about a place to stay she gave four options: "There are the fraternity houses but it's Friday night and I don't know if you saw *Animal House.* You can go back over the river to Norwich on the Vermont side if you're into Holiday Inn. You could stay here if you don't think $100 is out of line for a place to flop. Or you can try the Occom Inn down North Main

three blocks. They've *always* got room at the Occom.''
The cab driver, himself a young Dartmouth student, thought
it odd that we wanted a cab just to go three blocks. But
that was before he saw David take my pack and then virtually lift me into the backseat.

## 38

THUS BEGAN A NUMBING OPEN-ENDED STAY IN THE DANK concrete-floored basement of the Occom Inn, a classic rambling two-story white frame New England tourists' home on the edge of the Dartmouth campus, where there were showers and a dozen iron double-decker bunks made up with white sheets and drab wool army blankets as though ready for some natural disaster like an avalanche in the Whites or a flood of the Connecticut River. Except for some odd mute thirty-ish drifter we would nickname "Lurch" for the manner in which he bolted purposefully forward like a robot executing sharp military turns whether it be into the showers or around the coffee table in the upstairs living room, we had the bleak bunk room and years' worth of *Yankee* and *National Geographic* issues to ourselves. Our rent came to eight dollars each, per day, and every afternoon around three o'clock I would struggle up the stairs to the front desk and listen to yet another home remedy for crippled knees before paying in advance for another night's stay.

It was one day at a time—just like in AA and, for that

matter, just like hiking the AT—one stultifying day after
another when David slept as late as a nineteen-year-old
can, which is late indeed, while I lingered in the showers
and babied the knees and popped my Naprosyn and hobbled up to the Dartmouth Common to watch students fling
Frisbees or run their dogs or take the sun before I would
return and join Lurch in the living room to stare mindlessly
at the daytime soaps on the big color television. Eating at
Lou's Restaurant one day and, to relieve the monotony of
overpriced hamburgers, at a pizza joint the next. Reading
from the weather page of the local newspaper that on June
15 on Mount Washington in the White Mountains, where
arctic conditions can occur even in midsummer and there
are white crosses marking where scores of hikers have lost
their lives over the years, the temperature dropped to
twenty-seven degrees and winds hit ninety-four miles per
hour. And every day, out of loneliness and a despair that
ate at me like a cancer by the passing of each hour, there
would be a phone call to Susan and then a letter to her and
then more scribblings in my spiral-notebook journal.

Excerpts from the journal:

New $133 Merrill boots at Dartmouth Co-op for
Dave, crutches and drugs for me, God knows if we'll
need 'em. . . . *The Natural* playing all week at
movie, I've seen it and Dave not interested in baseball. . . . NH license tags: "Live Free or Die."
Never saw so many Saabs, Porsches, Mercedes, Vol-
vos. Rich Episcopalian outpost, only people friendly
to bony bearded Southerner in "On the Eighth Day
God Created Auburn" T-shirt are shop owners. . . .
Dave impressed by Dartmouth, "I gotta check out
this place." Jesus. Kid can't even pass English 101
at Sewanee. . . . Lurch tries to pick fight with Dave
for leaving light on late in bunk room and I tell Lurch
next day he better go easy with Dave: "You don't

want to hear what he did to a hiker when we were in the Smokies." . . . Niekro 11-4, 1.86 ERA, in All-Star Game. . . . Dave taken to jogging late at night, reading *Hamlet* and *Geographic*, even talking about how decorate apartment when returns Sewanee. . . . Got winter wear at PO, mailed back all else. . . . Last time we actually walked trail was into HF 10 days ago. Knees no better, hopes fading. . . .

On one of those afternoons, right in the middle of "General Hospital," I was called to the phone in the narrow hallway beneath the staircase leading to the guest bedrooms. It was Susan, from Atlanta, checking in but wanting me to know that there had been another death. This time it was Felton Covington, a dear old friend who had been the Southeastern sales representative for Simon & Schuster for at least thirty years and was known by authors all over the country as just about the best in the business (Cov was the one, in the final agonies of lupus and cancer, who had advised me at the literary awards banquet before David and I were to leave in the spring that he was into exercise; he had found a deal on an exerciser bike at Abercrombie & Fitch and "every morning at ten I have a boy who comes over and rides it for me"). Cov not only sold books but, a rarity among booksellers, he read them.

"That makes three," I said. "The AT is a jinx."

"You remember the time he sent us the sugar tongs?" she said.

"Refresh me. You mean we have some sugar tongs?"

"We had Cov over for dinner when we lived in the apartment. The phone rang. You had tickets to take David to an Auburn football game the next day. It was Susan on the phone and you went upstairs to talk because you expected the worst."

"Okay, yeah, I remember. She said as long as I owed her a penny I'd never see my boy again."

"Well, at least that she wasn't going to let him go to the game."

"And I ripped the goddam phone out of the wall," I said.

"Right. And Cov said if it was okay he'd be leaving."

"Okay. We talked him into staying for dinner and he tried too hard to be jolly."

"And the next day, without even a card, a gift-wrapped set of sugar tongs showed up from Neiman-Marcus," Susan said. "Sterling silver."

It was getting harder now for me to hide it from my wife that I was flagging, that maybe David and I had walked our last miles and stayed in our last shelter on the Appalachian Trail. A resigned despair was in my voice and in the letters she hadn't yet received. Tonight I would be watching the Miss Universe pageant and the next night the baseball All-Star game on television, I told her, and I was really getting an education out of the soaps and the game shows.

"Surely there's a bunch of good doctors up there," she said.

"Ah, shit, they'll tell me to do what I'm doing."

"Who was it, Yogi Berra? 'It ain't over 'til it's over.'"

"Yeah," I said. "I was telling David yesterday we ought to make like Vietnam. Declare a victory and get the hell out."

Quitting the AT, though, is something that David and I had never openly discussed. He would ask me a couple of times a day how the knees were coming and I would shrug and say maybe tomorrow and he, too, would shrug and go back to studying the AT guidebook for New Hampshire-Maine. We would drift by the old building housing the Dartmouth Outing Club, which maintained a long stretch of the AT running northeastward out of Hanover toward the forbidding Whites and Mount Washington, and hear from somebody hanging around or read from the AT Hikers' Log that some who had left Springer even later than we had already passed through. Privately I would remind myself that at the very best only one out of ten hikers who proclaimed that they were "GA-ME" ever made it to *the* mountaintop.

But then I met Phil Goad and that, more than anything else, is what finally broke my spirit. He came into the living room at the Occom Inn while the All-Star game was in the fourth inning—a tall, balding, sinewy fellow who looked a bit like the actor Robert Duvall of *The Great Santini* and *Tender Mercies*—tilting back his wrinkled army fatigue cap and crossing his scarred boots at the ankles as he plopped into a deep chair with soiled lace doilies. *Nope*, I thought, *he looks like one of those Australian mercenaries who would board C-130 cargoes in Vietnam and look straight ahead with hollow eyes and smoke acrid cigarettes while all around them teenaged boys screamed for their mothers.* Once when I asked one of those men how the war was going he said, with no emotion, "Like the bloody rest of them."

To draw his name out of Phil Goad was easy enough. It took the remainder of the game, pumping at him and quite obviously irritating him during commercial breaks, to assemble any sort of profile of him. From Sanford, Florida, actually, but working for the time being as a lab technician in Miami. He had the sort of job where he could work hard for a few months and then take off for adventures such as this. He'd left Springer in mid-April, moving alone all the way, and he was taking a couple of days' rest here so he could make Katahdin in two weeks.

"Two weeks?" I said. "My God, that's 440 miles."

"I've done it before," he said.

"What're you doing, running?"

"Just don't mess around."

"Why not take your time, though? They say it's pretty up there."

He said, "I don't want the same thing to happen that

happened last year. I got up there to Katahdin in good shape. But then I had an injury. And then I had to go home for some family problems. It took a total of three weeks for the turnaround.''

"The turnaround. You going Georgia-Maine-Georgia?''

"Would've made it last year but the delays cost me.''

"How far'd you get?'' I said.

"Erwin, Tennessee, middle of December. Too late to make it then.''

I was flabbergasted. I wasn't about to tell this Phil Goad about my troubles. Not a word would he squeeze from me. I said, "You got a contract or something? You know, some backpacking-equipment outfitter or something like that?''

"Oh, no. I don't care about that stuff.''

"Well, what the hell you doing this for?''

"Nobody's ever done the round-trip in a calendar year.''

"That's it? That's all?''

"Yeah.''

"I suppose you'll try the Pacific Crest Trail next.''

"Oh, hell, no,'' said Phil Goad. "I'll retire soon's I finish. Probably have a yard sale and get rid of all this junk. I'm tired of it.''

# 39

THE END CAME, FOR ALL INTENTS AND PURPOSES, ON A Friday the thirteenth. I had spent much of the day writing, on a borrowed typewriter at a laundry table in the basement, a 1,000-word Op-Ed Page ditty for the *Atlanta Constitution* about some of the characters we had met on the trail and about the bizarre trek up Madison Avenue for dinner with my agent and editor. "It won't win a Pulitzer, but it's worth a consolation prize of $150," I told David when he stirred awake early in the afternoon. I was so rusty that it had taken me six hours to write what I can usually accomplish in little more than an hour. When I dispatched David to town to mail the column and to fetch some hamburgers for us and to buy up some newspapers, I struggled up the steps to pay for one more night at the Occom and then, from the pay phone in the hall, called Susan with a situation report.

"Where are you calling from?" she said from her office.

"Same place."

"I called last night and they said you had left."

"Whoever answered didn't know, I guess."

"Is this it, Ace? Is this the call?"

"Not yet, kid," I told her. "You might think about *washing* the ashtrays, but don't put 'em out yet. There's a clinic around the corner and I'm going to break down and go over there in the morning. I want a second opinion. They tell me it's a hell of a clinic. They've probably seen more hikers' knees than anybody in America."

"How's David?"

"Resigned, I think. Ready for anything."

"Poor kid," she said.

"Which one of us are you talking about?" I said.

Later, after dark had enveloped another perfect New England day of high puffy cumulus clouds hanging in a motionless cobalt sky, I proposed cheesecake and coffee at Lou's Restaurant. We tarried there an hour, talking about everything except what was on our minds, and then I paid the tab and grabbed my crutches and we moved along the quiet main drag of Hanover. The moon was perfectly full now, hovering over the freshly mowed Dartmouth common like a soft spotlight written into a Hollywood script, and neither of us had to issue an invitation that we sit for a spell on one of the solid old park benches dedicated years earlier in the memory of some Dartmouth man who had made something of himself. There would be an occasional wisp of cool night breeze rattling the ageless elms. Now and then a jogger would huff across the green or an automobile would ease along the empty street or a distant howl would come from a fraternity house several blocks away.

We sat there, my son and I, and for a full ten minutes we didn't speak. I stroked at my beard. David took off his new boots and checked the irreparable damage all of the hiking had done to his toenails. We watched a fellow come out and, in the light of the full moon, begin tossing a Frisbee to his silver German shepherd. Two more weeks and it would be four months since the day my wife had let us out at Amicalola Falls, fresh and eager and fully loaded and ready to get on with the great adventure, and we had kissed and hugged her and the kid and then slipped into the woods. So much had happened to us—no, *between* us— that the profundities weren't yet ready to flow. We only knew that now the denouement had arrived.

"You'll go see a doctor in the morning?" David said to break the silence.

"First thing," I said.

"What do you think?"

"I'm thinking miracle drugs right now. A Joe Namath knee brace. Litter bearers. Some priest rattling beads. Oral Roberts. Where's Oral Roberts when I need him?"

"No, really."

"I think it's a no-go. I just want somebody else to say it."

"Dad," he said.

"Yeah?"

"I think you did pretty good."

"Well." *Am I my father's keeper?* was in his eyes again. Terror didn't accompany it this time, like it did the day he trashed the bourbon in North Carolina. He seemed ready now to launch into a soliloquy, a summation of what all of this had meant to him, and I was most prepared to let him have at it.

He said, "That day I turned on you and said all that stuff and we went back home so I could think things out? I don't think I've ever been so confused in my whole life. But you know what the real thing was? I didn't want us to turn out like you and Pop. You know, the love-hate relationship. You and Pop can't even talk to each other anymore. He was the hero of your youth, like you keep saying, but now y'all can't even agree on how to start a fire or make corn-bread. I mean, I'd really built up some hate for you, being so close to you all the time we walked, and that scared the hell out of me. It helped me when you told me about heroes and all of that."

"You got to remember, son," I said, "that Pop is the same man who once ran a one-man coal-mine operation in the Depression and had the gumption to tell the unions to go to hell, that he could do it all by himself, for better or for worse. And you got to remember that he drove a converted coal truck with a homemade flatbed trailer and a kerosene heater on the floor of the cab from Birmingham to Oregon and back in ten days. In the winter, over the Sierras, sleeping in the cab, living off of coffee and apple pie. He might be a pain in the ass these days, but by God there was a time. There was a time."

"I know that now," David said.

"Maybe I'll turn out to be the same way when I can't write anymore."

"Anyways, I've definitely changed because of the trek."

"How so? How do you see it?"

"Oh," he said, "taking care of business. First things first. Things you keep preaching about. I can see now, that's how I fucked up at Sewanee."

"Think you're ready now?" I said.

"It's about all I've been thinking about lately."

"I'm thinking it was probably good timing for you to take the leave of absence and do this so you could regroup. Right?"

"Definitely. I just wasn't ready for college."

"Going back ain't going to be easy, you know," I said. "Not for either of us. The booze is waiting for me. Kelley and Maggie and the gang at The Pub are waiting for you. You got to remember what Dorothy Hansen said about what happened when she came out of the woods. 'I walked the AT. How *dare* they tell me what to do?' Going into the woods is a hell of a lot easier than coming out."

We wandered back and forth across our lives like that for two hours on that park bench at the Dartmouth Common. I began to think that years from now we would both be able to say that it was there, on that airy night when

David was nineteen and I was forty-eight, that we nailed down a relationship which, if nobody made any particularly outrageous moves, should last forever. We talked helter-skelter about the people and places and things we had seen since March. We made solemn vows (I would try to make amends with my father and spend more time with Molly; he would try not to be such a perfectionist and might take up a discipline like jogging). I philosophized again, paraphrasing Hemingway's words about "going where you have to go and doing what you have to do," to make the point—particularly applicable to us and the AT—that the worst failure comes from not having tried.

"It's getting a little chilly, kid," I said.

"What time we got?"

"Midnight if the clock up there on the Admin Building's right."

"I think I might do some jogging," he said.

"May I advise Lurch what time to expect you?"

"Nah. I'll surprise him."

# 40

THE NEXT MORNING, A STEAMING SATURDAY SMACK-DAB in the middle of July, I rolled out of my cot in the basement bunk room of the old tourists' home and went about my business like a condemned man whose only hope was that maybe there had been a last-minute pardon or a power shortage. David snored softly. Lurch was gone somewhere. I numbly showered and, for whatever odd reason, spent ten minutes trimming my salt-and-pepper beard. I didn't bother to massage or bandage the knees, nor even to take up the crutches, on the grounds that they might as well see the wreckage plain and unadorned. I slipped into my blue hiking shorts and my cleanest dirty T-shirt and my sandals and walked the block and a half to the Hitchcock Clinic.

At ten o'clock, having signed a bunch of forms at the front desk, I found myself idly swinging my legs as I sat on an examination table to await the doctor. I tried not to look at myself in the full-length mirror across from the table. Within a few minutes the doctor came in. It was a woman, about my age, and she pulled up a stool in front of me and began to probe the knees with her fingers while I babbled. *It's me and my boy, see, Georgia-to-Maine. . . . Seems like every time I tried a fifteen-miler the knees went out. . . . Trying to keep up with a bunch of teenagers was foolish. . . . I thought maybe there were some knee braces y'all know about just so we can do Katahdin. . . . I used to play baseball. . . .* She nodded pleasantly through all of that, fending off a few spasmic kicks toward her when she found the spots she was looking for, and I finally shut up when it occurred to me that this woman had probably seen every hiker's knee there was to be seen. She was yet to say a word.

"Maybe there's a knee brace I don't know about," I said. "I mean, Joe Namath and Kenny Stabler, those quarterbacks, they got these knees like robots. Every play some elephant comes in on 'em and knocks the shit out of 'em and they get up smiling. Isn't there something like that? I mean, I should've come in here a week ago, but, you know."

"Your knees aren't your problem," she said.

"Ma'am?"

"It's your knees that *hurt*."

"Tell me. 'Hurt' won't cover it."

"The problem is with your thighs," she said.

"The thighs."

"You lack bulk in your thighs."

"Bulk. In my thighs." I thought for a second. "I'm skinny."

"You're skinny," she said.

"Sonofabitch."

She had a lot of patients waiting—kids with poison ivy, mean-eyed old curmudgeons in town for their weekly placebos, alcoholics wanting just one more I-promise-it's-the-last extension on their Librium prescription, ruddy-cheeked Dartmouth lads with "tennis elbow"—but she had enough time to explain and to console. "I've got a fourteen-year-old son and he loves to backpack," she said. "The same thing kept happening to him. He's a frail kid, or at least he used to be. What I did was put him on a Nautilus program. You know Nautilus. The exercise machines. Athletes use them these days. We put him to work on one that was designed for that one thing, to build up his thighs, and I tell you that after about six months that kid could almost *run* up and over Mount Washington. You've got the same problem he had. You're asking too much of your knees."

"But I gotta walk the rest of the trail," I said.

"You'll never make it."

"Come on. They got drugs and things these days."

"You're making me beg you not to go," she said.

"This Cherokee told me about mind over matter."

"I'm not going to touch that. I'm just telling you that you'd get up there in the Whites above tree line and the winds would get up to seventy miles an hour and you wouldn't even be able to crawl for water and there's no way in the world that anybody could come and get you. Not in a helicopter, nothing. And what if it snows? And your son gets sick? And you run out of food? That would make a wonderful heroic story but I don't want to read it. Look. Go home, do Nautilus, try it again and call me about this time next year. My boy would love to walk the rest of the way to Katahdin with you."

David, awake and pacing when I shuffled back to the Occom Inn with the news, was nonchalant. It was over. I called Susan and made airline reservations and turned in my crutches and we bought respectable lightweight sweaters for an airplane ride and gobbled some pizza and tossed what grub we had left over into a box in the bunk room for future hikers and squared the bill at the Occom and crammed everything into our packs. On the neat little twin-engine puddle-jumping commuter plane from Norwich, Vermont, to the Logan airport in Boston we chose seats on the left side so we could look at the White Mountains we might have walked to the end of the AT at Katahdin in Maine. On the mammoth Delta jet from Boston to Atlanta we chose seats on the right windows so we could see the Shenandoahs and the Smokies where we *had* walked. We were home before dark.

# Out of the Woods

FROM A BACKPACKER'S POINT OF VIEW, IT HAD BEEN A shabby performance. David and I lay about the house for three or four days after our return, not saying much to each other or to anybody else, nursing our psyches more than our bodies. Through all of that scrambling—the preparations, the dreams, the convalescences, the twenty-milers and the eight-milers—David could claim to have actually backpacked some 620 miles and I could only mumble "about a fourth of it" when the boys at Manuel's Tavern or the Old New York Book Store would ask. We're talking about three and a half months of "doing the AT" here. Phil Goad was up there in the Whites now, covering, in fifteen days, the mileage I hadn't managed in four months of hiking. Susan would try to perk me up by saying, of such speedsters as Goad, "It's also possible to run through the Louvre in an hour and say you've seen the great works of the Western world," but it didn't do much good. When I delivered David back to Birmingham we stopped for a lunch with my parents and I learned that my old man, who only two years earlier had been driving eighteen-wheelers to Texas at the age of seventy-one, rolling five-hundred-pound surplus aircraft tires into trailers and hauling them back to Birmingham, had finally raised the white flag: he had more or less retired to the basement, where he had a folding cot and a radio and a lifetime's supply of bourbon and beer, and Mama said he was paying somebody else to mow the lawn. *Am I through, too?* I would ask myself.

David moved back into his room at the apartment with his mother and his younger sister, and went back to sacking groceries at the Piggly-Wiggly until his return to Sewanee in late August, and I tried to return to normalcy with Susan and Martha in Atlanta. I had plenty of work to do—Internal Revenue had me surrounded on the matter of a large arrearage, missives were flying back and forth daily between me and New York as the novel went into its final hectic stages of editing and production, I needed to begin giving some form to *Me and the Boy*—but I found myself falling, as was David, into a malaise. Over the phone we would remind each other of what Dorothy Hansen had said to us back in March, at the Walasi-Yi Lodge during our first week on the trail: *I knew I could do anything in the world when I did the AT by myself . . . but I should have added, on my own terms.* I did a lot of puttering around the house, painting rooms and building a backyard fence and mowing the lawn and rearranging pictures, and then I began to sip around the edges after nearly ten months of giving no thought at all to whiskey. One afternoon Pat Conroy popped by the house, on a day when I had finally bent to the task of typing up my journals from the trek (the typescript came to thirty single-spaced pages of shorthand notes), and when he asked how it was going I told him, as I was telling everybody, "The book's in a lot better shape than my knees."

Life went on. Lisa graduated from Alabama and immediately took a job in marketing with *Southern Living* magazine and its book division, Oxmoor House, and began saving money for her first car and first apartment. Molly finally made a "B," missing an "A" by one point, but shrugged it off by saying it "was bound to happen." David loaded up his stuff and sputtered away in his VW squareback to try to redeem himself at Sewanee, where he only had to score a 2.2 (slightly better than a "C") to stay in school and retain his scholarships and loans, and somewhere in there I had a late-night call from the kids' mother during which she cried ("I just need somebody to talk to") about how they were systematically fleeing the nest. My piece about the Arkansas River finally appeared in the *Reader's Digest*, barely recognizable to me after all of their slashing and "editing," but I did, indeed, become acknowledged at last as The Writer in the Family. Phil Niekro finished the baseball season with a 16—8 record and a 3.09 earned run average and needed only three more wins to become the winningest over-forty pitcher in the history of the game. My knees hurt all the time and whenever I had occasion to trot I ran stiff-legged like a flamingo.

One weekend in the early fall, when the leaves were beginning to turn colors in north Georgia, I went up into the hills with Billy Winn and a pal of his named Bucky Parker (it was Billy who had first put the idea of the AT in my head) for a leisurely twenty-mile walk of the trail up to Blood Mountain. On the first day I saw Dorothy Hansen rocking her newborn daughter at Walasi-Yi. On the second day, during a driving rainstorm, we came across Jim Miner (of Suches and the washer and dryer and the Pall Malls) and he unlocked a cabin for us at Lake Winfield Scott. And on the third day we met one Laurence S. Lovejoy (The Hiking Machinist) of Westbrook, Maine. Suddenly all of my memories of the AT rushed over me in a flash.

Laurence Lovejoy was a beaten man. He would spend

one more night on the *gol-darned* Appalachian Trail, he
said, before kissing Springer Mountain and hitching to Atlanta and taking a bus back to Portland and "the *fahm*"
and then sending a wire to the ATC advising them that he
had finally walked every bloody mile of the AT and would
they please send him his "2,000-miler" patch so he could
go on about his business. He wore an army fatigue cap and
loose cotton trousers and a rumpled long-sleeved shirt—
better to keep the bugs away—and the cleats on his boots
were worn as smooth as pebbles. By about two o'clock the
next afternoon it would all be ended.

"*Stahted* in '72," he said.

"Did it in pieces," I said.

"Got to be an obsession."

"I know what you mean. I'm still pissed about not making it."

"Gonna be embarrassing if I didn't finish."

"So," I said, "what's been the best part? My boy and
I, it was the Smokies. Godamitey, I never saw anything
like it." I told him about the day of the hail-and-lightning
storms, and the Shelter-Belters, but he wasn't very impressed.

"Whites are prettier," Laurence Lovejoy said.

"We never made it that far."

"Smokies ain't much."

"Well," I said, "we came across a *bear* up there."

"You ain't seen anything 'til you've seen a *moose*. Up
in Maine."


DAVID AND I WERE STAYING IN TOUCH BY PHONE. HE WAS
sharing a room at Sewanee with a fellow his age named
George Phillip, an outdoors type from the Ozarks in Arkansas, and they seemed compatible. The VW refused to
wake up one morning, I learned from one of our long-
distance talks, but Dave had the ten-speed Schwinn I had

bought from one of the regulars at Manuel's. Kelley Vann, the blue-eyed angel of Huntsville, was now president of the German Club at the university. Maggie Thompson, spunky Maggie, was living in an off-campus apartment and was more the sister/adviser (reluctantly, I guessed) than the honey. I promised I would send a copy of the bound galleys of *The Sixkiller Chronicles* and he admitted that an "intimidation factor" was involved in his not having read the novel back in the spring, when he was chomping at the bit to leave on the AT and I was pounding out the novel, and in his flunking English 101 the first time around in spite of having a Verbal SAT score of a phenomenal 700. He was doing okay with his studies, he would always say, and he even had time to do a late-night two-hour stint as a disc jockey on WUTS, the laid-back little campus radio station that barely reached the interstate highway some ten miles away, and when I came up for Parents' Weekend in early October would I bring some of my albums—Don McLean, Willie Nelson, Randy Newman, Merle Haggard, Phoebe Snow, even Hank Williams—that WUTS didn't likely have? We would wonder what had become of hikers like The Irish Goat and Shawn Carson and Phil Goad, and I would say I was still looking for "the right voice" for *Me and the Boy* and he would tell me he had just "aced" an exam in math, one of the two courses he had managed to pass during his pre-AT semester.

Then, not two weeks before Parents' Weekend was to take place, I took another collect call from him. He was at the pay phone booth right around the corner from his and George's room. I wasn't just sipping around the edges anymore. I was buying rot-gut vodka by the fifth now, changing my hiding places every morning once Susan had driven off to the magazine, fooling her as little as my old man had "fooled" my mother for all of those years. Things were going to hell for me—on that day I had dashed off the chapter deadline with David's trashing the canteen of bourbon, the chapter I would denote as *Boubon Incident* on the chart tacked to the wall above my typewriter, while swigging vodka-and-Coke—and now I could see that David wasn't doing so hot himself. There had been an accident. He and Kelley had been returning from a weekend canoeing adventure in western North Carolina with a half dozen other Sewanee students when the driver lost the station wagon on a slick mountain curve and a lot of them had been hurt. He was near hysteria.

"I couldn't handle it," he was shouting. "I thought I was tough enough, but I was on top of her and I could see a lot of blood and I could see a bone in her leg. I lost it. I was crying. So was she. I didn't know what to do. The bone was sticking out of her leg, Dad."

"You hurt?" I said. Drunks call it one of those sobering moments.

"Bruises is all," he said. "I need you, Dad."

"I'll be there, son."

"Parents' Weekend means a lot more this time."

"Okay. I'm coming."


THE UNIVERSITY OF THE SOUTH—"SEWANEE"—IS A well-endowed sort of Harvard-of-the-South where a kid can spend four years without ever being asked what he intends to do for a living. The students are either rich or promising, or both, and this country is littered with lawyers and politicians and philosophers and writers (Walker Percy has a particular affinity for the place, his Uncle Alexander having been a major contributor, and Tennessee Williams left the whole of his $10 million estate to it sight-unseen, and then there is the blush-cheeked Episcopalian endowment of some $64 million) who first matriculated there, on The Mountain, at the feet of professors who hold forth at class while wearing austere black robes. Ninety percent of the teachers at Sewanee own Ph.D. degrees and sometimes, in one of the musty gothic classrooms of the ivy-draped campus, shrouded in the hills between Chattanooga and Nashville in the rolling land of Middle Tennessee, you will find three students involved in a ringing debate with the one be-gowned doctor of philosophy. This, then, was the world where David found himself. *What's a Hemphill doing here?* was a question I asked myself often.

The kid, I would find out that weekend, was having every bit as much trouble as I making the adjustment from the AT to the real world. Ahead of time I had set up appointments with two or three of his key professors. After a Saturday-morning brunch for Sewanee parents at Guerry Garth, a patch of green between ivy-clothed gran-ite buildings where I thought I had dressed properly (creased gray slacks, white oxford-cloth button-down, Bass Weejuns, the blue-striped cotton crewneck sweater bought at the Dartmouth Co-op in order to appear civi-lized on the flight back from Hanover to Atlanta that day when we aborted the hike) only to find that true Sewanee Papas wear identical uniforms of blue gold-buttoned blazers and rep ties and gray slacks and tasseled black loafers, I hustled across the trim commons to have a word, nevertheless, with the men and women who served David in this strange new world of his. What I found out was, to be brief, he was blowing it. Said his Spanish professor: "I keep waiting for David to blossom. But I think he ought to think about dropping Spanish to lighten the load. He was so *promising*, David. I'm, how do you say, *exasperated*." Said his English professor, Doug Paschall, who had been taken by his charm and was the nearest thing David had to an adviser: "I don't know about the 'intimidation' factor. Only David knows about that. But I can tell you that if he just showed up for class, did the work, threw something at the barn so we could talk about how much he missed it, he'd be fine. He'd be better than 'fine.' He'd be wonderful."

* * *

"THIS IS WUTS, UNIVERSITY OF THE SOUTH, SEWANEE,
Tennessee. Easy-listening time. Welcome to the parents
of Sewanee students. My name is David . . ." I had
brought a couple of dozen of the albums he knew I had
at home—the Randy Newmans and the Willie Nelsons
and the Hank Williamses and the Haggards and the Arlo
Guthries and the rest—but I had a feeling that David had
taken control of the microphone when I bolted awake at
dusk and heard James Taylor's "Blossom," a little-boy-
lost plea for somebody to hug away his lonesomeness.
Because now I knew that my son had missed, more than
anything, a good hugging now and then. That was my
son in 1984 and that was me, thirty years earlier, when
each of us was late-teens, suffering our first failures,
crying out for somebody to hang close and tight. *Help
me make it through the night.* Next, over the radio, he
played Arlo's "City of New Orleans."

Saturday night came and went. At the German House I
met the fabled Kelley Vann—a beautiful blond and blue-
eyed woman ("You must be 'Dad' ")—who hobbled into
the place on crutches and had no choice but to allow her
subjects to autograph her toes-to-hips cast. I may have been
drunk by the time I met her. I don't know. The morning
with David's professors had fucked me up and so had the
disjointed afternoon at the skeletal football field for the
game between Sewanee and a small college from Memphis
(Sewanee's "fight song" turned out to be the clog-dancing
favorite, "Rocky-Top") and the impressive pile of Tanqueray gin bottles in the room at Treszevant Hall where I
slept it off. I remember only that at some point in there—
between the hoitsy brunch of blue-blazered Sewanee Parents and the playing of "Blossom" over WUTS radio—I
got into a bitchy debate with a blue-nose about whether it

was best to walk the AT in sneakers or in Abercrombie & Fitch's finest.

By noon on Sunday I had dug into a basic Southern country breakfast of bacon-grits-eggs-biscuits at the City Cafe down by the railroad tracks, ridden the ten-speed bike to the Sewanee Tigers' baseball park (standing at second base, hung over, pretending to flip a throw against the wind to nail Country Brown of the Atlanta Crackers on a close play at first), banged on the door of Maggie's apartment to gain some insight on what the hell was going on between David and Kelley ("It's obvious he's head over heels in love"), thought better as I rode past Doug Paschall's house on Florida Drive to inquire further about why the kid was flunking out, and finally, out of patience, I biked back to the somnolent dormitory and leaned the Schwinn against the nearest post and creaked open the door. I found David up, his back resting against the white-painted concrete-block wall, admiring the Che Guevara poster he and George had enlarged from a mere photograph.

I walked past him to the couch, where I had slept the two nights before, and began to gather my things for the four-hour drive back to Atlanta. Every time I would throw a piece of dirty clothing into my bag he would turn another page of the book he was pretending to read. George, his roommate, was gone somewhere. David and I were mentally circling each other, waiting for the next move, both embarrassed by our own circumstances, and when we finally began to talk it was of peripheral matters. *Kelley's okay* and *Football up here isn't exactly like Auburn* and *How's it going with the novel?* and *Maggie's got a nice place* and the like. Finally I said, "I owe you for a fifth of Tanqueray."

"It's all right," he said.

"We aren't doing so hot, are we?"

"I guess not."

"Dorothy Hansen was right, I reckon."

"Yeah."

"Any way you can turn it around, Dave?" I said. "The two professors I talked to say you're losing it. Swimming in quicksand. 'All that promise,' they say."

"I know. I've got to get my ass out of bed, for starters."

"I've been the same place. We both know that."

"Maybe it was something in the water around Hot Springs," he said.

"That's it. I bet that was it." We laughed because there wasn't anything else to do.

We crawled on our knees, separately, toward the end of the year. Midterm grades arrived from Sewanee, showing two F's and a D and an Incomplete (in English) for David and by that time I was swimming in whiskey. On the day after Thanksgiving I got kicked out of the house by Susan and spent the weekend sleeping on the sofas of friends. Word came that David, embarrassed because he was unable to turn out perfect papers in English and Spanish and German, was skipping classes altogether so as not to be discovered. I finally listened to Bob Hannah ("Look, forget the atheism; they're there to save your ass, not your soul") and followed him meekly to a meeting of Alcoholics Anonymous and, to a roomful of strangers, wondering if Hemingway had ever done this in his time, told them, "My name is Paul, I'm an alcoholic." Christmas came to my sister's house in Birmingham, replete with aunts and uncles and cousins and children of cousins, and when David showed up for the dinner he was wearing a bow tie. So was I.

I don't know what you'll have heard from David lately, though I'm very hopeful the news is encouraging. We had a very extended visit some six weeks back—two or three long hours one afternoon—and I have to confess I came away from that session more rather than less bewildered; and rather abjectly dismayed. I felt that I was not at all making connections with him, despite the fact of some very straight talk from my side and some right intimate talk from his. And I watched him shuffle away with a great sense of anxiety filling my bosom. I know I wasn't any help, though I don't think I've ever tried harder with a student. That's not to say I've given up, or that I don't see any possible hope for transformation. But it didn't look to me like a very good stretch for him, coming up, though I'd be glad to be proved wrong. . . .

That note was written to me by Doug Paschall, the English professor at Sewanee, when I asked him to tell me what had happened to my son. Paschall knew all of the data about David—the SAT scores, the trek of the AT, the women ("Who *doesn't* know Kelley Vann?"), his father-the-writer, the difficulty any bright kid from a huge public high school has in adjusting to a demanding little university such as Sewanee—but even he couldn't predict what might happen next. "Nobody, I guess, enjoys confessing failure; but someone in my position [is] driven mighty close to that admission. I didn't 'register' with him, class or no class, time spent or not it's a worry for me. . . ." The teacher was clearly as confused as the father on the matter of David Hemphill.

But first, before he could pick himself up, he had to hit rock bottom. *Just like me and AA*, I thought. That time came soon enough for David. Not long after Christmas he abruptly appeared in the gift department of Rich's department store in Birmingham, a bewildered kid with the same black look I must have worn when *my* first dream had been shattered, and when his mother, startled, asked him what was wrong, he said, "Everything." He had flunked out of the University of the South.

Over the phone that night, wishing now more than ever
that he lived under my roof, I tried to commiserate as best
I could. Auburn in the fifties was a piece of cake compared
to Sewanee in the eighties, I told him. Yeah, he said, but
at least you went to class. *I was intimidated by Harvard,
too, until I got the hang of it.* Silence. *Maybe you're just
not ready for college. I mean, those SAT scores. Well, you
know, Hemingway said he didn't have time for college.*
He'd heard it before. *What did Kelley have to say?* He
didn't know how to tell her. There was no chance for a
successful appeal of his dismissal, he said when I asked,
and then for the next half hour we debated his options: join
the Marines ("they wrote the book on discipline"), scrape
up enough money for another attempt at a solo hike of the
AT ("to get it out of my craw"), get a job at Sewanee and
audit classes ("but I'd turn out to be the campus mascot"),
go back out to Colorado and work on the ranch ("I've
already done that") or take the old job at Piggly-Wiggly
and attend the University of Alabama-Birmingham (UAB)
until he could apply again at Sewanee.

"Pretty soon I'll be twenty," he said. "If I go back to
Piggly-Wiggly I'll be the dean of stock boys in Birmingham."

"You can't force college, Dave," I told him. "Lots of
times I've wished I'd waited. Auburn would've done me a
favor if they'd flunked me."

"I keep looking for a lesson somewhere."

"How's that?"

He said, "Something I learned on the trail that's transferable to the real world. That was the premise of the trek,
wasn't it?"

"Yes, it was," I said. "It certainly was."

When we rang off—it seemed that there was nothing
forced, anymore, about how we said "I love you" to
each other—I drifted out to our new screened porch. It
was a balmy January night, with a full yellow moon, and

I noticed that my JanSport pack and Pivetta boots, undisturbed since the weekend jaunt back to Blood Mountain in October, were gathering cobwebs and mildew. It seemed as though I had never worn that pack and those boots. It seemed as though the trek with my son had never happened. Was there, indeed, anything we had learned on the trail that was transferable to "the real world"? Or had we simply learned how to (or how *not* to) conduct a full-scale backpacking expedition? I wondered what had become of all of those wonderful bromides-to-live-by—"one step at a time" and "first things first" and "life is full of peaks and valleys" and "I'll climb that mountain when I come to it"—that we had intended to bring out of the woods and apply, like lessons learned in a classroom, to the rest of our lives. Did we have nothing more to show for all of the pain and time and expense of the trek than bruised hip bones and gnarled toenails and stretched Achilles tendons and some color slides and scarred boots and Dad's spiral notebooks and, if he ever finished it, Dad's book?

Presently, Susan sought me out on the porch. I filled her in on David's latest dilemma and told her what he had said about "transferable lessons" from the trail and about how I didn't see that we had learned a single important thing. She listened patiently as I told her, for example, that all I knew from the horrible crawl up Albert Mountain was that it is a horrible crawl up Albert Mountain. I motioned toward the pack and the boots on the porch, mute and haunting evidence that once I really had walked on the Appalachian Trail with my son, and reckoned that maybe we ought to hold a yard sale.

"Don't you dare," she said.

"Probably wouldn't bring fifty dollars, total, anyway."

"I mean don't dare talk about the walk like that." She was tired of all the slumping around and the talk of "failing" the AT. "So what if you didn't make it? So what

if it's been hard adjusting? You knew the odds when you
started out. How long's it going to take for you to understand what went on between you two out there? What
you did was cut out the bullshit that goes on between
most fathers and sons. You showed all of the warts and—
sonofagun—look what happened: you and David found
out that you not only love each other, you even like each
other. If that's not a 'transferable lesson,' I don't know
what is.''


I CAN'T AVOID ANALOGIZING THE ARRIVAL OF SPRING AND
the abrupt changes in the fortunes of David and me and
nearly everybody around us. It was as though seeds had
been planted in our lives—at Albert Mountain? on the day
of the bourbon? in the Shenandoah when he said he didn't
like me?—and now, having taken root during the gray days
of winter, they were suddenly bursting forth like so many
jonquils and dogwood and azalea. Hardly anything could
go wrong, it seemed, as the false spring of January gave
way to the real thing. My novel, *Sixkiller*, was bought for
a television miniseries even before its publication (and
somebody came along after that to renew the movie option
on my first novel); I hired on as writer-in-residence at
Brenau College, a small private women's school, right up
the road from Atlanta in Gainesville; and when I received
a gold poker chip from my AA group, signifying six
straight months of sobriety (''six months and a thousand
nights,'' they like to say at AA), I was surprised by a
graceful phone call from David's mother. Molly, the
youngest child from that first marriage, made the Junior
National Honor Society in spite of the single ''B'' on her
record. Lisa, the oldest, bought her first car and found her
first apartment and got happily involved as a youth worker
with the Episcopal church.

And then there was David. Something snapped, somewhere along in there; and although we thought it jolly to believe the AT had finally spoken, we were asking no questions. He went back to work at the Piggly-Wiggly (earning about $100 a week for twenty hours' work) and, again living in the apartment with his mother and his youngest sister, enrolled at the University of Alabama-Birmingham. "While bagging groceries is no great fun," he wrote me one day, "it provides a nice (and quite useful) contrast to 'integration by parts' and the philosophical romanticism of Søren Kierkegaard." He was making A's, and some B's, "taking care of business like you said," and he was fairly certain that he had settled on philosophy as his major. I fell in love with Kelley Vann myself when he told me their deal: nothing would happen for them if he didn't make it in college.

I had been sending him pieces of *Me and the Boy* as I wrote it, with the caveat that I would "take under advisement" any particular "violations of confidence you might have," but about his only complaint was the use of the word "boy" in the title ("although," he wrote, "I suppose it was true at the time"). He would send me essays he had written for his English Composition class. I would send him the *Appalachian Trailway News* where, in the March/April issue, for the third straight year, there was an item under "Hiking Partners" wherein John (Slow Joe) Harper was announcing plans for "northbound thru-hike in late March, averaging 12-15 miles a day." We were talking on the phone and writing long letters to each other two and three times a week now, often when there wasn't really anything to report, and for the first time in our lives we seemed to be relating more as friends than as father and son. One night on the phone I told him that I was learning more than how to stay sober at AA, that the meetings were "a novelist's paradise of broken lives," and he countered with his notion that maybe the experience on the AT was a prologue to his decision to become a philosophy major: "The Irish Goat, Don Rorer, even the Shelter-Belters; everybody out there was a philosopher." He made the wry observation that I had ended the year where I had begun it: in the company of strangers with vague backgrounds who only used their first names. We even survived—and prevailed—his last crack at teen-agery.

"You'd better talk to him," his mother said one day. "He just borrowed money for an old Porsche." *A Piggly-Wiggly stock boy with a Porsche*. I was livid. He had bought it from a Marine being shipped to Okinawa (the same one who had failed to recruit him?), and on his third day of ownership he had ripped out the transmission. *Is there no end to this*? But even in the fiery exchange of letters over this latest foolishness there was something between us that had never been there before.

> David: The dedication of *Me and the Boy* reads, "To David; for better, for worse, forever," but you're pushing it. . . .

> Dear Dad: Your words were entirely appropriate. Beyond this, all that I feel needs to be said is that I have needed you as my father for a long time and still do, not to prevent me from making mistakes for that would get me nowhere, nor to correct mistakes for your responsibility to do so has to a great extent, if not completely, ended. Instead I need your advice, support, praise and admonishment. . . . Keep prodding. Please . . .

> David: It's going to take about 120,000 words for me to say it to the world in great flowery gut-wrenching detail—and that's another reason why this book isn't going as easily as I had hoped—but I can state it to you in one simple declarative sen-

tence. I love you more than anybody or anything in
the world. . . . What I feel for you is not, "re-
sponsibility." It's love . . .

Finally, in the middle of the summer, almost a year
from the day we had come dragging home from New
Hampshire, there came a crisis. My old man—Pop, the
erstwhile King of the Road, adrift and bitter and swimming in whiskey now that he was seventy-four and
couldn't drive trucks anymore—had what the doctors
called a "mild stroke." They didn't even know his blood
type, because he had never been to a doctor in his life,
and at the hospital, he was hallucinating ("Hell, I just
drove in from Lubbock yesterday, I'm okay to go again")
and ripping the IVs from his sinewy arms and wishing a
nurse would slip him a beer. After a week of that, with
an admonition that if he drank again he would die, the
doctors gladly sent him home. Once again, as thirty years
earlier, I was appointed by my mother and my sister to
reason with him. *It's the son's place to go find him and
talk to him.* So I went to Birmingham and I purged the
house of cleverly stashed bottles of bourbon and I told
my father that I loved him.

"You know what really pisses me off, in a way?" It
was late on one of those sultry summer nights, when the
old man had been home for about a week, driving everybody crazy, and David and I had escaped to the backyard
swing. Fireflies played in the yard and our conversation
was interrupted by jet planes roaring over the house on
their final approach into the Birmingham airport. "They
checked his liver and said it was okay. That man's drunk
enough whiskey to fill Lake Michigan, but he's the one
with the good liver."

"You think he's quit for good?" David said.

"I do. It scared the hell out of him."

"You, too, I guess."

"Bet your ass," I said. "I like the ring of the three of us—'father, son, Holy Ghost'—but I'm not ready for him to be a Holy Ghost yet. I didn't realize that until this happened. I guess you've got to go through some shit with somebody to really appreciate 'em, you know?"

"I know," David said.

## About the Author

Paul Hemphill, writer-in-residence at Brenau College in Gainesville, Georgia, is the noted author of THE NASHVILLE SOUND, TOO OLD TO CRY, THE GOOD OLD BOYS, LONG GONE and THE SIXKILLER CHRONICLES. He resides in Atlanta, Georgia with his wife, the journalist Susan Percy.